Firesafety Concepts Tree

(A Qualitative Guide to Firesafety Strategies)

Committee on Systems Concepts for
Fire Protection in Structures 1980

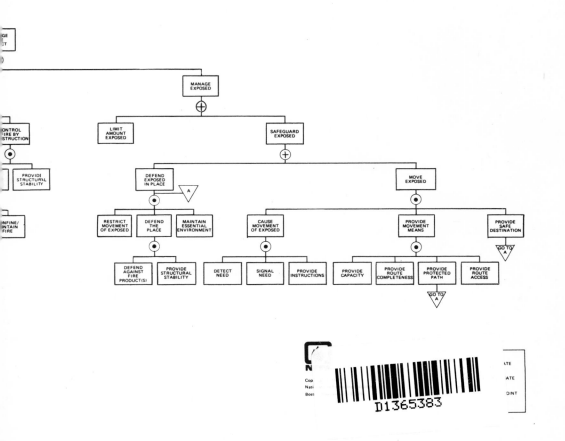

DESIGNING FOR FIRE SAFETY

Designing for fire safety

E.G. Butcher and
A.C. Parnell

JOHN WILEY AND SONS

Chichester · New York · Brisbane · Toronto · Singapore

Copyright © 1983 by John Wiley & Sons Ltd.

Library of Congress Cataloging in Publication Data:

Butcher, E.G.
    Designing for fire safety.

    Includes bibliographical references and index.
    1. Fire prevention.   I. Parnell, A.C. (Alan Charles)
II. Title.
TH9145.B87   693.82   82-6907

ISBN 0 471 10239 3   AACR2

British Library Cataloguing in Publication Data:

Butcher, E.G.
    Designing for fire safety.
    1. Fire prevention
    I. Title   II. Parnell, A.C.
    628.9′22   TH9145

ISBN 0 471 10239 3

Typeset by Photo-Graphics, Yarcombe, Nr. Honiton, Devon
Printed and bound in Great Britain by The Pitman Press, Bath

Contents

Foreword

All architects and teachers of architecture know that designing for fire safety is vitally important but have not always been clear on how to go about it. The fact that the subject may have seemed to be concerned principally with the fire resistant qualities of materials and with regulations which inhibit design freedom, has perhaps made it difficult to teach and discouraged full and enthusiastic consideration by designers at the conceptual stages.

During the last decade or so, as a result of research, much more has come to be known however, about how people, smoke and flames behave when there is a fire so that strategies for safe design can be taught and practiced. As these principally concern the occupants and the functions for which a building is designed and can be seen as being, to a certain extent, separate from the more tactical matters which dominated traditional 'fire precautionary' thinking (such as the choice of structural form and materials) the subject becomes more understandable and attractive to students and practicing architects alike.

What has been lacking however, is a book which brings together, in a readable and useful form, all the new thinking on the subject. This book fills that gap admirably. The Authors have been closely involved in all the recent developments in the field of Fire Safety and have distilled in an admirable way, their own extensive practical experience with that of others, and the results of research throughout the world.

As good design is now more than ever dependent upon the availability to the designer of the necessary knowledge in a usable form, this book should not only make for better buildings but contribute also to the saving of lives.

ALEX GORDON, C.B.E., LL.D., Dip.Arch.
Past President Royal Institute of British Architects

Preface

To many architects and building designers the fire precaution measures which have to be incorporated in a building design seem to impose onerous features dictated by a bureaucratic system and the real need for these measures is often not understood and therefore resented.

This book seeks to dispel this attitude and shows how all the required fire precaution measures can be put into a building design without any inhibiting effect, provided they are considered during the initial design stage and are included progressively throughout the development process.

The first part of the book explains how fires start, how they grow and how they spread inside and outside the building. It is shown that the building shape and size can affect all of these processes and possible ways of minimizing the dependence are indicated.

The second part deals with the practical aspects of incorporating fire precautions as an integral part of the building design. It takes the reader along the whole design path, starting at the original concept and eventually reaching the finalized design. Throughout that progress it shows, step by step, how and when the relevant fire precaution measure should be considered and in most cases gives alternatives which may be used to achieve the design requirement.

February 1982

E.G. Butcher
A.C. Parnell

Acknowledgements

In preparing a book of this nature information and ideas for presentation are obtained from many sources which are too numerous to mention individually but to our many friends and colleagues we offer our sincere thanks.

The material used in Chapter 5 of Part 1, which deals with Services, was supplied by Mr David Boughen, Mr Peter Pucill and Mr Philip Nash, while that used in Chapter 6 of Part 1, dealing with Insurance, was prepared by Mr B.R.J. Henman and Mr J.S. Davis, both of the Commercial Union Insurance Company. We wish to record our thanks for the great help given to us by these acknowledged authorities in their particular fields.

We must also acknowledge the help given by Mr Anthony Fergusson who, whilst in our employment, collected together much of the material which forms Part 2 of the book.

We are indebted to the following for supplying us with photographs or diagrams and for giving us permission to publish them:

The Director, British Constructional Steelwork Association Limited for the diagrams of Figures 2 and 7.

The Head, Fire Research Station, Borehamwood, and the Controller, H.M. Stationery Office for the diagrams of Figures 6 and Page 302 which are Crown Copyright.

The United States Steel Corporation for the photograph of Figure 26.

The Director, Fire Insurers Research and Testing Organization, Borehamwood, for the photographs of Figures 27 to 31.

Mr K.C. Bridges, until recently Commandant, Fire Service Staff College, Dorking, and the Controller, H.M. Stationery Office for the photographs of Figures in A1(6), which are also Crown Copyright.

Mr Stephen O'Shea, Apollo Manufacturing Limited, for the photographs in Page 239.

The National Fire Protection Association, Quincy, Massachusetts, for the Fire Safety Concept Tree referred to in Page 168 and printed inside the front cover.

Part 1

1
Ignition

1.1 General

The British Standard[1] definition of ignition is 'the initiation of combustion' and that of combustion is 'the consumption by oxidation, with the production of heat usually with incandescence or flame or both'.

Carrying this one stage further the definition of flame is given as 'A zone of oxidation of gas usually characterized by the liberation of heat and the emission of light'.

It is clear then that 'oxidation' is the important feature of 'combustion'. To a chemist the term 'oxidation' means more than just simple combustion and a definition of the wider aspects of oxidation can be stated as follows.

A substance is oxidized when:

(1) oxygen chemically combines with it;
(2) any non-metallic element or group of elements combines with it;
(3) hydrogen is removed from the substance;
(4) any metallic element or group of elements is removed from the substance;
(5) when positive ions have their positive charge increased;
(6) when negative ions have their negative charge decreased.

Only the first item in the above list constitutes 'combustion' but not all reactions between a substance and oxygen are so classed.

Combustion is a reaction between a substance and oxygen in which heat is given out, i.e. it is called an exothermic reaction, and enough heat must be given out either to maintain the temperature of the reactants, or to continuously increase their temperatures so setting up a chain reaction. In some cases the reaction between a substance and oxygen requires heat to be applied to maintain the reaction and the reaction stops when the applied heat is removed. This is not combustion.

3

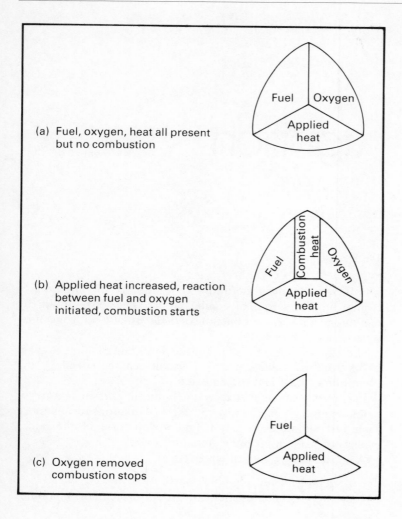

(a) Fuel, oxygen, heat all present but no combustion

(b) Applied heat increased, reaction between fuel and oxygen initiated, combustion starts

(c) Oxygen removed combustion stops

Figure 1 The combustion triangle.

In general, the combustible substance and oxygen can be in contact with one another without combustion starting. It will be necessary to apply heat to the mixture before the chemical reaction between the constituents starts, but if, once it has started, enough heat is given out to maintain or increase the reaction then combustion is said to have started.

The combustion process does not always involve the oxygen in the air. Two solids, one having combined oxygen in its make up, and the other being combustible, i.e. being ready to receive oxygen into combination, can be mixed together, heated up and combustion will take place between the components even if the oxygen of the air is excluded. Such cases of combustion are usually violent and sometimes explosive. An example of such a mixture is gunpowder (or black powder) which is a mixture of saltpetre (potassium nitrate), which has ample oxygen in its

(Figure 1 continued)

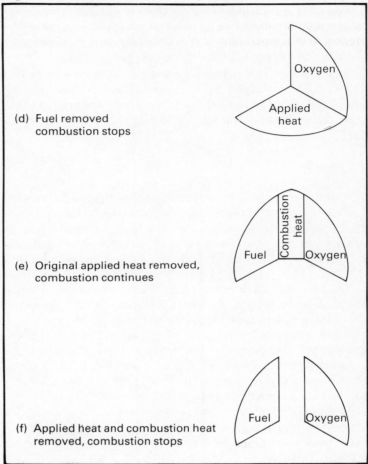

(d) Fuel removed
combustion stops

(e) Original applied heat removed,
combustion continues

(f) Applied heat and combustion heat
removed, combustion stops

make up, and charcoal and sulphur powders, both of which are ready to receive oxygen; the mixture when ignited burns so rapidly that it can be used as an explosive.

Thus combustion take place when a combustible substance and oxygen are brought together and heated until the two react together and give off heat.

The three parts of the combustion process give rise to the familiar 'fire triangle' but this is a little more complicated than is usually shown in the simple diagrams and Figure 1 shows the stages involved in starting and stopping combustion.

There may be a slight reaction between the fuel and the oxygen even at normal temperatures but this will be slow and the heat given off will be quickly dissipated without causing any rise in the temperature of the reactants.

In order to initiate combustion heat must be applied to the

mixture of fuel and oxygen so that the vigour of the interaction between them is increased until a stage is reached at which the heat given out by the now quite vigorous reaction maintains or increases the temperature and so the reaction is sustained without any further need for the applied heat.

When this stage is reached *ignition* is said to have occurred. In fact, a chain reaction has been started in which more heat is given out than is needed to sustain the reaction and the combustion grows in intensity or in range.

1.2 Ignition

It is a matter of common observation that flammable vapours and gases are very easily ignited when mixed with air or oxygen. In many cases all that is required is a spark or small flame, in other cases ignition is not so easy, a more general rise in temperature is needed, before the vapour/air mixture will ignite.

The lowest temperature at which this ignition occurs is called the *flash-point* and this in turn will depend on the *flammable limits* for any particular vapour/air mixture.

When a vapour/air mixture, or gas/air mixture is formed, ignition will only occur if the proportion of gas or vapour to air is within certain limits. If there is too much air and too little of the gas or vapour the mixture will not ignite and also if there is too much gas or vapour and too little air it will not ignite.

Thus there is an *upper* and a *lower* limit of flammability for gas/air mixtures and these differ markedly for various gases. (A list of a few of these gases showing the appropriate limits is given in Table 2.)

It follows that the flash-point is the temperature at which sufficient vapour comes off the liquid to make a vapour/air mixture–at the liquid surface–which is inside, or just above, the lower limit of flammability. It also follows that those substances which are gaseous at normal room temperature will ignite at room temperature because their flash-point will be much lower.

In general terms nearly all combustible materials burn as *vapour phase* reactions, that is to say they are reactions between two gases, one of which is usually oxygen. The combustible materials which are normally solid will, becaues of the high temperatures involved, either melt and then vapourize and burn, or decompose (by pyrolysis) and give off flammable vapours which will then burn. There are exceptions and there can be reactions between oxygen and solid surfaces which are vigorous and exothermic and so can be termed combustion. Carbon (which melts at a very high temperature–about 4000°C) is an example of the combustion of a solid and several of the well known metals also behave in this way. This combustion of a solid depends on a reaction with oxygen at the surface and so if the material is in a form in which a very large surface area, compared with the mass present, is presented to the air (or oxygen) then the resulting combustion will be the more vigorous. This means that the material must be in a very finely divided, or powder form and in these cases vigorous combustion is possible.

Ignition temperature

The exact value of the ignition temperature is a little hard to determine and indeed it is hard to define.

When a solid material, say coal or wood, is heated a chemical decomposition process starts which increases in vigour as the temperature is raised until a stage is reached at which the decomposition reaction is giving off more heat than is required to maintain a steady temperature.

At this stage the temperature of the body will increase without any further external heating being supplied, i.e. *self-heating* has started, and in a very short time obvious signs of ignition will appear, such as active smouldering or flaming.

In many cases the ignition temperature would be regarded as the temperature at which smouldering or flaming is first observed, but it is suggested by Wharry and Hirst[4] that it is more correct to regard the onset of self-heating as the true ignition temperature because at this stage smouldering or flaming must eventually follow unless an external agency starts cooling the body.

In Table 1 some approximate ignition temperatures are given based on the above definition of ignition and it is appropriate to

Table 1   Ignition temperatures of some common solid materials

Material	Ignition temperature	
	°C	°F
Coal	130	266
Hay	175	347
Newspaper	185	365
Sawdust	195–220	383–428
Jute	195	383
Cotton	230	446
Rayon	235	455
Wood	200–220	392–428
Magnesium	510	950

remind the reader that combustion of these solids (with the exception of magnesium) is all vapour phase reaction.

From the foregoing discussion it will be clear that the ease of ignition, or the 'ignitability' of a sample of a material will depend on how quickly the igniting source can raise the temperature to reach the ignition temperature of the flammable vapours given off by the material.

This is not a unique property of the material, but will depend enormously on the physical form of the material. The important feature is the ratio of surface area to mass. The higher this value for any material then the easier it will be to ignite. For instance, wood shavings with a high 'surface area/mass' ratio will ignite easily but the same material in block form, i.e. with a lower surface area/mass ratio will be difficult to ignite.

Ignitability is defined in the BS Glossary[1] as being 'the ability of a material to be ignited by a small flame, as determined in accordance with BS 476:Part 5.' This test has a very limited application and will be described later in Section 4.3 dealing with standard tests.

The ignition temperature of liquids will depend on the proportion of vapour and air present at the liquid surface. When the temperature of the liquid is such that enough vapour is given off and a combustible mixture (i.e. of the correct proportion, vapour to oxygen) can form at the liquid surface then the flash-point of the liquid is said to have been reached.

Table 2   Flash-points and boiling points of some common gases

Gas	Flash-point		Boiling point	
	°C	°F	°C	°F
Hydrogen	permanent gas			
Carbon monoxide	−195[a]	−319[a]	−190	−310
Methane	−170[a]	−274[a]	−161	−257
Ethylene	−130[a]	−202[a]	−104	−155
Ethane	−120[a]	−184[a]	−86	−123
Acetylene	−17	1.4	−84	−119
Hydrogen sulphide	−110[a]	−166[a]	−62	−80
Propylene	−110[a]	−166[a]	−47	−53
Propane	−104	−155	−42	−44
Vinyl chloride	<−22	−8	−14	7
Butadiene	<−7	<20	−4.5	24
Butane	−60	−76	−0.5	31
Ethyl chloride	−50	−58	12	54

[a]Approximate values: in general the flash-point will be below the boiling point and above the melting point. Acetylene is an exception to this rule because it sublimes at about 85°C, i.e. it passes straight from solid to gas, it has no liquid phase.

Table 3 Flash-points and boiling points of some industrially important liquids

Liquid	Flash-point		Boiling point	
	°C	°F	°C	°F
Petroleum (gasolene)[a]	−46	−51	40	104
Di-ethyl ether	−43	−45	34	93
Pentane	−40	−40	36	96
Acetaldehyde	−38	−36	21	70
Carbon-disulphide	−30	−22	46	115
Hydrocyanic acid	−18	−1	26	79
Naphtha[a]	−18	−1	70	158
Acetone	−18	−1	56	133
Benzine (petroleum ether)	−18	−1	38	100
Benzene (benzole)	−11	−12	80	176
Methyl acetate	−9	16	60	140
Methyl ethyl ketone	−6	21	80	176
Ethyl acetate	−4	25	77	171
Acrylonitrile	0	32	80	176
Cellulose nitrate (a solid)	4	39	—	—
Toluene	4.5	40	110	230
Dichloroethylene	6	43	59	138
Ethyl alcohol	13	55	78	173
Octane	13	55	126	259
Methyl alcohol (methanol)	18	64	66	151
Pyridine	20	68	115	239
Room temperature				
Ethylene chloride	21	70	83	182
Xylene	23	73	139	282
Butyl acetate	23	73	126	259
Amyl acetate	25	77	148	298
Butyl alcohol	28	82	118	244
Chlorobenzene	29	84	132	269
Styrene	31	88	154	309
Paraffin (kerosene)[a]	31	88		
Turpentine (white spirit)	35	95	160	320
Amyl alcohol	38	100	138	280
Acetic acid	45	113	118	244
Isopropyltoluene	47	117	176	349
Aniline	76	169	184	363
Nitrobenzene	88	190	211	412

[a]These liquids are a mixture of hydrocarbons and the flash-point and boiling point will depend on their constitution. The values given are the *lowest* normally encountered.

Thus the flash-point is defined as the temperature at which the vapour above a liquid will ignite when exposed to a small flame. If the boiling point of the liquid is low, i.e. only a little above room temperature or lower, then it follows that in ordinary conditions the vapour will ignite immediately a flame is presented to it. In the same way permanent gases which are combustible will also ignite at room temperature provided sufficient gas is present to form a combustible mixture with air.

Table 4 Limits of flammability of some industrially important gases and vapours in air

Gas or vapour		Flammability limits (percentage by volume)	
Name	Formula	Lower limit	Upper limit
Acetaldehyde	C_2H_4O	4.0	57
Acetic acid	$C_2H_4O_2$	5.4	—
Acetone	C_3H_6O	2.5	12.8
Acetylene	C_2H_2	2.5	80
Acrylonitrile	C_3H_3N	3.0	17
Amyl acetate	$C_7H_{14}O_2$	1.1	—
Amyl alcohol	$C_5H_{12}O$	1.2	—
Benzene	C_6H_6	1.4	7.1
Benzine (petroleum ether)	C_nH_{2n+2}	1.1	4.8
Butadiene	C_4H_6	2.0	11.5
Butane	C_4H_{10}	1.8	8.4
Butyl acetate	$C_6H_{12}O_2$	1.7	15
Butyl alcohol	$C_4H_{10}O$	1.7	18
Carbon di-sulphide	CS_2	1.2	50
Carbon monoxide	CO	12.5	74
Chlorobenzene	C_6H_5Cl	1.8	9.6
Coal gas		5.3	32
Dichloro ethylene	$C_2H_2Cl_2$	9.7	12.8
Diethyl ether	$C_4H_{10}O$	1.8	36.5
Ethane	C_2H_6	3.0	12.5
Ethyl acetate	$C_4H_8O_2$	2.0	11.0
Ethyl alcohol	C_2H_6O	2.5	12.8
Ethyl chloride	C_2H_5Cl	3.0	15
Ethylene	C_2H_4	2.75	28.6
Ethylene chloride	$C_2H_4Cl_2$	6.0	16
Hydrocyanic acid	HCN	5.6	40
Hydrogen	H_2	4.0	74
Hydrogen sulphide	H_2S	4.3	46
Isopropyltoluene	$C_{10}H_{14}$	0.7	
Methane	CH_4	5.0	15.0
Methyl acetate	$C_3H_6O_2$	4.0	14.0
Methyl alcohol (methanol)	CH_4O	6.7	36.5
Methyl ethyl ketone	C_4H_8O	1.8	11.5
Naphtha		1.1	4.8
Natural gas (approx.)		5.0	15.0
Nitro benzene	$C_6H_5NO_2$	1.8	
Octane	C_8H_{18}	0.8	3.2
Paraffin (kerosene)		0.7	5.0
Pentane	C_7H_{16}	1.4	7.8
Petroleum (gasolene)		1.4	7.6
Propane	C_3H_8	2.1	9.4
Propylene	C_3H_6	2.0	11.1
Pyridine	C_5H_5N	1.8	12.4
Styrene	C_8H_8	1.1	6.1
Toluene	C_7H_8	1.3	6.7
Turpentine (white spirit)	$C_{10}H_{16}$	0.8	—
Vinyl chloride	C_2H_3Cl	4.0	21.7
Xylene	C_8H_{10}	1.1	7.0

(A *permanent gas* is defined as a gas which cannot be liquefied by lowering its temperature at atmospheric pressure.)

Tables 2 and 3 list the flash-points (and boiling points) of a number of industrially important substances and Table 4 gives the limits of flammability for the same substances.

Tables 2 and 3 are arranged in order of flash-point temperature, and from this list it will be seen that for more than 70% of the substances the flash-point is below room temperature. This means that these vapour or gases will ignite immediately a flame is applied and they must, therefore, be regarded as very flammable.

Table 4 is arranged in alphabetical order since a grading in order of flammability limits is difficult.

There are, however, two features in the list which are worthy of note. The first is that in some cases a very small quantity of vapour (about 1%) is needed to make a flammable mixture with air. The second point is that for some substances the flammability of the gas/air mixture extends over a very wide range. For instance, a hydrogen/air mixture is flammable over the range 4% to 74% (of hydrogen) and an acetylene/air mixture can ignite over the range 2.5% to 80% of acetylene.

If there is a combination of:

(a)   a low value lower limit;
(b)   a high value upper limit; and
(c)   a flash-point below room temperature;

then the gas or vapour can be regarded as very hazardous.

Note that although Tables 2, 3 and 4 contain nearly 50 substances they must not necessarily be regarded as an exhaustive list of flammable materials. Other materials are listed in Chapter 2.

Summary

Ignition is the initiation of combustion which in turn is a self-sustaining process of oxidation. Ignition takes place in the following ways:

(a) If the substance is a gas ignition can only occur when there exists a gas/air (or gas/oxygen) mixture whose composition lies within the flammable range for that substance. A small igniting source (spark or small flame) will then start combustion.

(b) If the substance is a liquid ignition can only occur when enough vapour is given off at the liquid surface (or is present in the air) so that a vapour/air mixture is formed whose properties lie within the flammable range for that substance. For some substances this will be at room temperature or below, while for others the liquid itself may need to be heated before sufficient vapour is available. The flash-point is the temperature at which the liquid gives off just enough vapour to form this flammable vapour/air mixture. For temperatures above the flash point of the substance a small igniting source will start combustion.

(c) If the substance is a solid combustion will start when either:

(i) The solid is heated so that destructive decomposition starts and flammable vapours are given off. When these vapours form a flammable vapour/air mixture combustion can be started if a small flame is applied.

Most organic materials will come in this category. The size of the igniting source needed will depend on the physical form and shape of the material. If it is in a form which has a high surface area to mass ratio then only a small igniting source is required, but if the surface area to mass ratio is low a more prolonged heating will be needed. Wood shavings or paper are examples of a *high* surface area to mass ratio and logs are an example of a *low* surface area.

or

(ii) The solid is heated in air so that surface oxidation is initiated of sufficient vigour to be a self-sustaining reaction. Carbon and most metals are examples of this type of combustion and as will be expected a large surface area is required. This means, again, that a *high* surface area to mass ratio is needed and, in general, this means that the metal has to be in the form of a finely divided powder. An intense source of heat is required in most cases to ignite solids which burn in this way.

It should be noted that these two types of burning are not alternatives. A solid which burns in the way described in (i) does not burn in the way described in (ii) and vice versa.

In this section ignition has been discussed. Once ignited a substance can burn in several different ways. It may burn slowly so that it only smoulders, or, it may burn so fast that an explosion results. This feature–the rate of combustion–will be discussed in Chapter 2.

1.3 Ignitors

In general, combustion will not start (or ignition occur) unless an external agency applies a source of heat which may need to be large or small according to circumstances. The external source of heat will either initiate a reaction in a gas/air mixture (of the right proportions) or, it will raise the temperature of a solid or a liquid so that sufficient flammable vapour is given off to ignite or, it will start a surface oxidation process between a solid and atmospheric oxygen.

Exceptions

There are a few exceptions to this. Examples can be found in which self-heating (or a small oxidation reaction) can start at room temperature and this will progress until the material is hot enough to ignite itself. Oil soaked pipe lagging and rags soaked with oil or polish can behave in this way. The important condition here is that the heat developed by the small room temperature reaction is retained within the material so that the local temperature will rise and the reaction will accordingly increase in vigour and temperatures high enough to start combustion can result.

Although these exceptions are important and do cause fires most fires are, nevertheless, caused by the direct action of applied heat arising, for the most part, from every day effects and, in general, accidentally.

Causes of fires

In the *Fire Statistics* for the United Kingdom[2,3] the causes of fires in buildings are listed and analysed. In 1974 (the latest year for which figures are available at the time of writing) there were 101,522 fires in occupied buildings and of these, 54% (or 55,141 in number) were in dwellings.

The same records show that most fires are caused by electrical equipment of some kind (including wiring faults) and a look at the trend over the last ten years shows that the number (and percentage) of fires from this cause has increased from 25% in 1964 to 32% in 1974. Table 5 sets out these figures and lists the major cause of fires in buildings.

A further breakdown of the figures shows that the largest single cause of fire is the cooking appliance and since most cooking takes place in dwellings it is reasonable to consider fires in dwellings in this connection, particularly since Table 5 shows that more than 50% of all fires in buildings occur in dwellings.

Table 6 shows the relevant figures over the last ten years and it will be seen that in 1974 35% of all fires in dwellings in the UK could be traced to cooking appliances and 24% of all the fires were due to electrical cooking appliances. The comparable figures of ten years previous (1964) were 20% of all fires in

13

Table 5   Principal sources of ignition of fires in: (a) occupied buildings and (b) dwellings

	Number of fires					
Source of ignition	1964		1969		1974	
	Number	%	Number	%	Number	%
(a) Total fires in occupied buildings	71 884	100	90 856	100	101 522	100
Electric equipment and installations	17 752	24.7	25 008	27.5	32 735	32.2
Smokers' materials	7 600	10.6	8 718	9.6	9 085	8.9
Children playing (e.g. matches)	5 312	7.4	7 920	8.7	10 137	10.0
Gas appliances and installations	4 694	6.5	6 738	7.4	8 776	8.6
Oil appliances and installations	5 174	7.2	6 058	6.7	4 554	4.5
Solid fuel appliances and installations	5 202	7.2	3 960	4.4	2 156	2.1
Chimneys and flues (spreading beyond)	5 120	7.1	3 750	4.1	2 057	2.0
Rubbish burning	2 610	3.6	2 032	2.2	1 639	1.6
LPG and other fuel appliances	2 466	3.4	4 264	4.7	4 782	4.7
Malicious or intentional	1 136	1.6	3 872	4.3	8 300	8.2
Other specified causes	6 762	9.4	7 466	8.2	6 461	6.4
Unknown	8 056	11.21	11 070	12.2	10 840	10.7
(b) Total fires in dwellings	36 922	100	45 872	100	55 141	100
Electric equipment and installations	11 418	30.9	17 132	37.4	24 659	44.7
Smokers' materials	2 910	7.9	3 372	7.3	4 619	8.4
Children playing (e.g. matches)	1 490	4.0	4 102	8.9	4 624	8.4
Gas appliances and installations	2 990	8.1	4 648	10.1	6 689	12.1
Oil appliances and installations	3 110	8.4	3 478	7.6	2 430	4.4
Solid fuel appliances and installations	3 998	10.8	3 532	7.7	1 779	3.2
Chimneys and flues	4 198	11.4	3 078	6.7	1 691	3.1
Rubbish burning	104	0.3	204	0.4	171	0.3
LPG and other fuel appliances	770	2.1	1 406	3.1	1 465	2.7
Malicious or intentional	312	0.8	964	2.1	2 140	3.9
Other specified causes	1 830	5.0	2 870	6.3	3 272	5.9
Unknown	3 792	10.3	1 086	2.4	1 602	2.9

dwellings due to cooking appliances with 11% of the fires due to electrical cooking appliances.

In general terms the *ignitors* which cause accidental fires in buildings are several and varied, the most important known causes listed in Table 5 show that the general trend of increase applies to all the causes listed, with the exception of those due to solid fuel appliances, to chimney fires, and to rubbish burning.

There is some indication, from a preliminary look at the statistics for years later than 1974 that 'malicious or intentional' (i.e. arson) and 'children with matches' have increased more rapidly as causes of fire than the others listed in Table 5 and these must now be classed as among the major causes of fires in buildings.

In buildings, other than dwellings, which of course for the most part will be places of work, electrical installations are still

Table 6   Fires in occupied buildings caused by cooking appliances

Type of cooking appliance	Number of fires					
	1964		1969		1974	
	Dwellings	Other	Dwellings	Other	Dwellings	Other
Electric	4 340	394	7 696	704	13 568	940
Gas	2 498	1 154	3 736	1 380	5 011	1 301
Other Fuels						
LPG	32	54	56	162	96	155
Solid					53	25
Other	568	462	946	624	671	458
Totals	7 438	2 064	12 434	2 870	19 399	2 879
Total number of fires	36 922	34 962	45 872	44 984	55 141	46 381
	Percentage of number of fires					
Electric	11.7	1.1	16.8	1.6	24.6	2.0
Gas	6.8	3.3	8.1	3.1	9.1	2.8
Other fuels						
LPG	0.1	0.1	0.1	0.4	0.2	0.3
Solid					0.1	0.1
Other	1.5	1.3	2.1	1.4	1.2	1.0
Totals	20.1	5.9	27.1	6.4	35.2	6.2
	13.2		16.8		21.9	

the major cause of fire and the general frequency pattern of all the causes listed in Table 5 is very similar to that which applies to fires in dwellings.

There are many fires which do not occur in buildings. In 1974, in the UK, there were 175,000 (compared with 128,000 in buildings). Of these, outdoor fires 81,000 (46%) were confined to refuse and 52,000 (29%) were confined to grassland. This leaves 43,000 fires in other locations and just over half were in road vehicles (i.e. about 12% of all outdoor fires). The records are not complete in identifying the causes of outdoor fires. For this reason and because of the wide variety of locations concerned an overall statement of the most important cause of fires out of doors cannot be made.

However, in some particular categories, for instance in motor vehicles and in outdoor machinery and equipment, electrical causes are dominant. In road vehicles 7410 of the 21,929 fires (34%) could be traced to electrical causes and in outdoor machinery 1314 of the 4806 fires (27%) had a similar cause (electricity).

The fires listed and analysed in these records[3] are those which are attended by the County Fire Brigades. Fires to which the County Fire Brigades were not called are not included in this

15

statistical analysis since there is no method available to collect and collate this information.

Thus the numbers of small fires which did not become large or were extinguished by effective first aid action are not known; information which could be very important in any serious study of fire incidence. If it were possible to say how many small fires were prevented from becoming large *and why*, then it would be possible to make a study of the circumstances which were favourable for reducing the severity of accidental fires and the effectiveness of the fire prevention measures required in buildings could be assessed. Continued study of fire incidents and fire incidence is, therefore, important and it is to be hoped that eventually some of this information which is lacking may emerge.

References

1. British Standard 4422, Glossary of terms Associated with Fire. Part 1, The phenomenon of fire; Part 2, Building materials and structures, British Standards Institution, London, 1969.
2. *United Kingdom Fire and Loss Statistics, 1973,* Building Research Establishment, Watford.
3. *United Kingdom Fire and Loss Statistics, 1974,* Home Office, HMSO, London, 1978.
4. M. Wharry and R. Hirst *Fire Technology, Chemistry and Combustion*, Institution of Fire Engineers, 1974.

2
Fire severity

2.1 General

In the glossaries the term *fire severity* is not defined but for the purpose of this chapter it will be considered as being 'the condition of a fire (in a building) which is related to the maximum temperature reached and to the duration of burning.'

When defined in this way fire severity is the potential which the fire has to destroy or damage the building, the contents, and adjacent property. For this reason it is important to understand the mechanism which controls this potential and to study the ways in which buildings can be designed to minimize any possible fire damage.

Factors controlling fire severity

Fire severity has been defined above as depending on the maximum temperature reached in the fire and on the time for which that temperature persists.

These two factors are related to the fuel available and to the rate of burning of that fuel which are, in turn, determined by the quantity and type of fuel present (i.e. the building contents) and to the kind of building which contains that fuel.

This dependence can be indicated by Figure 2 which suggests that for deciding the fire severity the details of the building are as important as the combustibles contained within it. It must be understood that the factors which control the fire behaviour and thus control fire severity, are all inextricably interrelated.

Nevertheless, it is convenient to continue the more detailed discussion under the six headings contained in the boxes on the right-hand side of Figure 2. These are as follows:

(1) nature of the fuel;
(2) amount of fuel;

(3) arrangement of fuel;
(4) size and shape of room or compartment containing the fire;
(5) area and shape of windows;
(6) thermal insulation of walls and ceiling.

It should be noted here that the first three headings relate principally to the combustible contents of the building, while the last three relate to the building design.

2.2 The combustible contents

Nature of the fuel

The combustible materials which are to be found in buildings, be they dwellings, offices, factories, stores or warehouses, or other types of occupancy, will vary greatly in nature and composition. The important feature for the present discussion is how much heat will be released on burning and how quickly this release takes place.

The second of these, how quickly the heat is released, is not an unique property of the fuel but depends, in most cases, on the other factors listed in (1) to (6) above. On the other hand, the total amount of heat released on burning depends only on the nature of the material. It is referred to as the calorific value of the material and is the total quantity of heat released for the complete combustion of a specified quantity of the substance. The calorific values for a wide variety of commonly met materials are listed in Appendix 3 at the end of Part 1.

The combustible contents of a building are referred to as the fire load of that building and in the total fire load any combustible materials used in the building fabric must be included.

Because the fire load in any building will consist of a multiplicity of different materials, present in varying quantities, it is common practice to express the fire load in terms of the 'wood equivalent' and for the purpose of this conversion the calorific value of wood is taken to be 8000 Btu lb^{-1} (445 kilogram calories per kilogram). In Appendix 3 the 'wood equivalent' is also shown, expressed in 'pounds of wood for one pound of the material' (or in kilograms per kilogram of material). Also listed at the end of Appendix 3 are some typical value for a few composite items which may be found in buildings.

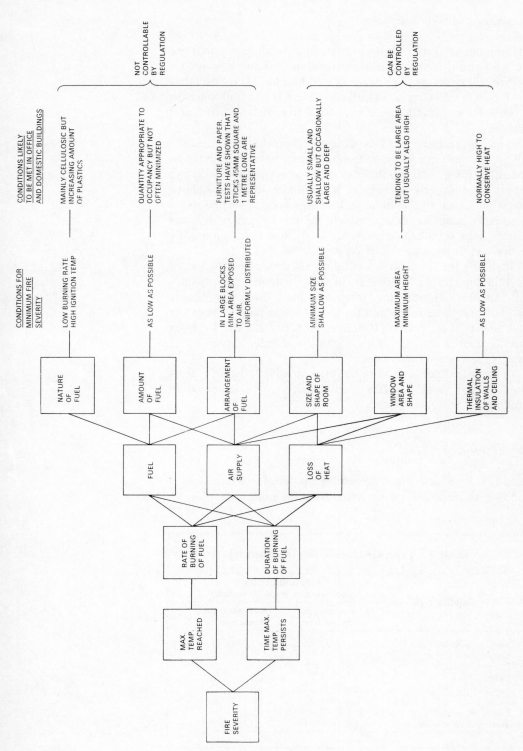

Figure 2 Factors affecting fire severity.

The amount of fuel or fire load

The amount of combustibles present in a building is called the fire load and it is an important feature in deciding how severe the fire will be if one does occur in that building. It follows that it will be a decisive factor in building design if that building is to be able to withstand the effects of a fire without structural collapse.

In any given building, it is almost certain that the fire load will vary from time to time; furniture and goods will move in and out of the building in the course of the normal everyday use of that building. For this reason, it is unlikely to be possible to assign an exact fire load to a building but, nevertheless, a reasonably accurate figure, which should for safety reasons approximate to the maximum value likely to obtain, can usually be decided by making use of Appendix 3.

Obviously the fire load in a building will depend on the size of the building, larger buildings will contain more combustibles than smaller. Hence, the total fire load does not enable comparisons to be made and for this purpose the quantity fire load density is used which is defined as being 'the fire load per unit floor area'. Again this quantity is usually expressed in terms of the wood equivalent.

As a general guide to the quantities involved, Table 7 gives some typical values of fire load density to be expected in buildings of various types.

Arrangement of the fuel

The way in which the combustible material contained in a building is disposed on or about that building can play an

Table 7   Typical values of fire load density

Building type	Fire load density (expressed as wood equivalent)	
	Pounds per square foot	Kilograms per square metre
Small residential	5	25
Institutional	5	25
Other residential	5	25
Office	5 – 10	25 – 50
Shop	up to 50	up to 250
Factory	up to 30	up to 150
Places of assembly	5 – 10	25 – 50
Storage and general	up to 100	up to 500

important part in the way in which a small fire, starting at one particular spot, will spread among the contents and so become a large fire.

If the various items which comprise the fire load are placed throughout the building so that there is a good separation between each item or groups of items, then obviously the fire spread will not be as rapid as if the items are closely packed.

If the items are tall, so that flames reach the ceiling quickly, then fire spread to other items, by reason of the rapid sideways movement of flames under a ceiling, will be accelerated. A similar effect is produced if combustible material is used to line the walls or combustible items are hung on the walls.

If combustible material is to be able to burn rapidly then it must be disposed so that as large a surface area as possible is exposed both to the air and to the igniting heat. Thus wood shavings will burn much more quickly than the same weight of wood in block or plank form. In the same way paper, when exposed to fire in single sheets, burns rapidly but stacks of paper, books on a shelf or files in cabinets, will burn much more slowly because the air cannot reach all the surface of the paper. The relevant factor here, which controls the rate of burning of a material, given an adequate supply of air, is the ratio of the surface area to the weight. A high value of this ratio means rapid combustion and a low value means slow combustion.

Yet another example of this is plastic foams; these have a very low weight, but because of their foam structure they have a high surface area, which gives a high area to weight ratio and so they burn very rapidly indeed.

However, while it is important to realize the contribution which the arrangement of combustibles will make to rapid fire spread, it must also be acknowledged that if the building is to be used adequately for its designed purpose, it may not be possible to arrange the combustible contents so as to achieve minimum fire development.

2.3 Details of the building

When a fire occurs in a building, two of the factors which control its severity are the air supply and the loss of heat. The general picture is shown in Figure 3, which shows a fire in a room or compartment; air is drawn in at low level, is entrained into the smoke and flame plume above and around the fire, and then air and smoke escape from the window at high level. Heat from the fire is lost through the open window and through the walls and ceiling of the room or compartment.

In the following discussion it must be understood that any reference to a window opening means an opening through

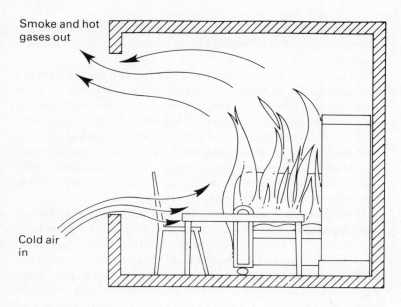

Smoke and hot
gases out

Cold air
in

Figure 3   Air flow into and
out of room on fire.

which air can reach the fire. It has to be assumed that any glazing present will fall away at an early stage of the fire. It might be argued that this does not always happen but unless there are other openings into the compartment through which air can enter the fire cannot develop until the glazing has fallen out. Any opening into a compartment, other than a window, will need to be closed by a fire resisting door or shutter and it is reasonable to assume that this must be closed. Consequently, the window is the only opening for air to reach the fire and since the discussion relates to a developing, or developed, fire the assumption must be made that the glazing has fallen away.

Size and shape of the windows

There are two kinds of fire behaviour which must be discussed here. When the window opening is small the amount of air reaching a fire will be limited, as the window opening is increased the rate of burning of the fire will increase because of the greater supply of air. This kind of fire behaviour is called a *ventilation controlled fire*.

As the window openings are increased still further, the stage is reached where the combustibles have a sufficient supply of air and any further increase will not cause a greater rate of burning. When this stage is reached the fire is said to be *fuel controlled*. That is, the rate of burning is now determined by the nature and disposition of the combustible material. Any increase in air

supply will now act to cool the fire because air will be entrained into the smoke and flame plume and will not contribute to combustion.

For the purpose of assessing the fire behaviour, as described above, it has been suggested[1] that fire load per unit window opening is the useful quantity to consider and it is shown in the same reference that, very approximately, the transition from ventilation controlled fires to fuel controlled fires takes place at a value of 160 kgm^{-2} for wood crib fires. Experiments have also shown[2,3] that furniture fires, of mainly wood framing and with traditional upholstery, are very similar in behaviour to the wood crib fires.

Experimental work[4] has also demonstrated that for ventilation controlled fires the shape of the window is important in that a factor $A\sqrt{H}$ describes the fire behaviour dependence on window opening, where A is the area of the window, and H is the height. This means that a wide squat window is better than a tall narrow window of the same area; with the former the rate of burning of the combustibles will be less than with the latter.

Size and shape of room

Under this heading the most important factor is the size of the room: the larger the area, the greater the total amount of combustible material that is available to be involved in the fire. As the room gets deeper so the fire gets hotter, because the cooling air flowing in and out of the window is unable to affect all the burning material. It follows then that for minimum fire severity the room must be as small as possible and as shallow as possible. These features may well often be quite contrary to the needs for the reasonable use of the building.

Thermal insulation of walls and ceiling

To the extent that fire severity can be related to the maximum temperature reached within the enclosure and to the speed with which that temperature is achieved, then it must be certain that a room or compartment bounded by walls and ceiling which have a low thermal conductivity will conserve the heat from the fire and so make heat available for a rapid increase of the fire temperature.

In contrast to the normal steady state, thermal insulation condition, the heating from a fire is a transient phenomenon and the depth of penetration of the heat into the walls and ceiling will be limited. The important feature is, therefore, the effect the fire will have on the inside surface layers of the room.

23

If the surface of the ceiling above the fire reaches a high temperature quickly, heat will be re-radiated from this surface back into the fire or down to adjacent combustible materials and the fire development inside the room will be significantly more rapid than if the ceiling temperature rise is slow. The former condition applies if the inside surfaces are lined with a material of low thermal conductivity and the latter condition will be the result if the ceiling and walls are of a material which both absorbs heat and conducts the heat away.

The physical properties of the material which are important in this respect are:

k the thermal conductivity
ρ the density
c the specific heat or thermal capacity

and the rate of rise of the surface temperature of a lining material, for a given heat input, is inversely proportional to the product of these three quantities, namely $k\rho c$. This product is called the thermal inertia.

The values of these quantities move, to some extent, in step. For instance, if the thermal conductivity is low, the density is also low, so that the product $k\rho c$ varies over a wider range than any of the individual values. Consequently; the rate of surface temperature rise is very sensitive to changes in their values.

Table 8 gives typical values of these properties for a few materials which might be used for lining walls and ceiling. The importance of this quantity $k\rho c$ has recently been studied by Thomas and Bullen[5] who suggest that a fire which takes 20–30 minutes to completely involve the contents of a room whose walls and ceilings are of brick and/or plaster construction would take only about one third of this time if the walls were insulated with a non-combustible lining of low thermal conductivity.

The same paper points out that this effect may depend on the combustible contents of the building and a recent experiment

Material	Thermal conductivity, k ($\mathrm{W\ m^{-1}\ K^{-1}}$)	Density, ρ ($\mathrm{kg\ m^{-3}}$)	Specific heat, c ($\mathrm{J\ kg^{-1}\ K^{-1}}$)	$k\rho c$ ($\mathrm{W\ m^{-2}\ K^{-1}})^2\ \mathrm{s}$
Brick	0.8	2600	800	1700×10^3
Chipboard	0.15	800	1250	150×10^3
Plasterboard	0.16	950	840	130×10^3
Birch plywood	0.11	700	1250	96×10^3
Fibre insulation board	0.053	240	1250	15×10^3
Expanded polystyrene	0.034	20	1500	1×10^3
Polyrurethane foam board	0.028	30	1260	1×10^3
Air	0.024	1.3	1000	0.03×10^3

Table 8   Thermal properties of some lining materials

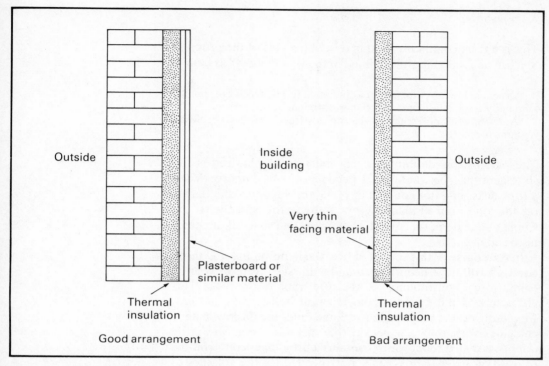

Figure 4   Sketch showing position of thermal insulation for fire safety.

using a fast developing fire (of, for instance, some polymeric materials) showed that the fire development was so rapid that the effect of the thermal properties of the walls and ceiling was not apparent.

All of the statements made above relate to non-combustible lining materials. A combustible lining which also has a low value of kpc will obviously have a very considerable effect on the rate of fire development inside a room.

The fact that the temperature rise due to a fire only penetrates a limited distance can be used to advantage in wall and ceiling construction. The wall and ceiling will almost certainly be of composite construction and for greater fire safety the thermal insulant should not be the material which forms the inside surface of the room (see Figure 4). The normal thermal insulation function of the construction will not be impaired if the insulating material is inside the sandwich, with the room lining of a material which has a high value of kpc, for instance, plasterboard.

2.4 Flashover

This is a term commonly used in describing part of the progress of a fire in a building. It is defined in the BS Glossary[6] as being:

> A stage in the development of a contained fire at which fire spreads rapidly to give large merged flames throughout the space.
> (*Note*: As a scientific term 'flashover' is applicable only to enclosed compartments).

The part of this definition which must be emphasized is the statement that the whole space becomes involved in fire. When a fire starts, one item or part of one item is ignited, the flames on this one item gradually grow and the fire spreads to the whole of this item, then to adjacent ones, and so to all the items in the room.

In the course of this spread of fire, the items on fire and those adjacent will have been heated and will have given off volatile combustible constituents as the fire rapidly spreads. This characterizes the *flashover* stage, which as its name implies, frequently occurs very suddenly. Some times the flashover stage coincides with some change in the enclosure, e.g. when the door to a sealed room which contains a fire is opened the inflow of fresh air gives the oxygen supply needed for the volatiles to ignite. Flashover in these circumstances is almost 'explosive' in nature.

On the other hand flashover can occur in rooms in which there is a sufficient air supply and the fire will grow quite

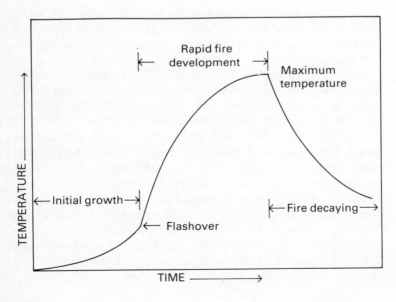

Figure 5   Diagram showing fire progress.

naturally until the whole enclosure is involved. This total involvement, even in this case, is quite sudden.

The graph of Figure 5 shows diagrammatically the stages of the progress of a fire in a building. The flashover is said to occur at the time when the temperature rise becomes rapid. Figure 5 is a very generalized picture. The actual curves are unlikely to be as smooth as drawn, but even so the stages indicated will be clearly recognizable.

The time at which flashover occurs varies enormously. The 'initial growth' period of a fire in a building can vary from less than a minute to several hours, depending on all of the six points discussed in Sections 2.2 and 2.3.

The important point about flashover is that, in general, escape from the room (enclosure, compartment) on fire is only possible in the initial growth stage, i.e. before flashover. Once flashover has occurred, the whole atmosphere in the room becomes untenable–even one breath will kill any occupant still inside.

2.5 Fire Resistance

Fire resistance is a term used to denote the extent to which a structure will resist the effects of a fire and the term has a very specific meaning as shown by the definitions given below.

The BS Glossary[6] defines it as follows:

(1) The ability of an element of building construction to withstand the effects of fire for a specified period of time without loss of its fire separating or load bearing function.

However, fires vary enormously in their severity and consequently it has been necessary to qualify[7] the above general definition:

(2) The ability of an element of building construction to satisfy for a stated period of time, some or all of the criteria specified in BS 476:Part 8[8]; namely, resistance to collapse, resistance to flame penetration, and resistance to excessive temperature on the unexposed face.

It must be stated here that a material cannot have a fire resistance, the term can only be applied to 'an element of structure'.

BS 476:Part 8, 1972 specifies a particular 'temperature-time' curve to be used in the furnace for assessing fire resistance and it also specifies that the element of structure shall be loaded and restrained in the same way as will apply when it is incorporated in its finished building and is in service. However, as is inevitable with all *standard tests*, the conditions specified in the

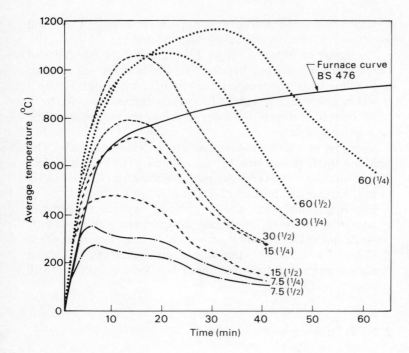

Figure 6 Temperature – time curves for fires and the furnace test (BS 476) compared. 60(½) means fire load density 60 kg/m^2 and ventilation 50% of one wall.

standard test for fire resistance cannot always reproduce the conditions likely to be met in 'real fire' situations.

In actual fires the temperature–time curve will vary considerably, so that one such curve cannot possibly be said to be representative. Figure 6 shows, for example, the measured temperature–time curves for a series of experimental fires using different fire load densities and with different window openings. On the same figure, the standard BS 476 heating curve is shown.

A further complication associated with the comparison between real fires and the furnace test is that the heat transfer from the flames to the element of structure may well be different in a furnace test than that which applies in the real fire situation. This has been discussed in detail elsewhere[9] but the important difference is that in the furnace test gas flames are used which are non-luminous; consequently, the dominant mode of heat transfer is convective until the furnace walls become red hot and start to radiate heat to the test specimen.

In a real fire, on the other hand, the flames are almost always luminous so that the radiation component of heating is important all through the fire period. The result of this is that the heat transferred to the element of structure in a fire is greater than in the furnace even if the real fire reproduces the temperature–time curve specified for the standard test. This effect is particularly marked during the early stages, for instance, during the first 20–30 minutes of the fire or furnace test.

Yet another difficulty in making the comparison is associated with loading and restraint. The standard lays down that the test specimen must be loaded in a way representative of service or design conditions. This probably means that a distributed load must be used, instead of point loading, and also the loading must not be reduced or affected by the deflection of the member during test. These conditions may well mean that 'dead weight' loading must be used making test operation difficult. However, by far the most unsatisfactory condition is that concerned with restraint. In service the element of structure will almost certainly be part of a continuous construction and consequently at its end points or edges will be heavily restrained.

This end, or edge restraint will markedly affect the load bearing potential of the structural member and in modern calculation methods the contribution of this restraint to the overall strength of the structure is given full cognizance. In the furnace test end, or edge, fixing representative of those applied in a continuous building are almost impossible to achieve and, generally, the fire resistance test is carried out with the end or edge unrestrained in an undefinable way.

It is clear, from the above, that the standard test for fire resistance cannot be expected to represent the behaviour of the structure when an actual fire occurs in the building. It is certainly not possible to say that because an element of structure has a fire resistance of, say, one hour as measured in the standard test, that the same element in a building will stay intact for one hour in a fire in that building.

Nevertheless, the standard test has a use in that it enables comparisons to be made as to the performance of different types of construction in fire conditions. Figure 7 illustrates the behaviour of steel in the furnace test.

Calculation of fire resistance

In spite of the limitations associated with the standard fire resistance test, there is an accumulation of experimental evidence which enables an estimation to be made of the fire resistance (as defined by the BS 476 test) needed in a building structure for that structure to be able to endure a burn out of the combustible contents without collapsing.

A study of all the available information, carried out by Margaret Law[10] showed that the fire resistance required in any building, as stated in the paragraph above, can be calculated using the formula:

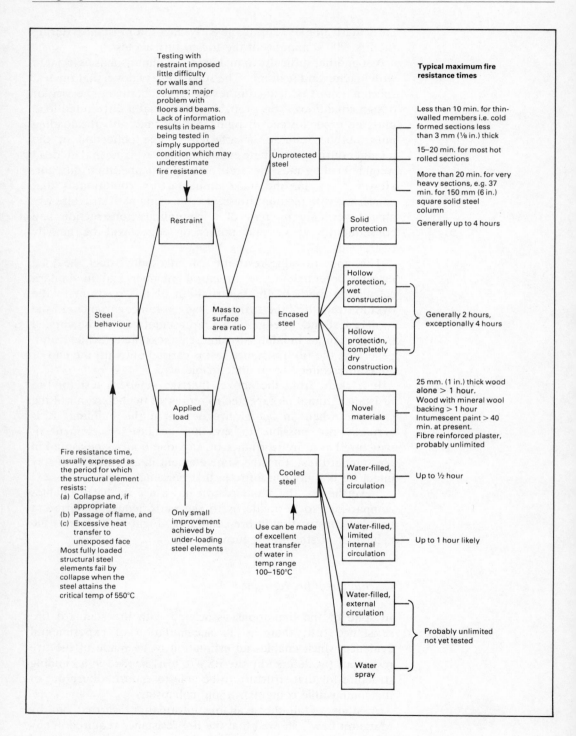

Figure 7   Behaviour of steel in furnace test.

$$t_f = \frac{L}{(A_w A_t)^{1/2}}$$

where t_f = the fire resistance period, in minutes.

L = the total fire Load, expressed as equivalent weight of wood in kg.

$A\omega$ = area of window opening, in m².

A_t = area of walls and ceiling, excluding windows, in m².

The results obtained from this formula gave very good correlation to the experimental results which extended to fire load densities as high as 150 kg m⁻² (30 lb ft⁻²) and up to values of t_f of nearly three hours.

It is possible to rewrite the above formula as:

$$t_f = \left(\frac{L}{A_f}\right) \frac{A_f}{(A_w A_t)^{1/2}}$$

where A_f is the floor area in m² and t_f is in minutes.

Thus, the fire resistance required for a building to survive a burn-out of its contents without collapse depends on the fire

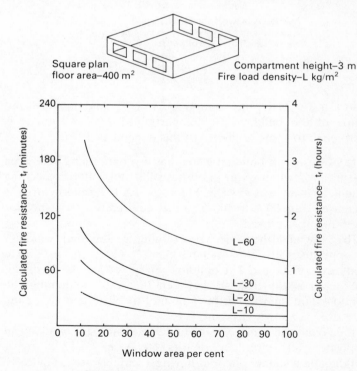

Figure 8 Variation of calculated fire resistance with window area and fire load density.

[Windows in two opposite walls and window area expressed as percentage of wall in which they are placed]

31

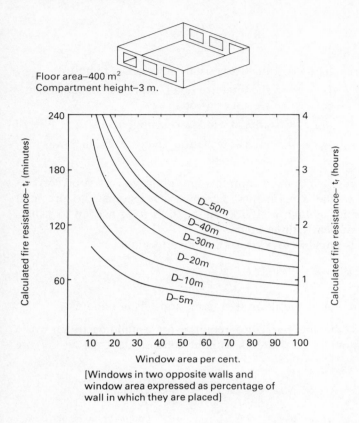

Floor area–400 m²
Compartment height–3 m.

Figure 9 Variation of
calculated fire resistance
with window area and
compartment depth.

[Windows in two opposite walls and
window area expressed as percentage of
wall in which they are placed]

load density L/A_f, the window area $A_\omega^{1/2}$, and the size and
shape of the building (or compartment) $A_f/A_T^{1/2}$ and it is
instructive to show examples of this dependence.

(a) Consider a building which has a square plan, floor area
400 m², has windows in opposite walls and a floor to ceiling
height of 3 m, as shown in Figure 8. As the window area is
increased from 25% to 100% so the required fire resistance for
the building is halved.

(b) Now take the same type of building, 3 m high, windows
in opposite walls, fire load 60 kg m^{-2} (12 lb ft^{-2}), with a
floor area of 400 m². The building will be rectangular in shape,
the depth is the distance between the walls containing the
windows and the width is the length of the walls containing the
windows, as shown in Figure 9.

(c) Again the same type of building, 3 m high, windows in
opposite walls, fire load density 60 kg m^{-2} (12 lb ft^{-2}),
building on a square plan but having a variable area. Figure 10
shows how the required fire resistance varies as the floor area is
increased.

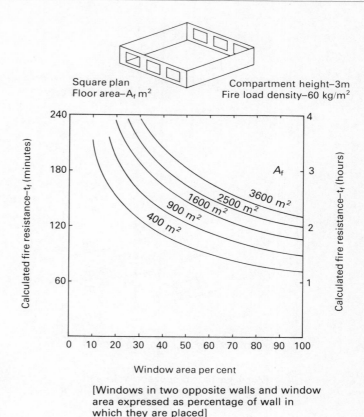

Square plan
Floor area–A_f m²

Compartment height–3m
Fire load density–60 kg/m²

Figure 10   Variation of calculated fire resistance with window area and floor area.

[Windows in two opposite walls and window area expressed as percentage of wall in which they are placed]

(d) Figure 11 uses a square plan building, windows in opposite walls, floor area 900 m², a fire load density of 60 kg m⁻² and shows how the calculated fire resistance depends on compartment height and window area.

The points raised in all these calculated examples confirm those discussed in sections 2.2 and 2.3.

It is reasonable at this point to ask how these calculations of fire resistance compare with those imposed by regulation. A full discussion on Building Regulations appears in Chapter 6 but in Figure 12 an example has been worked out which compares the calculated fire resistance with that imposed by regulation in the UK. In this calculation the same type of building has been used: square plan, variable area, floor to ceiling height 3 m, windows in two opposite walls, 50% and 25%, fire load densities 20 kg m⁻² (4 lb ft⁻²) and 30 kg m⁻² (6 lb ft⁻²).

The graph of Figure 12 shows the fire resistance period plotted against floor area. The lower solid curve is for a fire load density of 20 kg m⁻² (4 lb ft⁻²) and for a window opening of 50%. The next curve shown by heavy dashes is for

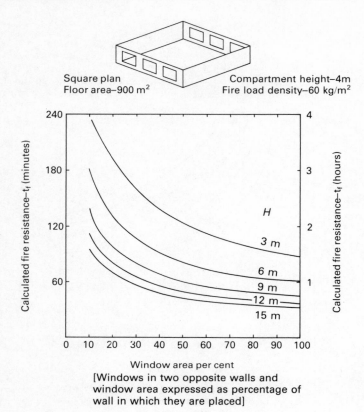

Square plan
Floor area–900 m²

Compartment height–4m
Fire load density–60 kg/m²

Figure 11 Variation of calculated fire resistance with window area and compartment height.

Window area per cent
[Windows in two opposite walls and window area expressed as percentage of wall in which they are placed]

the same fire load density, i.e. 20 kg m^{-2} (4 lb ft^{-2}), but for a window opening of 25%. The top, dotted curve, is for a higher fire load density, 30 kg m^{-2} (6 lb ft^{-2}), and for the original 50% window opening. The horizontal and vertical lines are the values imposed by Building Regulations for various heights of building.

It is clear from Figure 12 that there is no conflict between calculation and regulation bearing in mind that the latter works with a fairly broad brush.

References

1. P.H. Thomas, A.J.M. Heselden, and M. Law, Fully-developed compartment fires–two kinds of behaviour, *Fire Research Tech. Pap. No. 18*, HMSO, London, 1967.
2. E.G. Butcher, J.J. Clark, and G.K. Bedford, A fire test in which furniture was the fuel, *J. Fire Res. Org., Fire Res. Note No. 695*, 1968.

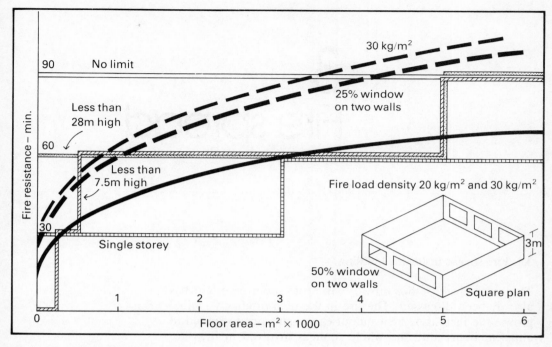

Figure 12 Comparison of calculated fire resistance – floor area curves with UK fire regulations. See text for explanations of curves.

3. C.R. Theobald, and A.J.M. Heselden, Fully-developed fires with furniture in a compartment, *J. Fire Res. Org., Fire Res. Note No. 718,* 1968.

4. Research on fires using models. P.H. Thomas, Inst. *Fire Eng Q.,* **21**(43), 197–219 (1961).

5. P.H. Thomas, and M.L. Bullen, The importance of insulation in fire growth, *Building Res. Est. Information Pap. IP 19/79,* August 1979.

6. British Standard 4422, Glossary of Terms Associated with Fire. Part 1, The phenomenon of fire, 1969.

7. British Standard 4422, Glossary of Terms Associated with Fire. Part 2, Building materials and structures, 1971.

8. British Standard 476, Fire Tests on Building Materials and Structures. Part 8, Test methods and criteria for the fire resistance of elements of building construction, 1972.

9. E.G. Butcher and M. Law. Comparison between furnace tests and experimental fires, *Paper No. 4, Proc. Symp. No. 2 on Behaviour of Structural Steel in Fire, Fire Research Station, Borehamwood, Herts, 24 January* 1967, HMSO, London.

10. M. Law, Prediction of fire resistance, *Paper No. 2, Proc. Symp. No. 5 on Fire Resistance Requirements for Buildings–A New Approach, London 28 September, 1971.*

3
Fire spread

3.1 Fire spread inside the building

The mechanism of fire growth within its room of origin has
already been discussed. The fire in the item originally ignited
grows, the increasing heat output causes this fire to spread to
adjacent items until the whole room is involved in fire, i.e.
flashover occurs.

If the room is large it is possible that the combustible contents
can be arranged in groups with a space between each group, as,
for instance, in a workshop or store and that by doing this, fire
will be prevented from spreading through the whole space so
that flashover will not result.

However, there are limits to the possibilities of preventing
fire spread by this means. If the material in each group burns
readily and rapidly or if it is possible for the flames to reach the
ceiling then the fire is almost certain to spread throughout the
whole space.

It is one of the most important principles of fire protection
that any possible fire shall be kept small and the various ways of
ensuring this are discussed below.

Compartmentation

Compartmentation is a way of keeping a fire relatively small by
dividing up a building into fire-tight cells or units by means of
fire resisting walls and floors. Regulations specify maximum
sizes for these fire-tight cells or compartments for the various
building types or occupancies.

The fire resistance required to ensure successful compartmentation can be calculated as described in Chapter 2 since it is
essential that the compartment shall survive a burn-out of its

combustible contents without the collapse of the fire resisting separating elements. The results obtained from this calculation should be compared with that laid down in the relevant Building Regulation. If the calculated value is higher than that required by regulation then it is suggested that the calculated value should be used for design purposes.

In practice the provision of real fire-tight cells is rarely possible if the building is to be able to fulfil its useful function. It will always be necessary for people to move about the building, i.e. from one compartment to another, and to allow for this, the fire resisting walls have to have doors in them.

To maintain the fire-tight cells these doors must be fire resisting and they must be closed at the critical time. This probably means that they must be self-closing. Where larger openings are required, e.g. for the movement of goods or equipment, fire resisting shutters will be necessary which must also be self-closing. If the self-closing feature of the doors or shutters is inconvenient, then 'hold open' devices may be fitted which automatically release the door, allowing it to close, when a fire alarm is set off.

The test for the fire resistance of doors and shutters forms part of the Standard Tests of BS 476. These are described in detail in Chapter 4. The standard of fire resistance required for doors and shutters will be similar to that required for the element of structure in which they are situated. An exception to this is for doors which open into protected shafts.

Vertical movement in the building will need to be by way of stairs or lifts and as part of the compartmentation of the building these will need to be enclosed in protected vertical shafts, the walls of which will need to be of the same standard of fire resistance as the rest of the building. As part of the protected escape route these spaces should not contain any combustible material and it is, therefore, suggested that if a fire breaks through a door into a stair or lift shaft (or service shaft) that fire will not spread to another floor of the building until it has in turn broken through a second door leading from the stair into the other floor. For this reason it is argued that these doors need have only half the fire resistance standard needed for the rest of the building.

Services, voids, and channels

In any building, services must be distributed around in both horizontal and vertical directions. This inevitably means that fire resisting compartment walls and floors need to be broken, usually by protected ducts in which the services are grouped together. For the main services, water, electricity, waste pipes, drainage, etc. the danger of fire spread can be minimized by fire stopping everywhere that penetration of a fire resisting member occurs and by the use of non-combustible pipes as far as possible.

Ducts associated with the distribution of ventilating air can pose problems since by their very nature the ducts will probably be common to and open into several compartments as part of their function of supplying or extracting air. Fire spread can occur by way of these ducts and to prevent this automatic fire dampers must be fitted everywhere a duct passes through a fire resisting wall or floor and, in addition, recirculating systems must be arranged to automatically exhaust to open air if any smoke is detected in the duct network.

However, the dangers associated with service distribution can usually be identified and appropriate protective measures arranged but there are other voids and channels which can occur in buildings which can enable fires to spread disastrously and which are sometimes not recognized.

Figure 13 (a) Sketch of New York Plaza external wall construction;

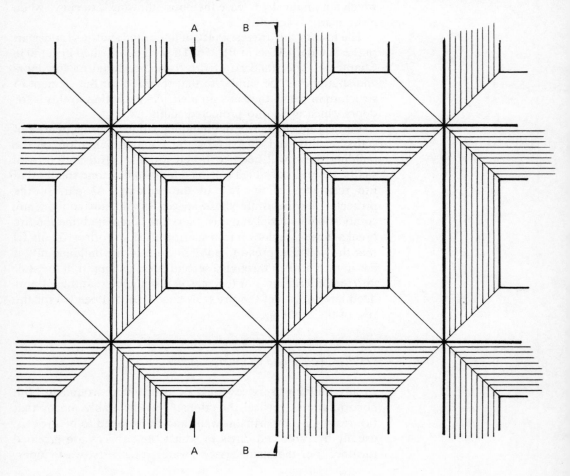

Channels can be formed between structural walls and decorative external cladding which could give a fire path from the bottom to the top of a building, these vertical spaces can communicate with horizontal voids, perhaps between a structural ceiling and a decorative false ceiling, to give further freedom for fire spread particularly if either of these spaces (i.e. vertical or horizontal) contain any combustibles. The presence of these interconnecting spaces may not always be realized and the building plans should be scrutinized carefully to ensure that such spaces, if they occur, are sealed off at sensible intervals.

There are plenty of examples of small fires becoming large because the presence of unknown spaces provided paths for rapid fire spread. Perhaps the most striking example is the fire which occurred in New York Plaza.[1]

This building of 54 floors had an external wall constructed in such a way that a lattice work of interconnecting horizontal and

Figure 13 (b) Sections of external wall construction.

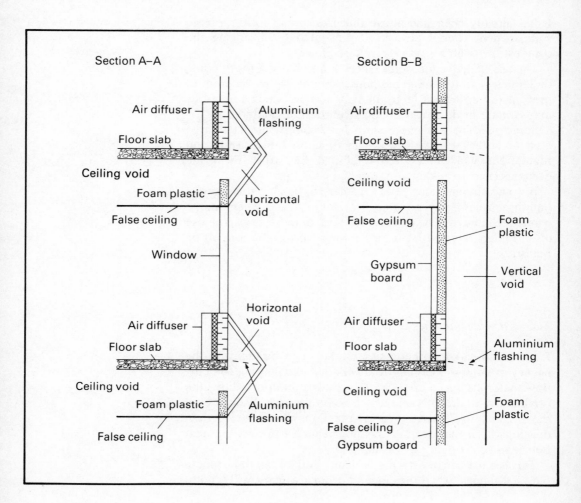

vertical channels was formed between the decorative external units and the structural wall. These spaces were continuous from bottom to top and across the whole width of the building. In addition, they communicated with horizontal ducts above false ceilings on every floors. In some of these sheets expanded polystyrene was disposed as thermal insulation. The dangers associated with this form of construction were apparently not appreciated, but it enabled a small fire which started in a ventilation duct unit to spread with alarming rapidity to involve a large part of this huge building causing extensive damage and fatalities.

The sketch in Figure 13 illustrates the construction described.

Active measures

It has already been said above that fire spread within a large compartment cannot always be prevented by arranging the combustible contents into discrete sections.

The use of active measures, such as sprinklers, CO_2 flooding or similar extinguishing methods, should be considered to prevent fire spread in large undivided areas which contain or may contain in the future, readily combustible material.

Some buildings must necessarily have compartments of large area in order to serve the design function satisfactorily and regulations will allow these areas to be larger for some occupancies if sprinklers are installed.

In some circumstances it is necessary to be able to assume a limiting size for any possible fire, for instance when smoke control schemes are being designed and, in these cases, the use of sprinklers is essential in order for such assumptions to be realistic.

Flames outside buildings

Fire can spread to other parts of the same building by the agency of flames emerging from windows and igniting combustible materials which are close to windows on floors above the original fire floor. This spread can be progressive. Flames from the original fire start a fire on the floor above which then develops until flames from this floor cause a fire on the next floor and so on right up the building.

This is a feature of extreme difficulty and it is an unfortunate fact that flames, when they emerge from a window will tend to

Figure 14   Fire in a large building in which fire spread by flames moving up the building face.

hug the face of the building and, in some circumstances, actually be sucked into open windows.

Examples of fire spreading by this means are all too common and Figure 14 shows one such example of a building totally involved in which fire spread was by the agency of flames outside the windows.

The behaviour of flames emerging from windows has been studied[2,3] and the interesting and important results have shown that the flame shape depends to a great extent on both the geometry of the building in which the window is situated and on the shape of the window.

41

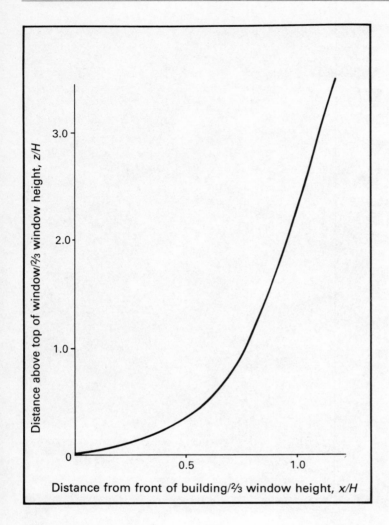

Figure 15 Shape of flame trajectory when there is no wall above the window.

The curve in Figure 15 shows the shape of the trajectory of flames emerging from a window above which there is no wall or building and it will be seen that the flames move upward at about the same distance from the front face of the building below as the window height. *For this position of window, the flame trajectory is independent of window width*, i.e. it only depends on window height.

This last statement contrasts with the situation when there is a vertical wall above the window from which the flames are emerging, which is the more important case for the present discussion.

The curves in Figure 16 show the shape of the flame trajectory for three shapes of window and from this it will be

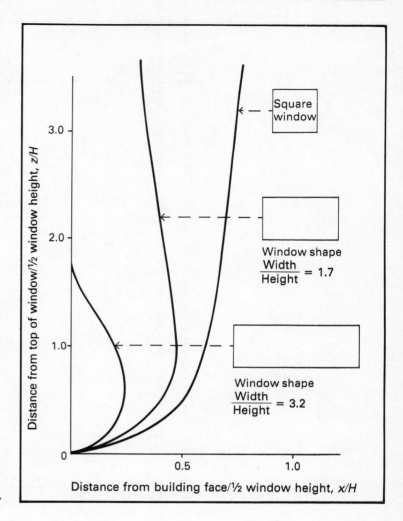

Figure 16 Shape of flame trajectory out of window when there is a wall or building above the window.

seen that the width of the window is as important in controlling the distance of the flames from the face of the building as is the window height. In none of the examples shown are the flames more than half the window height distant from the face of the building and for the broad window the flames actually return to the building face at a distance from the top edge of the window of just over ¾ of the window height.

The picture of the hazard associated with these flames would not be complete without some estimate of the temperature of the hot gases which constitute these plumes of flames and the investigations[2] to which reference has already been made make such estimates possible.

In Figures 17 and 18 two window heights have been taken as

43

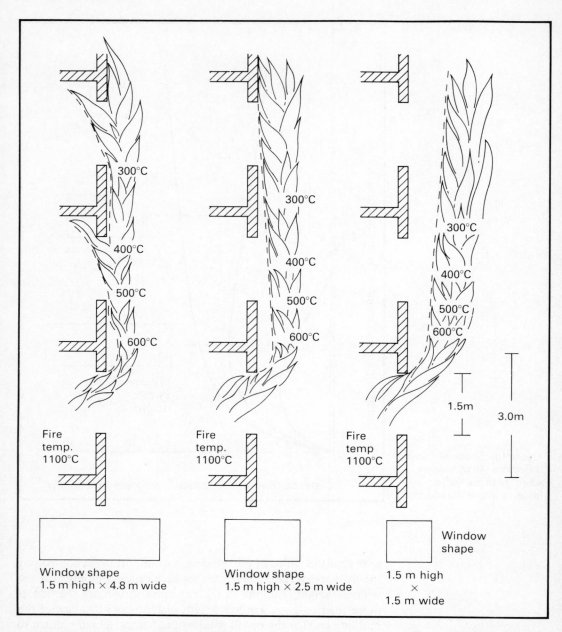

Figure 17 Flame profile and temperatures for windows 1.5 m high and different widths.

reasonably typical conditions likely to be found in modern buildings and the flame shapes and temperatures have been calculated for three window widths with each window height.

In Figure 17 the windows are 1.5 m high, the rooms in the building have been taken to be 3 m from floor to ceiling, and a fire temperature of 1100 °C has been assumed. Values are given for three window shapes, a square window and two rectangular ones.

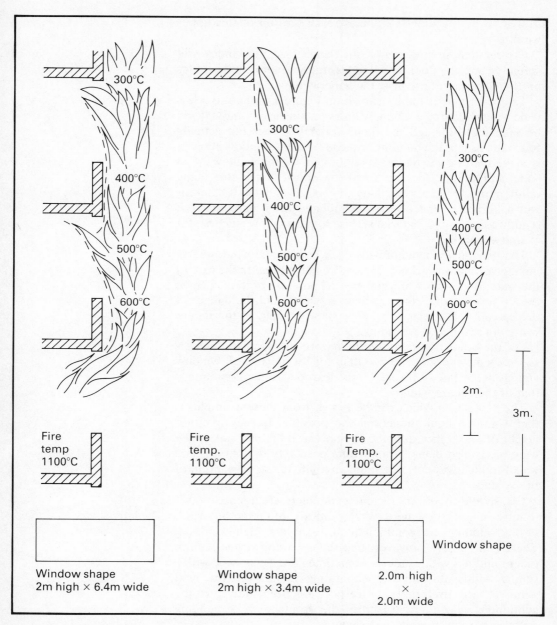

Figure 18 Flame profile
and temperatures for
windows 2 m high and
different widths.

The worst case shown is for the broadest window, 4.8 m wide
× 1.5 m high, and for this window shape it will be seen that the
flames out of the window have turned back to touch the face of
the building just below the sill of the window above and they
will then go in through the window opening and spread further
into the room when they reach the ceiling of this room.

At the sill of this window, i.e. at the point at which the flames
touch the building face, the flame temperature is 500 °C falling

45

to 400 °C by the time the flames reach the top of this upper window.

Clearly then, in this example the flames from the window will spread fire to the floor above unless there are no combustibles on this floor anywhere near the window opening.

The other two examples shown on Figure 17 relate to a less wide window and to a square window and in each of these it will be seen that although the flame trajectory does not actually touch the face of the building at the level of the window above it is, nevertheless, very close: about 0.25 m for the window 2.5 m wide and 0.5 m for the square window. Since the flame temperature at this level is between 500 °C and 400 °C there is still a hazard to the floor from radiated heat, particularly if readily combustible material is close to the window, such as, for example, curtains.

The diagrams shown in Figure 18, which are for windows 2 m high, give values which are even more dangerous. In the case of the wide window (6.4 m wide) the temperature of the flames at the sill level of the window above is 600 °C and the danger of fire spread is acute since for this shape of window the flames will go in through the window.

For the other two windows the hazard from radiated heat is still present, and more severe than for the 1.5 m high window and, as in the case of Figure 17, the least dangerous condition is that of the square window.

The conclusion which can be drawn from these examples is that windows should be as small as possible. Increasing either height or width increases the fire spread by flames out of the window. It also demonstrates quite positively that an upstand wall 1 m high will not contribute anything to the prevention of fire spread.

Clearly the conditions recommended here are not acceptable to most building designers. Wide windows, often the full width of the building are common features as are high windows. There is no doubt, however, that the conditions to be seen in older buildings with windows, sometimes 1 or 1.5 m wide with a similar width of solid wall separating them from the next window, are preferable in respect of fire safety, to the continuous glazing right across the frontage of a building sometimes seen in modern designs.

The examples given above relate to a fire temperature of 1100 °C which is the temperature assumed for the calculations of radiation dangers in building separation (which is considered in the next section). However, the dangers are present, albeit slightly less, when lower fire temperatures are assumed and Table 9 gives values for flame temperatures for lower fire temperatures for the two examples chosen in the above diagrams.

46

Table 9   Flame temperatures for three fire temperatures calculated for various window sizes and shapes

1 Window details	2 Flame temperature (°C)	Values of Z, the distance in mm along the flame profile, for flame temperatures indicated in Column 2		
		Fire temp., 900°C	Fire temp., 1000°C	Fire temp., 1100°C
1.5 m high 1.5 m wide	600 500 400 300	682 1281 2022 3040	886 1532 2238 3351	1146 1698 2471 3618
1.5 m high 2.55 m wide	600 500 400 300	616 1279 2216 3526	835 1607 2575 3877	1014 1872 2809 4213
1.5 m high 4.8 m wide	600 500 400 300	230 1167 2558 4218	621 1499 2879 4603	963 1970 3189 5031
2 m high 2 m wide	600 500 400 300	909 1707 2697 4053	1181 2043 2984 4469	1528 2266 3295 4868
2 m high 3.4 m wide	600 500 400 300	822 1706 2954 4702	1113 2148 2433 5184	1352 2497 3745 5618
2 m high 6.4 m wide	600 500 400 300	307 1556 3411 5623	828 1998 3839 6136	1284 2626 4253 6708

3.2 Fire spread between buildings

Fire can spread from one building to another in three ways, which may operate singly or in combination:

(a) By direct contact between flames from the burning building with combustible material on, or in, the exposed building that is by convected heat.

(b) By flying brands originating from the burning building landing on combustible surfaces of the exposed building.

(c) By heat radiated from the fire in the burning building falling on combustibles in, or on, the exposed building.

Each of these three processes is considered below.

Fire spread by convection

The transfer of heat by convection by way of the hot gases and

47

flames emerging from the burning building is relatively limited in range.

Flames and hot gases will escape from a burning building by way of the windows, or out of the collapsed roof. Those out of the roof will go straight up, unless deflected by wind, but even so, they are unlikely to impinge directly on to adjacent buildings. Flames out of the windows will spread sideways as well as upwards but the extent of this sideways spread is limited. The curves given in Figures 15 and 16 show that the sideways spread of flames emerging from a window is rather less than the height of the window.

It is clear then that fire spread by the direct impingement of flames or hot gases from a burning building can only occur when buildings are separated by a metre or two and then only if combustible material is present at, or on, the face of the exposed building.

Fire spread by flying brands

It is a matter of common observation that under the influence of the strong air movement above a fire red hot or burning pieces of material may fly off from the burning building. However, by themselves, these flying brands do not constitute a very great danger of fire spread. If they can be carried upwards by the air currents then they must be of fairly small mass, which in turn means that they can only contain a small amount of heat which is rarely sufficient to ignite other material. This is fortunate because flying brands can be carried over quite large distances from the original fire.

Nevertheless it is not possible to discount the dangers of flying brands completely. When there is also a considerable transfer of heat by radiation then the flying brand can become the pilot source of ignition and so cause combustion of the exposed material earlier than if the radiation only was present.

Fire spread by radiated heat

The danger of fire spread due to radiated heat from a burning building is severe and the danger can extend for a considerable distance, particularly when, as indicated above, the radiated heat combined with the flying brand.

In order to consider this danger, a knowledge is required of two major factors, which are:

(a) The levels of radiation which will ignite materials both on the outside of an exposed building and inside rooms due to radiation entering through a window.

(b) The level of radiation to be expected from a fire in a building.

Radiation levels for ignition

Experimental work carried out in the UK[4-7] and elsewhere[8,9] has provided a considerable amount of information about these points, particularly with regard to the ignition of wood.

Wood or wood based materials are probably the most commonly found combustible materials on the outside of buildings and the behaviour of these, when exposed to heat radiation, is representative of a large variety of building materials.

If wood is exposed to a high level of heat radiation, it will ignite spontaneously; the incident intensity of radiation required to cause this in the open is 0.8 cal cm^{-1} s^{-1} (177 Btu ft^{-2} min^{-1} or 33.5 kW m^{-2}). However, if there is a source of pilot ignition present, as for example might be provided by a flying brand, then combustion can start at a much lower intensity. For this case a radiation level of 0.3 cal cm^{-2} s^{-1} (66 Btu ft^{-2} min^{-1} or 12.6 kW m^{-2}) has been found to be the limiting value.

The above values are for open air conditions, but when radiation enters the window of a room and falls on combustible materials inside the level which will cause spontaneous combustion is lower than the 0.8 cal cm^{-2} s^{-1} quoted above. The precise value is complicated by such factors as the absorption of the window glass and the size of the opening but, assuming the worst condition, a room with one whole side occupied by window and the glazing destroyed by the heat very early in the fire, then spontaneous combustion of a piece of furniture near the window inside the room could occur after 20 minutes exposure to a radiation intensity of 0.3 cal cm^{-2} s^{-1}.

The ignition of the wall linings of the room will occur at a higher level of radiation and so the above values are the most critical. Bearing in mind that in 20 minutes the Fire Brigade would almost certainly be in attendance, it seems reasonable to say that building design and spacing must be such that the radiation likely to fall on an exposed building should not exceed 0.3 cal cm^{-2} s^{-1}.

The values given above for the important radiation levels are listed in Table 10 which compare them with some sensation levels so that an appreciation of their magnitude can be obtained.

Level of radiation from a fire in a building

The radiation emitted by a hot body varies with the fourth

power of the absolute temperature, so, for example, increasing the temperature from 700 °C to 900 °C nearly doubles the intensity of radiation and increasing from 900 °C to 1100 °C doubles it yet again.

Fires in buildings have temperatures which are within this range. Small fires with low fire loads may have temperatures which are about 800–900 °C but generally the temperature is 1000 °C or above, while 1200 °C is the highest value likely to be obtained from freely burning fuel. Increasing the fire load above a certain size does not increase the rate of burning (i.e. the fire severity) since access for air through the fuel bed will control this but it does increase the duration of the fire.

Some confirmation of these temperatures can be had from normal observation. Bodies at 700 °C look dark red, at 900 °C cherry red, at 1100 °C yellow, and above 1400 °C, white hot. Most building fires will appear to be in the range orange to yellow, implying a fire temperature of 1000–1100 °C and, indeed it has been found that the level of radiation intensity from building fires tends to the limiting value of 4.0 cal cm^{-2} s^{-1} (885 Btu ft^{-2} min^{-1} or 168 kW m^{-2}), i.e. that corresponding to a radiating body of about 1100 °C and this is taken as the normal standard for devising rules for building design and separation.

However, it is recognized that for low fire loads the temperature reached will only be of the order of 800–900 °C and for this temperature the radiation intensity will only be 2 cal cm^{-2} s^{-1} (442 Btu ft^{-2} min^{-1} or 84 kW m^{-2}). Such fire loads would be those below about 25 kg m^{-2} (5 lb ft^{-2}) and for those occupancies to which this would apply the lower level of radiation intensity is taken as appropriate. Table 7 (page 20) lists the occupancies taken from Building Regulations for England

Table 10 Comparison of various radiation intensities

Details	Radiation intensity in various units		
	cal cm^{-2} s^{-1}	Btu ft^{-2} min^{-1}	kW m^{-2}
At the fire	4.0	885	168
Spontaneous ignition of wood in the open	0.8	177	33.5
Ignition of wood with pilot flame present	0.3	66	12.6
Unbearable pain after one second exposure	0.5	110	20.9
Unbearable pain after three second exposure	0.3	66	12.6
Highest level which does not cause pain	0.025	5.5	1.05

and Wales and shows which of these will have the lower fire loads.

Reducing the risk of fire spread between buildings

General

From the discussion given above it is clear that the biggest danger of fire spread between buildings lies with the radiated heat and from the figures given it is equally clear that unless positive steps are taken to prevent it, there is a real possibility of the uncontrolled spread of fire through built up areas by this method of heat transfer.

The possible ways of preventing such fire spread are:

(a) to limit or reduce the intensity of the radiation;
(b) to limit or reduce the radiating area;
(c) to ensure that the distance between buildings is adequate to prevent fire spread.

The figures and values already quoted indicate quite positively that as far as fires in buildings are concerned nothing can be done to limit the intensity of the radiating source and in the following discussion it is assumed that this will be as stated in the previous section on fire spread by radiated heat.

Reducing the radiating area

Since fires in buildings are being considered, the radiating area will, in general, be the window in the external wall.

In this context the external wall will be thought of as having a given fire resistance, which will enable it to survive a burn out, and any part of it which has a fire resistance below the specified value must be considered to be a window or opening. Also, any part of the wall which has a combustible outside cladding must also be considered to be a window/source of radiation.

Starting then with an external wall which is fully fire resisting and imperforate, it is considered that this will completely contain any fire inside the building and since there are no openings, there will be no heat radiation hazard to neighbouring property.

However, buildings which can be built in this way are not very common and in most cases the need for windows will arise. Immediately a window opening has been made, the danger of radiation affecting adjoining buildings will arise and, obviously, the larger and more numerous the windows, the greater the hazard. Therefore, limiting the size and number of windows in the external wall is one way of controlling the danger of fire spread.

It has already been mentioned that, in this respect, the wood 'window' has a broad sense and in the relevant Building Regulations the term 'unprotected area' is used and is defined as follows:

> In relation to an external wall or side of a building the term 'unprotected area means: (a) a window, door, or other opening; (b) any part of the external wall which has fire resistance less than that specified for that wall; and (c) any part of the external wall which has combustible material more than 1 mm thick attached or applied to its external face, whether for cladding or any other purpose.

It will be normally assumed that the fire will spread quickly throughout the whole building so that all the window areas have to be treated as fully radiating parts of the building. This assumption has to be made if the building is not divided up in any way by fire resisting walls or floors and, of course, it represents the worst possible case.

In large buildings, where a fire will take some time to spread, it is unlikely that all the openings will simultaneously radiate the maximum intensity but in small buildings it is quite possible. So the assumption that all openings will radiate at once errs on the side of safety for larger buildings. In addition, some internal partitions, in spite of not being classified as fire resistant, do resist fire spread in the early stages and this factor will also add to the margin of safety.

However, if the building is divided into compartments by fire resisting walls and/or floors, then it can be assumed that a fire will be confined to the compartment in which it started. It is, therefore, reasonable to say that the radiation hazard of a building is limited to the hazard of the single compartment which has the largest area of openings.

Thus compartmenting a building is another way of reducing the radiating area for any given building.

Reducing the radiation by space separation

The second way to reduce the level of radiation by an exposed building is to increase the distance between it and a possible fire. For this purpose it is necessary to know the laws which relate radiation intensity and separation distance.

If a point source is emitting radiation then the intensity of the radiation at any other point is inversely proportional to the square of the distance between them, i.e. the well known inverse square law. However, if the source of radiant heat energy is not a point but an extended area (such as a window for instance) then this simple law does not hold and the intensity received at any point depends on the shape and orientation of the radiator with respect to the receiver.

The problem now becomes a geometric one and for any given shape and area of radiator a factor of proportionality can be calculated for any given position of the receiving point relative to that radiating area. This factor is denoted by the greek letter ϕ (phi) and is called the *configuration factor*.

If I_0 is the radiation intensity at the radiator (building on fire) and I_r is the radiation intensity at the receiver (adjacent building), then

$$I_r = \phi\, I_0$$

and ϕ will depend on the shape and area of the radiator, the distance between the radiator and receiver, and the relative lateral position of the two. Obviously, since I_r can never be greater than I_0, ϕ is always less than unity.

The configuration factors have a very important property, this is that they can be added or subtracted together. Thus, if a receiver collects energy from more than one radiating area then the total received is given by adding the appropriate configuration factors together to form the value for ϕ to use in the above equation.

Since in most buildings windows are rectangular in shape for the present discussion only rectangular radiators will be considered and the exposed point will be assumed to be on a vertical plane, parallel to the plane of the radiator.

The necessary calculations are difficult and beyond the scope of this book, but values of ϕ have been determined[10–12] and the additive and subtractive properties of the configuration factor enable the calculations to be modified so that all the radiating areas can be added together and the non-radiating parts subtracted from an overall simplified area called the 'enclosing rectangle'.

In considering the radiation received by the exposed building it is necessary to ensure that this never exceeds the value of 0.3 cal cm^{-2} s^{-1} and since the maximum radiation is received at a point on a line at right angles to the radiating rectangle drawn from the centre point of this reas, this is the position for the receiver assumed for all the calculations.

This gives the most hazardous condition and, in addition, the approximations which have to be made in the calculations also generally err on the side of safety and so a safety factor is built in to the tables used in assessing the space separation for buildings. For this reason it is considered that the additional hazard caused by radiation from flames out of the window can be ignored and a recent assessment of the magnitude of such an additional hazard has shown that the original calculations for space separation are valid even in these circumstances.

Position of building with respect to boundary of site

In practice, a combination of all the features discussed above is used. If the building can be placed a long way from other buildings, then there need be little restriction on the size or number of windows. However, if this distance has to be limited then the window area may need to be reduced but, if the building is compartmented then this reduction need not be so great.

When a building is being planned, the position of the potentially exposed building may not be known, i.e. it may not be built or even planned, so, for this reason, the site boundary has to be used as the reference position for the purpose of regulations.

A simple and obvious way of specifying the boundary distance is to make it half the calculated separation distance, so that if two smaller buildings, one the mirror image of the other, are then placed on opposite sides of the boundary, the distance between them is the correct separation distance. If the buildings are dissimilar, it may be that the building with smaller openings, and, hence, with a smaller boundary distance, may receive more than the agreed 0.3 cal cm^{-2} s^{-1} intensity of radiation if the other is on fire. To allow for such inequalities as these a larger fraction than half the building separation distance might seem to be appropriate for the boundary distance.

However, to ensure that in every situation no less than the correct separation would be attained there would be land wasted because in many cases excessive boundary distances would be obtained in order to cater for the fewer extreme cases. So, if the principle of placing buildings in relation to the site boundary must be accepted then some form of compromise is inevitable and the simple suggestion that the boundary distance is taken as one half of the separation distance is accepted and this idea is incorporated into the tables which are included in regulations.

3.3 Statistical information: trends in fire spread

In the fire statistics for the United Kingdom[13], published each year by the Home Office, some interesting information can be found regarding the likelihood of fire spread within and outside buildings.

There are currently about 100,000 fires occurring every year in buildings of all kinds and of these about 35% are confined to the item first ignited. A further 55% are confined to the room or compartment of origin and of the remaining 10% which break out of the room or compartment of origin 2.5% spread to other buildings.

Table 11   Fire spread inside and beyond building of origin

Occupancy	Year	Total no. fires	Confined to items first ignited		Confined to room or compartment of origin		Confined to building of origin		Spread to other buildings	
			No.	%	No.	%	No.	%	No.	%
All occupied buildings	1967	76 626	15 642	20.4	52 245	68.2	6 303	8.2	1 884	2.5
	1972	100 081	23 992	24.0	67 641	67.6	6 019	6.0	2 121	2.1
	1977	93 360	35 563	38.1	40 450	43.3	4 604	4.9	1 618	1.7
Dwellings	1967	39 266	7 581	19.3	27 667	70.5	3 751	9.5	246	0.6
	1972	52 868	15 320	29.0	34 058	64.4	3 170	6.0	309	0.6
	1977	51 026	20 858	40.9	21 581	42.3	2 739	5.4	311	0.6
Industrial buildings	1967	7 770	2 584	33.3	4 333	55.8	625	8.0	164	2.1
	1972	9 011	1 689	18.7	6 572	72.9	577	6.4	146	1.6
	1977	8 039	3 757	46.7	3 013	37.5	409	5.1	115	1.4
Distributive trades	1967	5 282	1 405	26.6	3 088	58.5	517	9.8	218	4.1
	1972	6 086	1 476	24.25	3 676	60.4	656	10.8	245	4.0
	1977	4 530	1 657	36.6	1 840	40.6	411	9.1	165	3.6

These figures are very approximate and are put down to illustrate the magnitude of the problem in general terms. The conclusion is that once a fire has broken out of the room or compartment of origin, there is a 1 in 4 chance that it will spread to another building. Thus, in the United Kingdom, there are about 2000 fires which spread out of the building of origin and involve another building.

This overall picture relates to buildings of all kinds but there is some difference in the figures if those relating to separate occupancies are studied.

Table 11 gives detailed figures of fire spread inside and outside buildings for the last ten years with separate values shown for the three occupancies: dwellings, industrial buildings, and distributive trades (i.e. including shops and wholesale warehouses). The breakdown of the overall figures for fire spread given in Table 11 shows some interesting points.

In all the categories shown, there is a slight increase in the proportion of fires which are confined to the item first ignited taken over the years 1967 to 1977. This is particularly marked for dwellings where the figures range from 19% in 1967 to 41% in 1977. This represents a nearly threefold increase in the number of fires in dwellings which are confined to the item first ignited because there is an increase of 12,000 in the number of fires in dwellings in the same period.

The other feature worthy of note concerns fires in dwellings which spread to other buildings. This percentage is constant over the years shown and stands at 0.6% of the total, compared with about 2% for industrial buildings and 4% for buildings associated with the distributive trades.

Table 12   Fire spread-compared with building age

Age of building (date of construction)	Percentage of fires which break out of room of origin (all types of buildings)	
	Single storey buildings	Multi-storey buildings
Pre-1920	15	26
1920–1949	15	24
1950–1967	11	15

At the same time, the percentage of fires in dwellings, which break out of the room or compartment of origin but which are still confined to the building of origin, is low. This must mean that the internal divisions inside a house are often substantial enough to contain the fire and that in many cases the space separation of fire resistance division between dwellings is sufficient to minimize fire spread to other buildings.

Another interesting feature can be extracted from the information contained in the Fire Statistics[14]. Table 12 shows the percentage of fires (for all types of building) which spread out of the room of origin for buildings of various ages. These figures would seem to indicate that buildings of more recent construction have a better standard of fire containment than those of earlier date. It is also worth noting that during the period 1950–67 legislation for building control was introduced which particularly affected multi-storey buildings.

References

1. W.R. Powers, Three dead, 30 injured and $10 million damage at New York office tower, *Fire,* **64** (792), 28–32 (1971).
2. S. Yokoi, Study on the prevention of fire spread caused by hot upward current, *Building Research Institute, Ministry of Construction, Report No. 34, Tokyo,* 1960.
3. T.T. Lie, *Fire and Buildings*, Applied Science Publishers, London, 1972.
4. D.L. Simms, Fire hazards of timber, *Record of 1st Annual Convention of British Wood Preserving Association, Cambridge, June 1951.*
5. D.L. Simms, Ignition of cellulosic materials by radiation, *Combustion and Flame,* **4** (4), 293–300 (1960).
6. D.L. Simms and D. Hird, On the pilot ignition of materials by radiation, *Fire Res. Note 365, J. Fire Res. Org.,* 1968.
7. R.C. Bevan and C.T. Webster, Radiation from building fires, *National Building Studies Tech. Pap. No. 5,* HMSO, London, 1950.

8. K. Kawagoe, Fire behaviour in rooms, *Japanese Ministry of Construction, Building Res. Inst. Rep. No. 2, Tokyo, Sept.* 1958.
9. M. Bergstrom, P. Johannesson, and G. Marsson, Fire research, some results of investigations, *Statens Provningaustalt Meddelande* 122, Stockholm, 1957.
10. M. Law, Heat radiation from fires and building separation, *Fire Res. Tech. Pap. No. 5,* HMSO, London, 1963.
11. J.H. McGuire, Heat transfer by radiation, *Fire Res. Spec. Report No. 2,* HMSO, London, 1953.
12. D.C. Hamilton and W.R. Morgan, Radiant interchange configuration factors, *US National Advisory Comm. Aeronautics, Tech. Note 2836, December,* 1952.
13. *United Kingdom Fire Statistics,* Home Office, HMSO, London.
14. R. Baldwin and L.G. Fardell, Statistical analysis of fire spread in buildings, *Fire Res. Note 848,* 1970.

4
Fire effect

4.1 Products of combustion

Constituents of smoke

The smoke produced at a fire will vary enormously, both from fire to fire and from time to time in the same fire, and consequently it is only possible to speak in very broad terms.

The plume of hot gases above a fire will have many constituent parts, which will generally fall into three groups:

(a) hot vapours and gases given off by the burning material;
(b) unburned decomposition and condensation matter (which may vary from light coloured to black and sooty);
(c) a quantity of air heated by the fire and entrained into the rising plume.

The combustion of the solid materials in a fire involves the heating of those materials, usually by the adjacent burning material and hot volatile combustible vapours are given off; these ignite so that above the fire there rises a column of flames and hot smoky gases, which because its density is lower than the cold surrounding air, will have a definite upward movement. As a result, the surrounding air is entrained into the rising stream and mixes with it (Figure 19). Part of this entrained air will supply the oxygen needed for the combustion of the gases evolved by the decomposing fuel and flames will be produced.

At the height of the tips of the flames the column of rising hot gases (which includes the entrained air) invariably contains much more air than is required or used for the combustion of the fuel gases but by this time the excess entrained air has been heated and well mixed with the hot smoky products of combustion and so forms a large inseparable component of the smoke.

Rate of production of smoke

Compared with the total volume of air entrained by the fire the volume of the fuel gases is relatively small and it is, therefore, possible to say that *the rate of production* of smoke by a fire is approximately the rate at which air *is entrained in (and contaminated by) the rising column of hot gases and flames.*
   This rate of air entrainment will depend on:

(a) the perimeter of the fire.
(b) the heat output of the fire;
(c) the effective height of the column of hot gases above the fire (i.e. the distance between the floor and the bottom of the layer of smoke and hot gases which form under a ceiling).

It has been shown[1] that the mass of gas entrained by a fire (and, therefore, the quantity of smoke produced) can be estimated using the following relation:

$$M = 0.096 P \rho_0 y^{3/2} \left(g \frac{T_0}{T} \right)^{1/2}$$

The meanings of the symbols used above are given in Table 13. The numerical values given in the third column of Table 13 are typical for a common fire situation when the flames in the smoke plume extend up to the layer of smoke under the ceiling and it is appropriate to use these for the approximate calculation of the rate of smoke production unless other information is available for a particular circumstance.

Table 13   Meanings of symbols and typical values of quantities used

Symbol	Meaning	Typical numerical values which may be used to calculate smoke quantity
P	perimeter of fire	as appropriate (expressed in metres)
y	distance between floor and bottom of smoke layer under ceiling	as appropriate (expressed in metres)
ρ_0	density of the ambient air	1.22 kg m^{-3} at 17° C
T_0	absolute temperature of ambient air	290 K
T	absolute temperature of flames in smoke plume	1100 K
g	acceleration due to gravity	9.81 m s^{-2}
M	rate of production of smoke	in kg s^{-1}

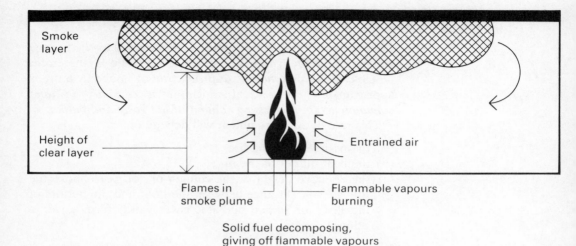

Smoke layer

Height of clear layer

Entrained air

Flames in smoke plume

Flammable vapours burning

Solid fuel decomposing, giving off flammable vapours

Figure 19   Production of smoke in a fire.

Using the numerical values listed, the expression for estimating the rate of smoke production reduces to:

$$M = 0.188Py^{3/2}$$

This reduced expression shows clearly that the rate of smoke production is directly proportional to the size of the fire (P and dependent upon the height of clear space (y) above it. The graphs of Figure 20 show the values to be expected for the rate of smoke production for values of fire size (P) and clear height above the fire (y) which might be expected if a fire occurred in a building.

The values for the size of the fire are shown as either:

(a) the perimeter of the fire (in metres); or
(b) the length of the side of a square fire (in metres).

The values for the rate of smoke production are shown as kilograms per second and the volume rate (in cubic metres per second) for smoke at a temperature of 500 °C is also indicated.

The conversion of the mass rate of production of smoke to a volume rate can be made by calculation using the following information:

(a) the density of air at 17 °C is 1.22 kg m^{-3}
(b) the density of air (as smoke) at T °C is

$$1.22\left(\frac{290}{T + 273}\right) \text{ kg m}^{-3}$$

(c) the rate of smoke production is kg s^{-1} can be changed into m^3 s^{-1} by dividing by the density appropriate to the smoke temperature.

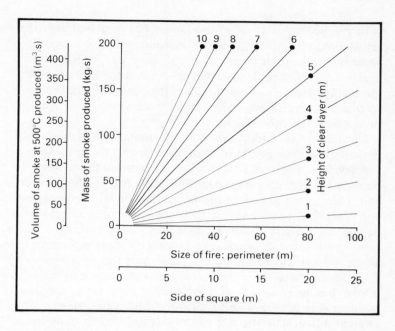

Figure 20   Smoke produced by fires.

Equivalent values for mass rate of smoke production and volume rate in various units are given for a typical range of values in Table 14.

Table 14   Conversion of mass rates of flow into volume rates of flow

Mass rate of flow		Volume rate of flow			
		m³ s⁻¹		ft³ min⁻¹	
kg s⁻¹	lb s⁻¹	at 20°C	at 500°C	at 20°	at 500°C
200	440.8	163.9	436.9	346 930	925 350
100	220.4	81.9	218.5	173 460	462 780
90	198.4	73.8	196.6	156 310	416 400
80	176.6	65.6	174.8	138 940	370 230
70	154.3	57.4	152.9	121 570	323 840
60	132.2	49.2	131.1	104 205	277 670
50	110.2	41.0	109.2	86 838	231 290
40	88.2	32.8	87.4	69 470	185 110
30	66.1	24.6	65.4	52 103	138 517
20	44.1	16.4	43.7	34 735	92 557
10	22.0	8.2	21.8	17 346	46 278
9	19.8	7.4	19.7	15 631	41 640
8	17.7	6.6	17.5	13 894	37 023
7	15.4	5.7	15.3	12 157	32 384
6	13.2	4.9	13.1	10 420	27 767
5	11.0	4.1	10.9	8 684	23 128
4	8.8	3.3	8.7	6 947	18 511
3	6.6	2.5	6.5	5 210	13 852
2	4.4	1.6	4.4	3 473	9 256
1	2.2	0.8	2.2	1 735	4 628

In the general case of a developing fire in a building, the calculation of smoke quantities becomes almost impossible because the conditions are changing in a way which cannot usually be predicted. It has been shown that the rate of smoke production depends on the size (i.e. the perimeter) of the fire, so that as a fire grows and its boundaries spread, the rate of production will also increase.

On the other hand, the rate of smoke production also depends upon the height of clear space above the fire. As the fire develops, the smoke layer collecting beneath the ceiling will become thicker, the clear space above the fire will be reduced and, therefore, the rate of smoke production will become less and less. The magnitude of these two opposing effects will depend on the circumstances prevailing in the building at the time and there will, of course, be other factors operating to affect the amount of smoke produced as a fire develops, not least among these being the increase in heat output as the size of the fire increases. It is certain that even for a specified building it is not possible to quantify these variables and any attempt to calculate the rate of smoke produced or to design a smoke control system based on a general set of conditions is not realistic. However, one of the primary principles of fire protection is to make provisions in a building which will either limit the fire size or restrict its spread.

In a large building the installation of sprinklers will usually be specified, in which case, it is possible to assume that the fire will be limited to a size which is approximately a 3 m × 3 m square. This assumption is justified by records which show that in a high proportion of fires in sprinklered premises the fire is controlled to a size approximating to the sprinkler head spacing. Consequently, in most smoke control designs sprinklers are specified as a firm requirement and the above fire size is assumed in any consideration of smoke control measures.

Quantity of smoke produced

When the assumption is made that the fire size will be limited to a 3 m × 3 m square (or its equivalent circle 3.8 m in diameter), the rate of smoke production can be calculated from the above equation or found directly from Figure 20, but Table 15 gives typical values which have been calculated on the basis that the heat output from the fire is such that the flames will extend into the layer of smoke and hot gases which will form underneath the ceiling but above the fire.

The equation and Figure 20 give the smoke quantities in kg s^{-1}. The volume occupied by these hot gases depends on their temperature; close to the fire where the temperature may be as

Table 15 Rate of production of smoke from a 3 m × 3 m fire

Height of clear layer (distance between floor and bottom of smoke layer) (m)	Rate of smoke production				
		Smoke volume at 500°C		Smoke volume at 20°C	
	kg s^{-1}	m^3 s^{-1}	(ft^3 min^{-1})	m^3 s^{-1}	(ft^3 min^{-1})
2	6	13.1	(27 710)	5.0	(10 550)
2.5	9	19.6	(41 570)	7.5	(15 826)
3	12	26.2	(55 420)	10.0	(21 180)
4	18	39.2	(83 135)	14.9	(31 653)
5	25	54.5	(115 466)	20.7	(43 962)
6	33	71.9	(152 415)	27.4	(58 030)
8	51	111.2	(235 550)	42.3	(89 680)
10	71	154.8	(327 920)	58.9	(124 850)

high as 500 °C, 1 kg of smoke will occupy about 2 m^3 but a long way from the fire, where the smoke may have cooled to only slightly above ambient temperature, 1 kg will only occupy about 0.8 m^3.

In Table 15 the mass rates of flow have been converted to volume rates of flow for these two temperature conditions. It is clear from Table 15 that the volumes of smoke produced from quite a small fire are very large, and it is important to realize how quickly a building can fill with smoke.

When the level of the smoke layer which forms underneath the ceiling in a building extends downwards and reaches head level the occupants can be considered to be in extreme danger. This situation can develop very quickly, and in Table 16 the

Table 16 Approximate times for a 3 m × 3 m fire to fill a building with smoke down to a given distance from the floor

Building height (m)	Building area (100 m^2)			Building area (1000 m^2)			Building area (10000 m^2)		
	Distance of smoke from floor (m)			Distance of smoke from floor (m)			Distance of smoke from floor (m)		
	3	2	1.5	3	2	1.5	3	2	1.5
	(Time in seconds)			(Time in minutes)			(Time in minutes)		
4	4	11	17	0.7	1.8	2.8	6.9	18.4	28
5	7	14	20	1.2	2.3	3.3	11.5	23	33
6	9	16	22	1.5	2.6	3.6	15	26.5	36
8	12	19	25	2.0	3.1	4.1	20	31	41
10	14	21	27	2.3	3.5	4.4	23	35	44
15	17	24	30	2.8	4.0	4.9	28	40	49.5

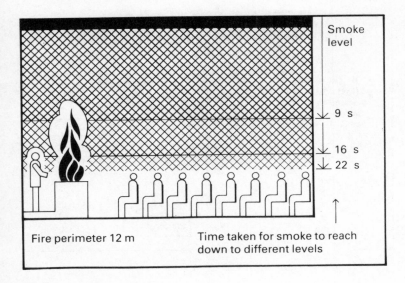

Smoke level

9 s

16 s
22 s

Fire perimeter 12 m   Time taken for smoke to reach
                             down to different levels

Figure 21   Smoke levels in a small room: height, 6 m; floor area, 100 m².

approximate times are given in which the smoke developed by a small fire (3 m × 3 m) will fill or partially fill buildings of various sizes. A glance at the figures in Table 16 shows that in all but the largest building, the time to fill a room with smoke down to shoulder level is short, very short indeed in some cases.

Consider the smallest room in the table, one whose floor area is 100 m². A room of this size and (say) 6 m high, which was set up as a small lecture room, could easily hold up to 100 people. If a fire occurred at the demonstrator's bench at the front (say, because of fractured glass apparatus causing a flammable liquid spillage, perhaps benzene, resulting in a flash fire), it would quickly spread and have a perimeter of 12 m in a very few seconds. Table 16 shows that such a fire in a lecture room of that size would fill it with smoke down to shoulder height (1.5 m) in 20 seconds. This will be before most people in the room have realized there is a fire, let alone started the escape movement. This is a startling illustration of the kind of dangerous situation which can very quickly develop because of the very large quantities of smoke which are developed by even a small fire (see Figure 21).

The calculations made for Table 16 are only approximate in that they ignore the time taken for the smoke to flow along under the ceiling until it reaches the boundary walls. This time is short; depending on the smoke temperature, the speed of the leading edge of the smoke layer may approach 1 m s^{-1}. Thus, compared with the time taken for the smoke layer to deepen it is reasonable to ignore it. Making this assumption, the time taken for a building of any size to fill with smoke may be calculated using the following relation derived by Hinkley[1]:

$$t = \frac{20A}{Pg^{1/2}} \left(\frac{1}{y^{1/2}} - \frac{1}{h^{1/2}} \right)$$

where

t	=	time taken in seconds
A	=	floor area of the building, room or compartment (m^2)
P	=	Perimeter of the fire (m)
y	=	the distance from the floor to the lower surface of the smoke layer (m)
h	=	the height of the building, room or compartment (m)
g	=	acceleration due to gravity (9.81 m s^{-2})

Quality of smoke.

The smoke produced by fires varies enormously in nature and content. It will vary in appearance from light-coloured to black and sooty, containing unburned decomposition and condensation products arising from the destructive combustion of the fuel. This variation is illustrated in the following examples. For convenience, the smoke density is expressed in terms of visibility, but the main features of this term are discussed in detail later in this section. Given a small domestic lounge, of size 1250 ft³ (35 m³), then 1 lb (0.5 kg) of wood burning would produce enough smoke to reduce the visibility to about 3 ft (1 m), i.e. it would be impossible to see a hand at the end of an outstretched arm. This is quite a small bundle of firewood!

A similar comparison can be given for commonly used building materials[2]. In Table 17 the result of burning a piece of

Table 17 Smoke produced by various building materials

Material	Thickness (mm)	Visibility in metres when sample is burnt in 34 m³ room	
		Flaming combustion of sample	Smouldering combustion of sample
Plasterboard	9.5	17	15
Fibre insulating board	10.7	18	2.7
Chipboard	12.7	2.7	1.5
Birch plywood	6.4	4.2	2.3
Hardboard	3.7	4.2	2.2
Melamine faced hardboard	3.2	4	3.3
PVC faced hardboard	5.7	3	3.8
Rigid PVC	1.6	2.8	3
Polyurethane sandwich board	13	4.7	4
Glass fibre reinforced polyester (flame retardant)	3.3	1.5	1.6

building board 220 mm × 220 mm is shown, in a room of size 34 m³, for some 20–40 minutes. Again the results are expressed in terms of visibility. These examples serve to show that the variation in smoke produced is not only due to the use of different materials, but can also depend upon how the material burns.

Some of the constituents of the smoke will be gaseous and colourless (i.e. air, carbon monoxide, carbon dioxide, etc.); other constituents will be condensed vapours finely dispersed as droplets to form an opaque cloud (ranging from water vapour to tarry condensates); and, the final type of component will be the dispersed solid matter (like soot), formed by the combustion of the fuel, which is too fine to remain as ash but which is dispersed into the energetically rising cloud of smoke.

In discussing the quality of the smoke there are two aspects to consider. These are: (1) the obscuration of light caused by the smoke and the consequent hazard of impaired visibility; and (2) the toxic nature of the constituent gases and vapours which present very real danger to life. These two aspects of the quality of smoke will be treated separately.

Smoke density:

Density is an important feature of smoke quality because it reduces visibility and so hinders the progress of a person escaping from a fire. If the person (or persons) concerned is in an unfamiliar place, reduced visibility can very quickly cause dangerous conditions.

The reduction of visibility depends on the composition and concentration of the smoke, the particle size and distribution, the nature of the illumination, and the physical and mental state of the observer. Smoke density can be measured objectively by determining the reduction in the intensity of a light beam as it passes through a smoky atmosphere. This objective measurement can then be related subjectively to the reduction in visibility. The objective measurement of smoke density is usually expressed either in terms of the *light obscuration* or the *optical density* of the smoke.

(1) *Light obscuration*: is a measure of the attenuation of a light beam when it passes through an atmosphere of smoke. If I_0 is the intensity of an incident parallel beam of light and I_x is the intensity received by an optical measuring receiver (e.g. a photocell) after having passed through a path length (of smoke) x, then obscuration S_x, expressed as a percentage, is

$$S_x = 100\left(1 - \frac{I_x}{I_0}\right)$$

(2) *Optical density*: The reduction of light as it passes through smoke will obey a logarithmic law. For instance, if in passing through 1 m of smoke the intensity of a parallel beam of light has fallen by 50% then when this same beam of light passes through a second 1 m of the same smoke its intensity will have fallen by 50% of 50%, i.e. to 25% of the incident light, and, after passing through a third 1 m it will have fallen to 50% of 25%, to 12½% of the incident light. This is known in optical work as Lambert's law of absorption. It can be expressed mathematically and is used to define the optical density (OD) of smoke as the negative logarithm (to base 10) of the fraction of light which is transmitted through smoke of path length x, or:

$$OD_x = \log_{10}\left(\frac{I_0}{I_x}\right)$$

Thus the optical density of 1.0 means that 90% of the incident light has been obscured.

Relation between 'obscuration' and 'optical density'

The two different ways of expressing the objective measurement of 'smoke density' may at times seem to be confusing but they are related and 'percentage obscuration' (S_x) can be converted into 'optical density' (OD_x) by using the relation

$$OD_x = 2 - \log_{10}(100 - S_x)$$

provided the same path length in smoke is used for the measurements of S_x and OD_x, and in this respect it should be noted that neither the light obscuration nor the optical density are absolute measurements of smoke density since they are both related to a path length of light in smoke.

It can be shown, however, that there is a direct relationship between optical density and path length in the form of the relation

$$OD_x = \frac{x}{y}OD_y$$

where x and y are different optical path lengths.

Although there is no formally agreed standard it is common practice to use a light transmission path of 1 m in making objective smoke density measurements thus the comparison between several sets of measurements is facilitated.

The direct relationship between 'optical density' and 'path length' is important in considering all aspects of smoke density and in particular when suggesting smoke dilution. For instance, if a smoke has an optical density of P for a 1 m path length and

Table 18 Corresponding values of light obscuration, optical density, and visibility

Light obscuration (for 1 metre path length), S_x (%)	Optical density (for 1 metre path length), OD_x	Visibility (m)
5	0.02	50
10	0.05	20
20	0.10	10
30	0.15	6.6
40	0.22	4.5
50	0.30	3.3
60	0.40	2.5
70	0.52	1.9
80	0.70	1.4
90	1.0	1.0
93	1.15	0.87
96	1.40	0.72
99	2.0	0.5
99.9	3.0	0.33
99.99	4.0	0.25
99.999	5.0	0.2

if that same smoke is diluted with n times its own volume of fresh air (and well mixed) the optical density per metre of the resulting diluted smoke will be P/n.

In Table 18, values are given for the optical density related to a range of values of 'percentage obscuration'. All the figures given relate to the same optical path length of 1 m.

Visibility in smoke

The subjective indication of smoke density is concerned with how far people can see through smoke, and this may well be the most important feature which decides the hazard presented by a given amount of smoke.

Visibility in smoke depends on many conditions, some of which are functions of the smoke, others, features of the environment, and others characteristics of the observer. These conditions can be placed into three groups:

(a) Smoke: colour of smoke; size of smoke particles; density of smoke; physiological effect of the smoke (i.e. its irritant nature).
(b) Environment: size and colour of object being observed; illumination of object (intensity of light and whether back or front lighting).

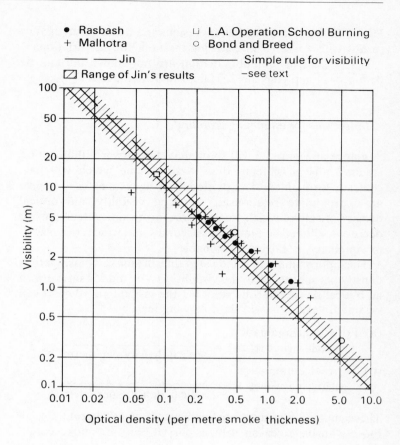

Figure 22   Comparison of visibility measurements.

(c) Observer: physical and mental state of observer; whether in the controlled conditions of a laboratory investigation or whether in the panic or near-panic state of a real fire.

Information about the last group is the most difficult to obtain and, indeed, it must be recognized that all the information generally available relates to the 'laboratory investigation'.

Such information as is available is shown in the graph of Figure 22 which compares the visibility measurements made (for forward illumination) by the various workers when these are reduced to comparable values of optical density, and in view of the variables which must exist in this kind of work the agreement is remarkably good. Both Rasbash[3] and Malhotra[4] reported variations of up to 25% in the visibility recorded by the same observer for the same conditions, but on different occasions. Jin[5] reports variations of up to 30% depending on the several factors such as intensity of illumination and smoke colour. The difference in visibility between front lighting and rear lighting of the observed object is according to Jin about 250% or 2½-fold, rear lighting giving the greater visibility. In

Figure 22 the line of dashes represents the mean value of Jin's results with a wide band showing the range of his variations.

His results for rear illumination are not shown but can be deduced by applying the 2.5 factor indicated above.

A simple rule for estimating visibility[6]

A glance at Figure 22 will show that (for forward illumination results) it is possible to draw a single line which will pass centrally through the data plotted. This line can be used to give an approximate relationship between visibility and optical density of smoke which for most fire protection discussions or decisions will be adequate in its accuracy and which, because of its simplicity, is extremely valuable.

This approximate line indicates that in smoke whose optical density per metre is 1.0, the visibility is 1 m and for smoke with an optical density per metre of 0.1 the visibility is 10 m. It can be stated very simply in the following terms:

(a) For front illumination
$$\text{visibility (in metres)} = \frac{1}{\text{optical density per metre}}$$

(b) For rear illumination
$$\text{visibility (in metres)} = \frac{2.5}{\text{optical density per metre}}$$

These simple formulae are well worth remembering for all those who have reason to consider visibility in smoke conditions.

Practical values

The foregoing discussion of the relation between optical density and visibility may seem academic if the reader has no idea of the values of optical density likely to be experienced and the following approximate values may be worth noting.

It is generally accepted that the dense undiluted smoke produced at a fire will have an optical density per metre of 10 or even greater. This, according to the simple rule stated above, will mean a visibility of some 10 cm (or 4 in) which is compatible with the remark 'unable to see a hand in front of one's face' but which would more truthfully be described as a 'nil' visibility. At the other end of the scale, it can be said that the minimum visibility acceptable on an escape route will be at least five metres (16 ft) which, again, using the simple approximate relationship, will correspond to an optical density per metre of 0.2.

These are two important levels of smoke density of which a building designer needs to be aware and, again, according to the theory outlined above, in order to convert smoke whose optical density per metre is 10 to smoke of optical density per metre 0.2, it will be necessary to mix the original dense smoke with 50 times its own volume of fresh air.

Toxicity of smoke

All smoke from fires will contain gases which are toxic and if exposure to smoke is prolonged its effect may be lethal. In some cases even short exposure can have fatal results. Carbon monoxide is always found in smoke from fires and this gas has been identified in many post-mortem examinations (up to 40%) as being present in lethal amounts. Although it is only one of many potentialy toxic constituents present in fire smoke, it is nearly always present in much greater concentrations than others and it is for this reason that most fatalities are due to (or ascribed to) its effect.

Several workers have identified the toxic components present in smoke from fires. Bunbury[7] has listed about fifty compounds given off by the destructive distillation of wood and Woolley[8] has investigated the toxic products of the combustion of plastics.

The more common compounds found in fire smoke are listed in Table 19[9] together with an indication of their source

Table 19 Toxic compounds which may be produced by the combustion of various materials

Toxic gas or vapour	Source material
Carbon dioxide, carbon monoxide	All combustible materials containing carbon
Nitrogen oxides	Celluloid, polyurethanes
Hydrogen cyanide	Wool, silk, leather, plastics containing nitrogen. Cellulosic plastics, rayon
Acrolein	Wood, paper
Sulphur dioxide	Rubber, thiokols
Halogen acids (hydrochloric acid, hydrobromic acid, hydrofluoric acid, phosgene)	Polyvinyl chloride, fire retardant plastics, fluorinated plastics
Ammonia	Melamine, nylon, urea formaldehyde, resins
Aldehydes	Phenol formaldehydes, wood, nylon, Polyester resins
Benzene	Polystyrene
Azo-bis-succino-nitrile	Foamed plastics
Antimony compounds	Some fire retardant plastics
Isocyanates	Polyurethane foams

Table 20 Concentrations of various toxic gases which will be either dangerous for short exposure, or the maximum allowable for prolonged exposure

Compound	Maximum allowable concentration for prolonged exposure (parts per million)	Concentration dangerous for short period exposure (parts per million)
Carbon dioxide	5000	100 000
Ammonia	100	4 000
Carbon monoxide	100	4 000
Benzene	25	12 000
Hydrogen sulphide	20	600
Hydrocyanic acid	10	300
Hydrochloric acid	5	1 500
Sulphur dioxide	5	500
Nitrogen dioxide	5	120
Hydrofluoric acid	3	100
Chlorine	1	50
Phosgene	1	25
Phosphorous trichloride	0.5	70
Acrolein	0.5	20
Bromine	0.1	50

materials. This table is not by any means complete but it is sufficient to show the great variety of toxic compounds which may be present in smoke.

In assessing the possible toxic effect of any substance in fire smoke concern must be for the acute poisoning action due to exposure for short periods to high concentrations of the substance. Maximum acceptable concentrations of the toxic gas for prolonged exposure are more the concern of those interested in the hazards present in industrial atmospheres.

A very approximate relationship between these two concentrations can be deduced as is shown from the figures given in Table 20 below. The values for the two cases are only approximate and the compounds are listed in order of toxicity, the least toxic at the top of the table.

It will be seen that the concentration regarded as 'dangerous for short exposure' is about twenty times the maximum allowable for prolonged exposure.

In no case is the ratio less than 1:20 and in some cases it is considerably more, which suggests that when the concentration which is dangerous for short exposure is not known taking a factor of twenty times the maximum allowable for prolonged exposure will give a result which errs on the safe side.

Table 21   Amounts of carbon monoxide and hydrogen cyanide given off by the combustion of 1 kg of various substances

Substance	Carbon monoxide			Hydrogen cyanide		
	kg	m³ at 20°C	m³ at 300°C	kg	m³ at 20°C	m³ at 300°C
Cellulose (cotton)	0.50	0.4	0.8	—	—	—
Wool	0.23	0.18	0.37	0.12	0.1	0.19
Nylon	0.44	0.35	0.7	0.11	0.09	0.18
Acrylic fibres	0.3	0.24	0.47	0.26	0.21	0.42
Polyurethane foam	0.55	0.44	0.88	0.035	0.028	0.056

The figures given in Table 20 show that very small quantities of the toxic product of combustion are required to produce lethal conditions even for short exposure. For instance, it has been stated[15] that exposure to an atmosphere containing 1% of carbon monoxide (CO) will give loss of consciousness in under 5 minutes and, could therefore, cause death in a very short time. Rasbash[10] has given values of CO concentration measured in some experimental fires and figures of up to 10% have been recorded.

In order to emphasize still more how toxic fire smoke can be and to give some idea of the quantities of toxic gas that can be produced by the combustion of various materials, the masses and volumes of two such gases (carbon monoxide and hydrogen cyanide) produced by burning 1 kg of the material are given in Table 21.[9]

The figures given in Table 21 must only be regarded as approximate since the exact quantities of the two gases produced may depend on the particular conditions which applied when the material was burnt. However, the significance of the figures given in Table 21 is that, since it is most likely that much more than 1 kg of any of the fairly common substances listed will be involved in a fire, the volumes of toxic gas produced can be many cubic metres and, so, even having regard to the large amounts of smoke and hot gases generated in a fire, *concentrations of toxic gases of the order of those listed in Table 20 can be quickly exceeded.*

Subjective nature of toxicity effects

This short section dealing with the toxicity of some of the products of combustion should not be concluded without the warning that the effects that exposure to toxic gases will have on any particular person may well depend to a considerable extent on the mental and physical condition of that person. For this reason, any statement about allowable or dangerous concentrations of toxic gases must be taken as indicating orders of magnitude rather than as precise figures. It could well be that in the mental stress conditions of an actual fire situation, toxic concentrations lower than those given above could have unfortunate if not fatal results.

4.2 Effect of heat on material properties

General

In a fire the building fabric in the space containing the fire will be subjected to severe heating and the ability of the various parts of the building structure to resist the effects of this heating and still be able to perform the required supporting or separating function is important. The building designer must be able to ensure that the building is adequate in this respect.

The behaviour of any part of the building under the effect of heating will depend on both the thermal and mechanical properties of the material(s) which are used in the structural elements and it is the purpose of this part of the chapter to examine the relative importance of these properties.

Thermal expansion

This property is important when a building element is constructed of several components since, if the expansion of the components is different then local fractures may occur because of the effect of differential thermal expansion.

This effect has been known to cause failure even under the temperature variations of the normal ambient conditions and its importance in the fire situation is much greater.

Table 22 sets out the coefficients of linear thermal expansion for a variety of materials commonly used in buildings. The precise value of the coefficient will depend on the temperature range over which the measurements were made and on the constitution of the sample tested, particularly for non-homogenous substances such as brick or concrete. Where possible values appropriate to the temperature range 100 °C to 500 °C are given in the table, but in most cases it is necessary to show a range of values. In general the coefficient of expansion increases with temperature so that the higher values shown may correspond to the higher temperature, but in many cases much

Table 22   Coefficients of linear expansion of various materials used in building construction

Material	Coefficient of linear expansion per °C $\alpha \times 10^6$
Brick	3 – 9
Cement and concrete[a]	10 – 14
Granite	6 – 9
Limestone	4 – 9
Marble	3 – 15
Masonry[b]	4 – 7
Portland stone	3
Sandstone	5 – 12
Slate	6 – 12
Woods { along grain	2.5 – 9.5
{ across grain	32 – 61
Aluminium	20 – 30
Duralumin	23 – 27
Brass	19
Steel (mild)	10 – 13
Stellite	13 – 16
Stainless steel	11 – 16
Bronze	16 – 29
Copper	18 – 20
Lead	25
Magnesium	26
Nickel	10 – 14
Zinc	27
Plastics[c]	$\alpha \times 10^5$
Epoxy	3 – 9
Cellulose acetate	8 – 16
Cellulose nitrate (celluloid)	9 – 16
Nylon	8 – 10
Melamine formaldehyde	2 – 4
Methyl methacrylate (acrylic)	9
Phenol formaldehyde (bakelite)	1.5 – 8
Polyester	1.8 – 2.5
Polyethylene (polythene)	15 – 30
Polypropylene	6 – 8
Polystyrene	6 – 8
Polytetrafluorethylene (teflon)	5.5
Polyvinylchloride (PVC)	5 – 6
Urea formaldehyde	2.2 – 3.6

[a] The thermal expandion of concrete will depend on the cement, the water content, the aggregate type and the age. In general terms concrete with gravel aggregate has a higher value for α than concrete with limestone type aggregate and those with expanded slag, expanded shale and expanded clay have even lower values of α.

[b] The values of α for masonry will also depend on the constitution of the blocks. Concrete masonry will show variations similar to those reported in the footnote above and pumice concrete masonry may show considerable shrinkage at temperatures above 300°C.

[c] The thermal properties of plastics will depend on the resin and on the proportions of filler and plasticizer used. Where trade names have been used in the table they are intended to give a commonly used name for the more exact chemical name. The same, or similar, product may well be available under other trade names.

of the variation will be due to differences in the composition of the material.

The coefficient of linear expansion, α, is the factor shown in the equation:

$$L_{T_2} = L_{T_1} [1 + \alpha (T_2 - T_1)]$$

where

L_{T_2} is the length of the component (in any units) at the temperature $T_2(°C)$, and L_{T_1} is the length of the component (in the same units) at the lower temperature $T_1(°C)$.

The information given in Table 22 is sufficient to enable an estimate to be made of any likely trouble from differential thermal expansion when two or more different materials are used in close association with one another in the structure, cladding or internal lining of a building.

There are two points about the values given in Table 22 which are worthy of comment. One is that the thermal expansion of concrete and steel are almost the same which accounts for the usefulness and success of concrete as a surrounding medium for steel whether the latter is in girder form or as reinforcing rods. The second point is that all forms and types of plastics have a much larger coefficient of thermal expansion (larger by a factor of 10 or more) than other materials found in buildings.

Thermal conductivity, thermal capacity, and thermal diffusivity

The importance of thermal conductivity and thermal capacity (or specific heat) in relation to their effect on fire severity has already been discussed in Chapter 2, but they are also important in the assessment of building behaviour when exposed to fire.

However, the two effects are to some extent in opposition. When a fire occurs in a room lined with material of low thermal conductivity the temperature reached by the fire will be high because little heat is able to escape but the heat penetration into the material structure of the building will be less because of this low conductivity and so the effect of the fire on the structure will be reduced.

In the discussion in Chapter 2 it is pointed out that the important quantity in deciding the temperature reached by the surface of the wall or ceiling lining is the thermal inertia, which is the product of the thermal conductivity, the thermal capacity (or specific heat), and the density. This quantity is usually written as $k\rho c$.

The temperature of the structural element will obviously rise faster if the material has a high thermal conductivity, i.e. more heat will flow in from a given fire condition; but also the quantity of heat required to heat up the material is also important, this is the specific heat, or thermal capacity, and in this case the material which has a low specific heat will get hotter more quickly for a given heating condition (i.e. a fire) than one with a high specific heat.

Thus, the important factor in deciding the heating up of the building structure or fabric is obtained by dividing the thermal conductivity by the 'volumetric thermal capacity' which is the product of the specific heat and density. This quantity, *k/pc*, is called the *thermal diffusivity*.

The calculation of the temperature rise in a solid when subjected to heating at its surface (i.e. the condition which obtains when a fire heats an element of the structure) is too complicated and difficult to set out here and for information on this reference should be made to a standard text on heat conduction in solids.[11] It is sufficient to realize here that the thermal diffusivity (*k/pc*) is an important factor which will give some indication of how fast the structure will heat up in the event of a fire. Values for this quantity for some materials found in buildings are set out in Table 23.

The two quantities, thermal conductivity and density, are not completely independent; in general terms it is possible to say that for many materials used in buildings *k* and ρ are almost proportional. The exact relationship between the two quantities is shown in the graph of Figure 23 from which it will be seen that for low density materials the change in *k* is much less than in ρ.

Figure 23 Relation between thermal conductivity *k* and density ρ.

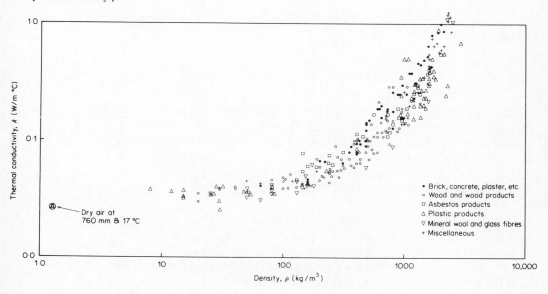

Table 23   Values of thermal properties for various building materials[a]

Material		Density, ρ (kg m^{-3})	Thermal conductivity, k (W m^{-1} K^{-1})	Specific heat, c (J kg^{-1} K^{-1})	Thermal diffusivity, $k/\rho c$ (m^2 s^{-1})
Asbestos insulating board		750	0.12	850	1.9×10^{-7}
Asbestos-cement sheet		1600	0.40	860	2.9×10^{-7}
Sprayed asbestos (light)		80	0.043	816	6.6×10^{-7}
Sprayed asbestos (dense)		240	0.075	816	3.8×10^{-7}
Asphalt		2250	1.20	1250	4.3×10^{-7}
(bitumen with mineral filler)		1600	0.43	1250	2.1×10^{-7}
Brickwork		1000	0.24	850	2.8×10^{-7}
		2600	0.86	850	3.9×10^{-7}
Concrete		800	0.23	960	3.0×10^{-7}
		2400	1.83	960	7.9×10^{-7}
Cork granules		115	0.052	2000	2.3×10^{-7}
Cork slab		145	0.042	2000	1.45×10^{-7}
Fibreboard		300	0.057	1670	1.13×10^{-7}
Glass wool (mat)		25	0.04	840	1.9×10^{-6}
Hardboard	medium	600	0.08	1250	1.06×10^{-7}
	standard	900	0.13	1250	1.15×10^{-7}
Mineral wood	felted	50	0.039	840	9.3×10^{-7}
	semi-rigid	130	0.036	840	3.3×10^{-7}
Perlite	loose granules	65	0.042	830	7.8×10^{-7}
	plaster	600	0.19	830	3.8×10^{-7}
	gypsum	1280	0.46	840	4.3×10^{-7}
Plaster	light weight	400	0.079	820	2.4×10^{-7}
	sand and cement	1570	0.53	820	4.1×10^{-7}
Plasterboard	gypsum	950	0.16	840	2.0×10^{-7}
	perlite	800	0.18	840	2.7×10^{-7}
Plastics, cellular					
Expanded polystyrene		20	0.034	1500	1.1×10^{-6}
Polyurethane foam board		30	0.028	1260	7.4×10^{-7}
Polyvinylchloride rigid foam		25	0.035	1500	9.3×10^{-7}

This relationship between k and ρ is reflected in the values of thermal diffusivity given in Table 23. For a wide range of commonly used building materials the variation in the value of $k/\rho c$ is small. It is only at the two extremes, i.e. for very good insulators (plastic foam, mineral wool, etc.) and for very good conductors (metals) that the values of this quantity are markedly different.

The significance of this is that for very good insulators the heat from the fire will not penetrate deeply into the structure and at the other extreme, metals when used in buildings will quickly be at uniform temperature throughout their mass as the heat from the fire penetrates their enclosing material.

Table 23   Continued

Material	Density, ρ (kg m^{-3})	Thermal conductivity, k (W m^{-1} K^{-1})	Specific heat, c (J kg^{-1} K^{-1})	Thermal diffusivity, $k/\rho c$ (m^2 s^{-1})
Plastics, solid				
Bakelite (phenol formaldehyde)	1300	0.17	1300	1.0×10^{-7}
Cellulose nitrate (celluloid)	1370	0.17	1500	8.3×10^{-7}
Cellulose acetate	1350	0.21	1550	1.0×10^{-7}
Nylon	1140	0.25	1670	1.3×10^{-7}
Perspex, lucite, Plexiglas, Oroglas, methyl methacrylate	1200	0.21	1465	1.2×10^{-7}
Polystyrene	1070	0.08	1340	5.6×10^{-8}
Polythene (polyethylene)	925	0.29	2220	1.4×10^{-7}
Teflon (polytetrafluoroethylene)	2200	0.25	1050	1.1×10^{-7}
Wood, across grain				
Softwood, deal	610	0.125	1250	1.6×10^{-7}
Hardwood, oak	770	0.160	1250	1.7×10^{-7}
Hardwood, teak	700	0.170	1250	1.9×10^{-7}
Wood, along grain				
Softwood, deal	610	0.215	1250	2.8×10^{-7}
Hardwood, oak	770	0.290	1250	3.0×10^{-7}
Plywood	700	0.11	1250	1.3×10^{-7}
Wood chipboard	800	0.15	1250	1.5×10^{-7}
Wood wool slab	500	0.10	1050	1.9×10^{-7}
Cast iron	7000	46	570	1.15×10^{-5}
Steel, mild	7800	41	500	1.05×10^{-5}
Stainless steel	8000	25	470	6.6×10^{-6}
Aluminium	2700	200	860	8.6×10^{-5}
Copper	8940	390	380	1.1×10^{-4}
Lead	11340	35	126	2.4×10^{-5}
Brass	8500	104	223	5.5×10^{-5}

[a] The values given in this table must be regarded as approximate only. However, they are accurate enough to give the relative magnitudes of the quantities under discussion.

U-values[12]

In considering normal thermal insulation properties of a building the term U-value is often used. This is more correctly known as thermal transmittance. It is a property of the particular piece of material used for the application being considered and it is a measure of the ability to transmit heat under steady flow conditions. It is especially useful when composite constructions are proposed in that it is possible to use it to calculate an overall thermal behaviour. However, its usefulness is mainly for the steady state condition of normal building use and it is not appropriate to the heating found in the fire situation.

Mechanical strength

Concrete

The behaviour of concrete when heated, as for instance in a fire, will depend on the aggregate used, on the moisture content, on the cement to aggregate ratio, and on the applied load.

Compressive strength. The very high compressive strength of concrete is the property which makes this material so important in building design and this property is generally exploited to its full extent. However, most concretes lose strength on heating. Up to temperatures of 200 °C only a slight reduction occurs but at temperatures of 500 °C and above all concretes deteriorate rapidly.

Precise figures concerning concrete strength at high temperatures cannot readily be given because the results obtained by various workers differ because of dependence on testing method (size of specimen, rate and method of heating and loading), on concrete age, on the quality of the cement paste, and on the condition of the particular type of aggregate used.

Table 24   Compressive strength of concrete at high temperatures[a]

| Concrete type | Compressive strength (% of initial strength) | | | | | | | |
| | 200°C | | 400°C | | 600°C | | 800°C | |
	Stressed	Unstressed	Stressed	Unstressed	Stressed	Unstressed	Stressed	Unstressed
Carbonate aggregate (limestone)	99	92	95	85	85	77	62	40
Siliceous aggregate (gravel)	100	97	87	81	56	34	—	20
Lightweight concrete (expanded clay, etc.)	98	94	96	91	86	74	48	42
Sand + gravel aggregate; cement/aggregate ratio 1 : 6	99	92	86	71	61	20	—	—
Sand + gravel aggregate; cement/aggregate ratio 1 : 45	96	89	78	64	41	10	—	—

[a]Owing to the effect of several factors (method of test, size of specimen, method of heating, method of loading, quality of aggregate, etc.) the figures in this table must only be regarded as approximate. They do, however, indicate the general pattern of the behaviour of concrete at high temperatures.

For instance Petterson[13] reports that concrete with Jura Limestone as aggregate increases in strength (by about 20%) for temperatures up to 400 °C and then shows a rapid deterioration. However, it is more generally agreed that the general pattern of the behaviour of concrete at high temperatures approximates to the figures given in Table 24.

Temperatures as high as 600 °C are rarely attained by concrete throughout its whole mass even in severe fires and for this reason concrete often maintains its integrity and strength even after being attacked by fire.

Concrete, when subjected to heat, undergoes a colour change which is irreversible so that after a fire, or a fire test, some information is readily available about the temperatures reached by various parts of a concrete structure. These colour changes are thought to be due to small quantities of ferric oxides in the aggregate which on heating becomes dehydrated or react with the lime in the cement paste. The changes occur at fairly well defined temperatures which are indicated in Table 25.

Table 25   Colour changes which take place when concrete is heated

Details of colour or other change	Temperature for change to take place (°C)
Development of pink, red or reddish brown	300
Pink or red fades, reverts to almost normal grey; some coarse aggregate may remain red; concrete becomes friable	650
Development of buff colour	1000

Observations made on concrete after exposure to heat can, by noting the above changes, give information about heat penetration into a concrete mass. Table 26 gives the results of a set of such observations made after exposure in a standard furnace test which lasted 1 hour, 2 hours, and 4 hours respectively. It is clear from the figure in Table 26 that even during a severe fire test (4 hours) the temperature at which concrete loses its strength (650 °C) has only been reached at a depth of just under 2 in (50 mm) from the heated surface. Thus the strength of the main bulk of a concrete member which is 6 in (150 mm) or more in thickness will not have been affected by a severe fire.

Table 26 Depth of heat penetration into concrete during exposure to fire tests – results obtained by noting position of characteristic colour changes

Test period (h)	Surface temperature at end of test (°C)	Distance from surface of colour change position corresponding to temperatures					
		300°C		650°C		1000°C	
		inch	mm	inch	mm	inch	mm
1	950	2.25	57	0.75	18	0	0
2	1050	2.75	79	1.0	25	0.25	6
4	1150	4.75	120	1.75	44	0.5	13

In all the above discussion the term strength is intended to mean compressive strength. The tensile strength of concrete alone is not high, even at normal temperatures, and to increase this tensile strength steel reinforcement is used.

As will be seen in the next section steel loses its strength at high temperatures. It is generally considered that the critical temperature for structural steel is 550 °C. At this temperature its tensile strength has reduced to 50% of the design strength.

In the tests whose results are reported in Table 26 a temperature of 550 °C was reached at a distance of 1 in (25 mm) from the heated surface in the 1 hour test, at 1.4 in (35 mm) in the 2 hour test and at 2.25 in (57 mm) in the 4 hour test, so that provided the concrete remains in place and provided the reinforcing steel has a concrete cover of the appropriate thickness then the reinforced concrete will retain its tensile strength for the period of time which corresponds to the thickness of cover.

In Building Regulations a greater thickness than those given above is specified in order to introduce a safety factor.

Spalling

Concrete is subject to a form of damage due to excesive heat which is known as spalling. This takes the form of the breaking off of pieces or layers of the material, sometimes with explosive violence. The photograph in Figure 24 shows a severe example of spalling and it will be seen that in this case the concrete covering to the reinforcement has spalled away leaving the latter exposed directly to any further heating.

It has been suggested that spalling is caused by one or more of the following causes:

Figure 24   Example of spalled concrete.

(a) excessive compression or restraint of the material;
(b) the formation of high pressure steam in the material;
(c) splitting of the aggregate used in the concrete mix.

Spalling by reason of (a) above can be regarded as an example of differential thermal expansion. In a fire the surface layers of the concrete are heated relatively quickly while the inner mass stays cool. If the unequal expansion in adjacent layers of the material cannot be relaxed because of restraint by, for instance, the steel reinforcement then the surface layer, which is hotter and has therefore developed the highest internal stress due to expansion, may spall off.

Spalling by cause (b), the development of high pressure steam, can be explained by suggesting that the heating of the concrete is rapid and initially moisture in the heated surface layers will migrate inwards, driven by a low steam pressure, until a stage is reached when part of the concrete has so much water in it which can no longer move quickly enough through the concrete pores to relieve the steam pressure developed. Thus this steam pressure will build up until the forces are great enough to cause lateral fracture of the concrete and a layer spalls off.

Spalling by cause (c), the splitting of the aggregate, is due to the thermal instability of the small solids, which, with the cement paste form the concrete mass. The tendency to this effect is most marked in siliceous aggregates, i.e. in flints and gravel, the carbonate aggregates, i.e. limestone, are less prone to this kind of fracture and the lightweight aggregates, i.e. foamed slag, crushed brick, expanded clay, well burnt clinker, etc. are even less likely to be subject to aggregate splitting.

Other factors are important as well as the type of aggregate. For instance, for mixes using the same aggregate, the likelihood of splitting increases with the strength and stiffness of the cement paste and also with the size of the aggregate particles. It is probable that spalling due to aggregate splitting will be most serious with strong concretes in which large size aggregate particles have been used.

The effect of spalling on the fire resisting properties of a concrete construction will vary considerably. On the one hand it may be mild with only slight surface damage which will not impair the strength or separating function of the concrete member, but on the other hand the layers which spall off may be large enough to expose the reinforcing steel rods or the structural steel in which case the fire resisting property of the whole structure will be suddenly at risk.

In order to prevent this it is common practice to surround the main steel reinforcement by a secondary reinforcement, usually composed of a wire mesh, whose purpose is to hold the concrete up to the steel reinforcement, i.e. to prevent the spalling off of the thermal insulating layer of concrete which can have a disastrous effect.

Where concrete is used as an encasement of steel beams or columns a similar arrangement of secondary reinforcement is advisable.

Brick and blockwork

Brick and blockwork constructions are for the most part used in walls which may or may not be load bearing but which will always have a separation function.

Clay will usually be the material used in the manufacture of bricks which can be solid, hollow or perforated. Blocks used for this purpose are produced under a variety of trade names but are, in the main, comprised of light weight or aerated concrete, and as with bricks, they may be solid, hollow or with specially shaped cavities.

The compressive strength of bricks and blocks at elevated temperature follows a similar pattern to that already reported for concrete. For temperatures up to 400 °C there is only a slight deterioration in compressive strength, at 500 °C the strength starts to decrease, and at 600 °C and above this decrease becomes rapid.

However, in very general terms it is possible to say that brick and blockwork constructions behave well in fire conditions possibly because the numerous joints prevent thermal stresses from building up over long distances or large areas. Solid clay bricks are better than an equivalent thickness of perforated or cavity. bricks, the improvement expected in thermal insulation due to the air cavity being insufficient to compensate for the loss of solid material.

In their manufacture, bricks are subject to high temperature and the aggregate used in blockwork is also produced using high temperatures. The manufacturing process for both will also have involved a slow cooling stage so that residual stresses which could cause brick or aggregate splitting in fire conditions will have been relaxed in the heating and cooling in their production.

Under fire conditions load bearing walls will deflect towards the fire, due to the greater expansion of the surface layers nearest the heat source (i.e. the fire) and the failure of such a wall will frequently be due to excessive distortion caused by this effect rather than by loss of compressive strength in the material.

When hollow clay or concrete blocks are used in floor construction the behaviour in fire conditions will be similar to that noted for walls. Again the floor will deflect towards the heat source and this effect is almost certain to be the cause of ultimate collapse.

Nevertheless, walls and floors, whether constructed of solid or hollow bricks or blocks, can form an effective fire resisting structure and, depending on details of their construction, can survive a severe fire.

Steel

Steel is a most important material which is used in building construction but on its own it will be quickly weakened when exposed to fire. In use, therefore, measures must be taken to protect it from the effect of heat.

There are two main functions for steel in buildings. It can be used as a steel framework composed of beams and columns to provide the main structural strength for the building or it can be used as reinforcement to provide the tensile strength for concrete constructions.

There are very many different varieties of steel and each will have its own special characteristic. For this reason it is only possible to discuss the behaviour of steel in fire conditions in broad terms.

In the context of building construction there are, in general, four types of steel to consider. Structural steel forming the building framework, i.e. beams and columns, is usually of mild steel but exceptionally a stronger alloy steel will be used.

The steel rods in concrete reinforcement will also usually be of mild steel although occasionally alloy steel is used. Steel cables and rods used to prestress concrete members will be of a strong high tensile variety and may be one of three types: (a) alloy steel which is self-hardening; (b) cold drawn steel; or (c) heat treated steel.

Under fire conditions the behaviour of these types of steel is different. As the temperature rises cold drawn and heat treated steels lose their strength more rapidly than self-hardening and mild steels. In addition on cooling self-hardening and mild steel regain practically all their original strength but cold drawn and heated treated steels lose part of their strength permanently when heated above 300–400 °C. This return to initial strength is an important feature when reinstatment or the stability of the structure is being considered.

Typical values of the ultimate strength for three types of steel are given in Table 27.

| Temperature (°C) | % of strength at room temperature (20°C) Type of steel | | |
	Mild steel	Cold drawn prestressing	High strength alloy bars
20	100	100	100
100	102	97	98
200	115	94	102
300	112	80	97
400	82	55	82
500	55	34	60
600	30	16	38
700	20	8	20

Table 27   Variation with temperature of ultimate strength for three types of steel used for concrete reinforcement

It will be seen from Table 27 that mild steel increases in strength by a little over 10% as the temperature rises to 200 °C, at about 350 °C its strength is the same as at room temperature but as the temperature rises still further the strength falls rapidly until at 550 °C it only has half this strength.

Structural designs are commonly based on 50% of the ultimate strength and so for mild steel 550 °C could be and is regarded as the critical temperature above which failure becomes likely. High strength alloy bars behave in a similar way, the strength at room temperature is maintained until about 300 °C, it then falls quite rapidly and at 550 °C it has reached about 50% of the cold strength. Again for this steel 550 °C must be regarded as the critical value.

In contrast, cold drawn prestressing steel loses its strength more rapidly. It has lost 20% of its cold strength at 300 °C and 50% at just over 400 °C, so for this type of steel 400 °C must be regarded as the critical temperature.

Although no figures have been given in Table 27 for heat treated steels their behaviour in fire can be taken to be similar to that of cold drawn steel, i.e. they have a critical temperature of about 400 °C and, most importantly, both cold drawn and heat treated steels do not regain their initial strength on cooling.

Steel is a good conductor of heat and has a low heat capacity so that when exposed to a source of heat, i.e. a flame, a uniform temperature will be quickly achieved by the steel throughout its whole mass. In fire conditions temperatures of 800 °C to 1000 °C will be quickly reached even in a small fire so that if steel members are exposed to these temperatures the critical temperatures of 550 °C or 400 °C will be reached early in the fire. Thus exposed structural steel members can only be used in buildings if they are placed in positions where they will be protected from flame impingement, for instance as members external to a building and shielded from flames which may emerge from the windows. For all other positions structural steel members must be protected from the effects of heat.

Protection of structural steelwork

The traditional and by far the most common method of protecting structural steel is to encase it in a material which will act as a thermal insulator.[14] Other, less common methods are: (1) to use water to cool the steel member; or (2) to use an intumescent coating.

The rate at which the temperature of structural steel rises when exposed to a fire depends on the mass of the steel and on the surface area exposed to heating. Thus it is important to know the exact position proposed for the steel work if the conception of the ratio of surface area to steel mass is to be used to estimate the fire behaviour of the structural member. For instance a free standing column or fully exposed beam will present a greater surface area to heating than one which has one side abutting onto or built into a wall or floor.

More information about this factor is given in the section below.

Encased steelwork.

There are four methods of encasing steel structural members in order to provide fire protection. They are:

(a) Solid protection

The common material used for solid protection is concrete and in all cases it is advisable to provide secondary reinforcement (i.e. a steel mesh or similar arrangement) in order to hold the concrete in position and prevent spalling.

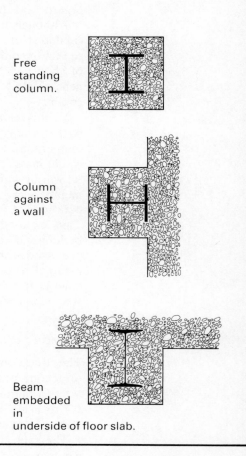

Free standing column.

Column against a wall

Beam embedded in underside of floor slab.

In the examples which have been illustrated (Figure 25) the thickness of the insulation required to give the steel structural members of the specified level of fire resistance depends on the mass of steel and on the heated area of the steel. For lighter weight sections of steel a *thicker* layer of insulation is needed than with a heavier section.

Figure 25 Diagrams of steel encasement. There are four methods (parts (a) – (d)) of encasing steel structural members in order to provide fire protection.

(b)   Profile protection

The protection used
for this will most likely
be a sprayed on
formulation such as
mineral wool fibre.
Again it may be advisable
to use a wire mesh
embedded in the insulant
in order to hold it in
place.

Free
standing
column.

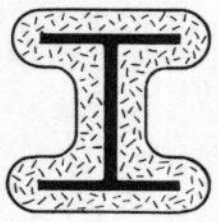

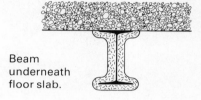

Beam
underneath
floor slab.

(c)   Hollow protection

A non-combustible board
material will probably
be used for this
insulating construction.
Special attention must
be given to the method of
fixing to ensure the
board stays in position
throughout the fire.
The heads of any nails
or screws must be
protected from exposure
to heat.

Free
standing
column.

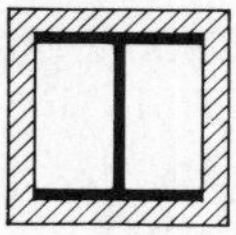

Beam
underneath
floor slab.

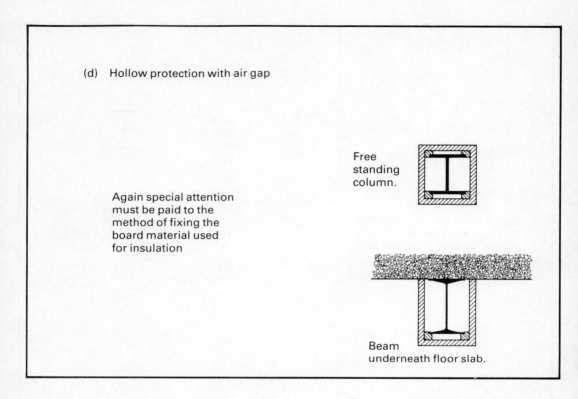

(d) Hollow protection with air gap

Again special attention
must be paid to the
method of fixing the
board material used
for insulation

Free
standing
column.

Beam
underneath floor slab.

This dependence is expressed in terms of the ratio of the cross-sectional area divided by the perimeter of the steel section (A/P) but in some publications there is now a tendency to use the inverse (P/A) since this gives more convenient numbers for tabulation. In the published tables of fire resistance test results[15,16] early work was carried out using steel section sizes:

8 in × 6 in × 35lb ft^{-1} RSJ columns

and

10 in × 4½ in × 25lb ft^{-1} RSJ for beams

but following metrication in the steel industry later test results[17] have included steel section sizes of:

203 mm × 203 mm × 55 kg m^{-1} universal column for columns
and
 406 mm × 178 mm × 60 kg m^{-1} universal beam for beams.

In the earlier tests beams were tested with a span of 10 ft and in the later work a span of 7 m has been used although the BS 476: Part 8, 1972 (Test methods and criteria for the fire resistance of elements of building construction) allows a minimum span of 4 m.

The tables giving notional fire resistance values for steel members with various forms of protection which are appended to regulations and given in other publications[18] are based on the later steel sizes given above; where earlier test results have been used a reassessment has been made to take account of the smaller steel size.

These tables of notional fire resistance values are too large and numerous to quote here and the reader is referred to the relevant publication[17] or to the appropriate regulations.

It must be emphasized again that the fire resistance values given in these published tables relate to the steel sizes which have been adopted as standard for this purpose. For lighter steel sections a thicker layer of insulation will be needed and for heavier sections a thinner layer may be sufficient.

In order to give some guidance about the thickness of insulation required for steel sections of different size one of the following empirical relations may be used:[14,19–22]

$$\frac{t_1}{t_2} = \frac{x_1 A_1/P_1}{x_2\,A_2/P_2}$$

where

t	=	fire resistance time,
x	=	thickness of the protective covering or coating
A	=	area of cross section of the steel member
P	=	perimeter of the protected section (through which heat can enter the steel)

and the suffixes 1 and 2 relate to the tested construction and to the construction to be assessed respectively. Alternatively

$$R = 60\left(\frac{215.2W}{D\rho} + \frac{C}{25.4}\right)h$$

where

R	=	fire resistance time (in min)
W	=	weight of steel (in kg m^{-1})
D	=	perimeter of protection, at the interface between protection and steel through which heat is transferred to steel (in mm)
ρ	=	density of insulation (in kg m^{-3})
h	=	thickness of insulation (in mm)
C	=	constant (for sprayed mineral fibre or cementitious mixtures for recommended value of C is 0.5 where ρ is in the range 240 – 320 kg m^{-3}).

Both these relationships are related back to fire test results for the comparison or in order to determine the value of the constants used. For this reason it is suggested that they should only be used for assessments when the size of the steel being studied is not very different from that used in the fire test. For steel sizes which are very different special fire tests will probably be necessary.

Water cooling for structural steel

The use of water to keep structural steel cool in case of fire provides interesting possibilities and the method has been used in several large buildings.

There are three possible variations of the method: (1) to fill the hollow steel sections of the structural steel with water in order to increase the heat sink effect already provided by the steel itself; (2) to interconnect all the hollow steel column and beam sections and provide a circulatory system of water cooling; or (3) to install sprinkler type devices which spray water on to the surface of the steel members to cool them.

In the simple non-circulatory system of (1) above the water is not replenished and so the level of the water is likely to fall during a fire and the steel member may need to project above the level at which its structural function ends in order to ensure that the structural parts likely to be exposed to fire are always full of water. An alternative is to connect all the columns to a replenishment tank so that any water that is boiled off is readily replaced. In both cases, however, the steam generated in the member at the fire may expell water violently at the top of the column and the prevention of this is difficult. A major disadvantage of the non-circulatory system is that if the fire occurs near the top of the column the water in the lower part of the steel member can play no part in keeping the steel cool. This type of system is only likely to be acceptable in simple low fire load buildings.

There are several types of circulatory systems ((2) above) and the most common is one which acts as a large gravity feed heating system. Several buildings using this system have been erected and Figure 26 shows one such example. All the steel members have to be fully interconnected at both ends and steam separating tanks are required in addition to the replenishment tanks. The whole system is designed on the idea that one part will be heated while other parts remain cool.

Careful analysis of the likely flow patterns should be carried out in order to ensure that there are no stagnant areas where circulation could be non-existent.

As an alternative to the gravity action circulation in the fully interconnected system can be maintained by pumps and also

Figure 26   The United Steel Building, Pittsburgh USA.

single columns or small groups of columns can be given a circulation system by means of pumps. This improves the flow in the steel members but places reliance on mechanical pumps.

The last method ((3) above), using sprinklers installed in such a way that the whole of the steel surface is cooled by the water spray, has the advantage that the water is only in contact with the steel when and where it is needed but it has the difficulty that maintaining a cooling film of water on the steel surface can be prevented by local surface irregularities or by relatively small pieces of foreign matter.

As far as is known no buildings have been constructed using this method of water cooling.

In all the examples quoted for water cooling of structural steel there are many difficulties associated with, for instance, corrosion, freezing, additional pipework, and sufficient water supply. It is essential therefore that careful attention be given to all aspects of the proposed design and reference to the available literature should be made.[23–25]

Intumescent coating

The use of a coating, which on the application of heat will foam and form a stable thick insulating cover for the structural steel, appears attractive, particularly as it is applied to the steel in the form of a coat. However, at present the materials available give only a relatively short period of fire resistance, typically 30 to 40 minutes and require several on site applied coats to achieve even this. The ordinary intumescent paint is not suitable for this purpose and a special formulation[26,27] which will remain adhered to the steel throughout the duration of any fire is needed. One objection to this method of protection is that there is a danger of mechanical damage to the coating during the normal use of the building in which case there would not be a complete cover of insulation available should a fire occur.

Aluminium

This material and its alloys is not used extensively for structural purposes but it may sometimes be used as part of an element of structure which has a separating function. Some knowledge of its mechanical and thermal properties is therefore needed.

It will make only a small contribution to the fire resistance of any part of the structure because it is unable to withstand the direct action of a fire.

The melting point of pure aluminium is 660 °C but this is reduced to about 600 °C for most of its alloys although some of these have melting points as low as 500 °C. The critical temperature is about 250 °C so that if it is used structurally a thick layer of insulating material would be needed for its protection.

The mechanical strength is considerably less than that of steel by a factor of 5–10 fold. It has twice the value of thermal expansion and a thermal conductivity about five times that of steel. The heat capacity of the two, steel and aluminium, is very similar. It is not intended to imply that aluminium and its alloys have no place in building construction. On the contrary, for many applications it has most valuable properties but it must be understood that it will not resist direct attack by fire and flames.

Wood

Timber is one of the oldest structural materials used in buildings and it still finds many applications in the present day. There have been many technological advances in treatment, preparation, and component assembly so that wood and wood products are used extensively in buildings both structurally and in other applications such as cladding, interior finish, and component construction (e.g. doors and windows, etc.)

It has many advantages such as a high strength to weight ratio, a low thermal expansion, and a low thermal conductivity, and although it is combustible it can, nevertheless, achieve a reasonable level of fire resistance.[28,29]

When wood burns it forms a layer of charcoal on the burnt surface which helps to insulate and protect the unburnt wood below the charred zone. The low thermal expansion means that the char layer stays in place even with continued heating and the low thermal conductivity helps the undamaged timber below the char retain its strength. The rate at which timber chars will depend on the heat radiation intensity which it receives from the fire[30] and for very intense fires this rate of charring can be as high as 4 mm depth in one minute.

However, when subjected to the heating conditions which apply for the Fire Resistance Test specified in BS 476:Part 8, 1972, it has been found that wood chars at an almost constant rate of between 30 mm and 50 mm depth per hour, depending on the species, for each face exposed but when all faces are exposed a rather different rate may apply.

The variation of the charring rates have been studied[31] and a brief indication of the range of value expected when a solid timber column is tested in the fire resistance furnace is given in Table 28. Table 28 shows that Hemlock has a lower charring rate than the other three species tested, of these other three Douglas fir was marginally the best. The effect of load appears to be small, the values of charring rates for the three examples differ by amounts which could be attributed to experimental variations. The shape of the column section is shown to be

**Table 28   Charring rates of timber measured
in fire resistance tests;[31] variation with:
(a) species; (b) load; (c) section shape**

(a)	Species	Charring rate (mm h^{-1})
	Western Hemlock	33
	Douglas fir	39
	European redwood	42
	Western red cedar	42

(b)	Load (% of design load)	Charring rate (mm h^{-1})
	100	39
	50	41
	25	36

(c)	Section shape ratio (width/depth)	Charring rate (mm h^{-1})
	1.0	44
	1.7	34
	2.7	34

important. A square section gives the largest charring rate which becomes lower and of constant value as soon as the section shape departs from square.

When the timber used is of laminated construction the type of glue used introduces another variable and different rates of char apply for heating normal to the laminations compared with heating along the glue lines.[31]

There is now enough information available about the behaviour of wood in fire for it to be possible to predict the fire resistance of any given construction for any load condition using a procedure set out in BS 5268[32] and in CP 112[33] and if the use of timber is proposed in any building design then an analysis on the lines set out in these papers should certainly be carried out.

Plastics or polymeric materials

Plastics in many forms and for a variety of purposes are currently used in building construction but as yet they seldom serve as part of the supporting structure except in some secondary way, as for instance, as cladding or trim.

There are many different types of plastic and indeed new forms almost daily. For this reason it is not possible to give a complete list of all the types likely to be used in buildings nor to quote typical values for mechanical properties. It is, however, useful to indicate how heat affects them.

Table 29   Classification of plastic or polymeric materials

	Uses	Plastic	Possible hazard
Thermoplastic			
High density	Sheet, mouldings, extrusions	Acrylics (Perspex, etc.) Polyvinylchloride Nylon Cellulose acetate Polypropylene Polyethylene Polycarbonates	Flaming droplet hazard
Low density	Flexible foam, rigid foam	Polyurethane Polyruethane Polyethylene Polystyrene (expanded) Polyisocyanurate	Burns very rapidly with flaming droplet hazard
Thermosetting			
High density	Sheet, mouldings, extrusions, laminates	Phenolics, phenolformaldehyde (Bakelite, Formica, etc.), Melamine formaldehyde Polyesters	Burns as a solid
Low density	Flexible foam, rigid foam	Urea formaldehyde Polyester	Burns rapidly as a solid

Plastics fall into two general groups, as follows:

(1) Those which soften and eventually melt on the application of heat — these are known as *thermoplastic* materials.
(2) Those which have been solidified by the application of heat and which do not soften or melt when heat is reapplied. These are called *thermosetting* materials.

A thermoplastic material will lose its mechanical strength and its physical shape very quickly when heat is applied and in a fire it will burn as a molten material. A thermosetting material will retain its mechanical strength and its physical shape in a fire until the decomposition which precedes ignition occurs.

Using this method of classification Table 29 can be drawn up which gives examples of the various types of plastic together with their use and possible hazard. In very general terms most thermoplastic materials will soften at temperatures in the range 100 – 150 °C. Many plastics, including the thermosetting materials, will decompose in the range 250 – 400 °C, and pilot ignition will take place between 300 °C and 500 °C.

All plastics are to some degree combustible and it is important to consider the nature of the dangers which their use may cause.

Many plastic materials are now available in two forms or grades, a standard grade and a fire retardant grade, this latter

Table 30   Calorific content of various
materials

| Material | Calorific content | |
	Btu lb^{-1}	Wood equivalent (lb per lb or kg per kg)
Polyurethane	16 500	2.06
Polyvinylchloride	9 250	1.15
Nylon	10 000	1.25
Polyester	10 000	1.25
Wood	8 000	1.00
Coal	14 000	1.75
Rubber	17 000	2.12

grade having in its formulation some kind of inhibiting compound, probably as part of the filler component, whose purpose
is to render the final material less readily combustible.
However, the effect of this treatment is to make the plastic less
easily ignited, but when exposed to a fully developed fire then it
will still burn readily. The treatment does not make the
particular plastic non-combustible.

In considering the fire potential, the important feature is how
quickly does the plastic release its total calorific content and this
is undoubtedly related to the particular physical form of the
plastic concerned.

There is not a great deal to be learnt from a study of the
calorific content of various materials as Table 30 shows. From
Table 30 it will be seen that plastic materials are not markedly
different from other very familiar substances in their heat
content so other features have to be considered. When a
material is in a form such that it has a lot of surface area
exposed it will certainly burn more rapidly than the same
material in a solid form (for instance wood shavings compared
with wood planks). So a foamed plastic, since it has more
surface area exposed will almost certainly burn more readily
and more quickly than the same plastic in a solid or sheet form
and the obvious fact is that very many plastic materials are used
in the form of a foam and so will burn very rapidly and release
their heat content very quickly. In this respect physical form
may be more important than chemical composition.

In buildings some of the greatest hazards from the use of
plastics arise in two areas: (1) when the plastic is used as the
internal lining of the wall or ceiling with the danger of rapid fire
spread across the surface; and (2) as a thermal insulating
material in the form of plastic foam of one variety or another.

In this latter application large quantities of the material can be disposed in ducts or other concealed cavities and so be a latent hazard of extreme proportions. Building designers must note the possibility and take such precautionary measures, such as fire stopping, as are necessary.

None of the accepted standard tests is completely satisfactory for the realistic assessment of the fire behaviour of plastic materials. All of the parts of BS 476 have been developed for the testing of traditional materials and their use for plastic materials often presents difficulties. The parts 508 A,C, and D of BS 2782 are frequently criticized on the grounds that they are not truly representative of fire conditions in that they only use a small igniting source.

Nevertheless until more realistic tests are developed the above tests have to be used as far as possible in order to obtain some assessment, however unsatisfactory, of the fire behaviour of plastic materials.

4.3 Standard tests

General

In order to ensure that a material or element of structure can be safely used in a building and survive the effects of a fire without adding to the fire severity there must be some means of assessment.

The Fire Tests drawn up, for the UK, by the British Standards Institution and in other countries by the relevant national testing authority seek to provide this need but because of the extreme difficulty of translating the real fire conditions into the form of a standard it is not possible to be certain that the tested behaviour gives a realistic picture.

There is no such thing as a standard fire; all fires are different, some are more severe than the Standard Test and some are less severe. When a part of a structure is placed in a test furnace or a specimen of material in the apparatus for the smaller fire test, that piece of the building is not mounted or supported in exactly the way it will be in the building and this can make a vast difference to the behaviour of it.

In the Furnace Test or other fire tests a standard rate of heating is imposed and a definite mode of heat transfer to the test item is applied and both of these conditions will almost certainly be very different from those existing in any fire.

When a fire occurs the size of the room or compartment, the ventilation, the fire load (its type and quantity) all affect the fire severity and none of these can be satisfactorily represented in a standard test.

It follows that the Standard Fire Tests leave much to be desired in showing how any material or part of a structure will behave in a real fire but to devise a standard test procedure which can simulate the real fire with all the large number of variables which inevitably apply is a very difficult task and until a great deal more development work has been done the present Standard Tests must be used.

It must be realized and accepted that the Standard Tests do not predict the behaviour in real fires but they can be said to form the basis for comparison and will show, for instance, that A will be better than construction B in a fire but that neither will be as good, say, as structure C.

Even though this limitation in the interpretation of the Standard Test Results must be agreed, nevertheless when test results are combined with experience gained, over many years, about how various different constructions have behaved in real building fires a reasonable basis for the assessment of any material or structure can be said to exist.

The important Fire Tests are those given in the several parts of BS 476 and these are described below. Other small scale tests for specific materials are described in a later section.

Fire Resistance Test BS 476: Part 8, 1972

This is a large scale test and is appropriate for elements of building construction, as follows: walls and partitions (load bearing and non-load bearing), floors, flat roofs, beams, suspended ceilings protecting beams, door, and shutter assemblies, and glazing.

The furnaces used are large items of capital equipment and are shown in Figures 27–29. In all of the test furnaces shown in Figures 27–29 the test assembly can be loaded when appropriate.

For columns the height the furnace can accommodate is 3 m. For walls, partitions, doors, shutters, and glazing the largest assembly which can be tested measures approximately 3 m wide and 3 m high. For floors and flat roofs a specimen 7 m long and 3.5 m wide can be erected in the horizontal furnace. In the same furnace a beam 7 m span can be tested. For smaller floors, flat roofs or beams this furnace can be subdivided.

The test assembly should be constructed and mounted as nearly as possible in the same way as will apply in use. If it is loadbearing it should be loaded, before heating, so that the stresses produced are the same as those which the full size element will carry when designed according to the relevant Code of Practice or British Standard. This load must be maintained constant during the whole test.

Figure 27   Furnace for
testing columns.

Figure 28   Furnace for
testing walls, partitions,
doors, shutters and glazing.

Figure 29 Furnace for testing floors, flat roofs and beams.

In addition to the loading the element shall be supported or restrained at its edges or ends in a way which is similar, as far as is possible, to the condition which will obtain when the element is used in the building. During the test the temperature of the furnace is controlled according to a pre-determined temperature – time relationship which gives the temperatures shown in Table 30. Tolerances in terms of the area under the curve of mean furnace temperature are specified as follows:

During first 10 min of test ± 15% of area under standard curve
During first 30 min of test ± 10% of area under standard curve
After the first 30 min of test ± 5% of area under standard curve

Additionally the temperature must not depart from the standard curve by more than ± 100 °C after the first 10 min of test.

There are three criteria which the element must satisfy during the test.

Table 31 Temperature rise in test furnace at various times										
Time (min)	5	10	15	30	60	90	120	180	240	360
Temperature rise in furnace (°C)	556	659	718	821	925	986	1029	1090	1133	1193

(1) *Stability*. The specimen must not collapse during the heating period. For load bearing constructions there is a reload requirement in which the load is reapplied after the heating has stopped and the element has cooled down, i.e. after 24 hours.

For floors, flat roofs or beams there is a limit to the allowed deflection. The construction will be deemed to have failed if the maximum deflection is greater than $L/30$, where L is the clear span.

(2) *Integrity*. No cracks or openings shall appear in the test element through which flames or hot gases can pass. When testing for integrity the upper part of the furnace must be maintained at a positive pressure of 15 ± 5 Pa (1.5 ± 0.5 mm water gauge).

(3) *Insulation*. The *mean* temperature of the unexposed face of the test specimen must not rise more than 140 °C above the initial temperature or any *point* more than 180 °C above the initial.

The result of the test for any element of construction is given as the period, expressed in minutes during which all three of these criteria are satisfied except that:

(a) for columns only the stability requirement is appropriate;
(b) for doors, shutters and glazing the insulation requirement is waived but there may be a need to measure the radiation received from the unexposed face in order to assess how near combustible articles can be safely stored.

Classification according to this standard test is required: in Table 1 to Regulation E1 of Building Regulations for England and Wales and Northern Ireland and in Schedule 9, Table 5 of Building Standards for Scotland.

Surface Spread of Flame Tests for Materials BS 476, Part 7, 1971

In this test a reasonably large scale apparatus is used to determine the tendency of materials to allow flame to spread across their surface, and it is applied to materials which may be used as internal linings for the walls or ceilings in a building.

The test consists of supporting a sample of the board or sheet material, of size 900 mm × 225 mm, fixed to a non-combustible backing and held in such a position that one face of the material is exposed to radiant heat from a vertical furnace panel 900 mm square. The apparatus is shown in Figure 30.

As will be seen in the photograph the face of the specimen is vertical with its long dimension horizontal. It is mounted at the edge of the radiant panel and at right angles to it. Thus the

Figure 30　Spread of flame
apparatus.

intensity of the heat radiation falling on the face of the
specimen board varies from a maximum at the radiator panel
end to a minimum at the end remote from the radiant source.

The BS specifies that the heat radiation shall vary along the
panel according to the values given in Table 31. The radiation is
measured by radiometer discs cemented to an asbestos board at
intervals of 75 m and this board is then mounted in the place
which will be occupied by the specimen under test. The
tolerance on the radiation intensity values set out in Table 31 is
given in the Standard in terms of the millivolt output from the
radiometer discs but it varies from approx $\pm$ 3.0 kW m^{-2} at
the hot end to $\pm$ 0.6 kW m^{-2} at the cool end.

**Table 32　Specified radiation intensities along the face of the test specimen in
the surface spread of flame test**

Distance from hotter end of specimen (mm)	75	150	225	300	375	450	525	600	675	750	825
Radiation intensity (kW m^{-2})	37.0	31.0	25.5	21.0	18.4	15.1	13.4	11.7	10.5	8.8	7.5

Immediately the specimen is exposed to the radiant heat (as above) a vertical luminous gas flame is applied to its hotter end for 1 min. The movement of the flame front along the specimen is observed and the test is terminated after 10 min.

Depending on the results of these observations the materials are classified into four classes as follows:

Class 1   flame spread after 1½ min 165 mm max.
  Very low flame   (tolerance for 1 specimen 25 mm)
  spread   flame spread after 10 min 165 max.
        (tolerance for 1 specimen 25 mm)

Class 2   flame spread after 1½ min 215 mm max.
  Low flame   (tolerance for 1 specimen 25 mm)
  spread   flame spread after 10 min 455 mm max.
        (tolerance for 1 specimen 45 mm)

Class 3   flame spread after 1½ min 255 max.
  Medium flame   (tolerance for 1 specimen 25 mm)
  spread   flame spread after 10 min 710 max.
        (tolerance for 1 specimen 75mm)

Class 4   all surfaces which exceed the class 3 limits
  Rapid flame
  spread

The surface flame spread properties of wall and ceiling linings are controlled by reference to these classifications, in Regulation E15 of the Building Regulations for England and Wales and in Regulation E15 of the Scottish Regulations.

Fire Propagation Test for Materials BS 476, Part 6, 1968

This test is the most recently developed Standard Test in the BS 476 series and it is designed to improve the indication of the properties of materials in fire conditions.

The Surface Spread of Flame Test gives information about the rate of horizontal movement of a flame front across the surface of a material but the Fire Propagation Test takes into account other factors, such as, the ease of ignition, the calorific content of the material, the rate at which this heat is released on combustion, as well as the thermal properties of the material.

The Surface Spread of Flame Test is perfectly satisfactory for distinguishing between a good material and a bad material but it is insensitive in separating good materials into their correct order of performance. The Fire Propagation Test has been designed to overcome this deficiency.

It is a box test in contrast to the open test of surface spread of flame and the apparatus is simpler and smaller than this latter.

The combustion chamber of the apparatus is constructed of asbestos board 12.5 mm thick (density $1.3 - 1.45$ g cm^{-3} and the inside dimensions are 190 mm × 190 mm × 90 mm wide.

One of the larger faces constitutes the specimen holder into which the sample of material being tested is inserted. The size of the sample is 228 mm × 228 mm and the specimen holder is adjusted to take any thickness of material up to 50 mm.

In the face opposite to the sample being tested is a mica observation window and below this window in the same face there is an air inlet port 95 mm wide and 25 mm high. On the top face of the combustion chamber there is a chimney (made of steel plate 1 mm thick) which is 38 mm diameter and 190 mm long over which is placed a cowl containing two thermocouples to measure continuously, during a test, the temperature of the fire gases.

The heating in the combustion chamber is both gas and electric. A row of gas jets (14 in number) is located at the bottom of the chamber and using a carefully metered gas supply these jets play on the bottom of the specimen for the duration of the test (20 min). Two pencil type electric elements are supported horizontally, one above the other, symmetrically in the chamber at centres 64 mm apart and 45 mm from the face of the specimen. These electric elements are switched on 2 min 45s after the start of the test at 1800 watt and the power is reduced to 1500 watt after the test has been going for 5 min; the power is then maintained at this level until the end of the test.

The measurements made during the test are of the fire gases using the two thermocouples in the chimney cowl. Temperature measurements are taken at ½ min intervals for the first 3 min of the test, then at 1 min intervals from the fourth minute to the tenth minute, then at 2 min intervals from the twelfth minute to the end of the test.

The test result is obtained by taking a standard curve, produced by carrying out the test with a sheet of asbestos board 12.5 mm thick in the specimen holder and then an index of performance is calculated for any other sample by taking an average of the difference between the temperature for the sample and for the standard asbestos board for the three periods indicated above. The exact expression for the calculation is given below:

$$i_1 = \sum_{1/2}^{3}\left(\frac{\theta_m - \theta_c}{10t}\right) \quad i_2 = \sum_{4}^{10}\left(\frac{\theta_m - \theta_c}{10t}\right) \quad i_3 = \sum_{12}^{20}\left(\frac{\theta_m - \theta_c}{10t}\right)$$

$$I = i_1 + i_2 + i_3$$

where

I = index of performance and i_1, i_2, and i_3 are subindices

106

t = time (in min) from the beginning of the test

θ_m = temperature (in °C) of the mean curve for material at time t

θ_c = temperature (in °C) of the calibration curve of the apparatus.

(In the calculation only positive values of $(\theta_m - \theta_c)/10t$ should be used.)

The values of the index, I, may range in descending order of merit from 0 (for a non-combustible material) to a high value approaching 100 for a very combustible material. Since the total index I is made up of three parts it is possible to determine from these three components how rapidly or otherwise the heat is released from the specimen.

In regulations a material graded as class 0 is sometimes allowed as an alternative to a non-combustible material. This grading of class 0 relates to a performance in the Fire Propagation Test and at the time of writing to meet the class 0 requirement a material must have a total index I not greater than 12 and an index for the first three minutes i_1 not greater than 6.

It sometimes appears confusing for a material to be specified as needing to be both class 0 and class 1 and in this respect it is important to remember that these refer to different tests: Class 0 is determined by the Fire Propagation Test results, and class 1 is determined by the Surface Spread of Flame Test.

A class 0 grading for materials is specified in Clauses E7(4), E7(5), and E15(1) in Building Regulations for England and Wales and for Northern Ireland, and in clauses E15(1) in Building Standards for Scotland.

Ignitability Test for Materials BS 476: Part 5, 1968

This test is a small scale bench test originally forming the preliminary part of the Fire Propagation Test but which is now a standard test in its own right.

The test is intended to identify easily ignitable materials of low heat content for which the performance in the Fire Propagation Test (BS 476: Part 6, 1970) does not necessarily indicate the full hazard. It is intended for rigid or semi-rigid building materials but it is not suitable for fabrics.

The sample of material used for this test is of the same size as that used in the Fire Propagation Test, 228 mm × 228 mm. This is held in a vertical position and a gas jet, whose size and position is closely specified, is applied to the centre of the test panel for 10 s, after which it is moved away and subsequent duration of flaming, if any, is noted to the nearest second.

Three samples of the material are tested and if any specimen flames for more than 10 s after the removal of the flame or if burning of the specimen extends to the edge within this period then the material is classified as 'easily ignitable' and its performance indicated by the letter 'X'.

If no specimen flames for more than 10 s after the removal of the test flame and burning does not extend to the edge within this period then the material is classified as 'not easily ignitable' and its performance is indicated by the letter 'P'.

There are no requirements under Building Regulations or Building Standards in the UK for a performance rating using this test but it is certain, nevertheless, that a material which obtains an 'X' classification needs to be used with very great care in any building.

Non-Combustibility Test for Materials BS 476: Part 4, 1970

This test is also a small scale bench test. It consists of lowering a small sample of the material into a pre-heated electric furnace and observing any rise of furnace temperature or flaming of the specimen.

The specimen size is 40 mm wide, 40 mm breadth, and 50 mm high and if the thickness of the material is less than the height of 50 mm then the required height is made up of layers of the material with the layers held in the horizontal position. For the test the specimen is placed in a steel wire mesh holder and lowered into the furnace.

The test apparatus consists of a tubular electric furnace with an internal diameter of 75 mm, with its axis vertical, a height of 150 mm, and an overall wall thickness of between 10 and 13 mm. It is heated by electrical windings round the outside of the tube which is then enclosed in an insulating surround. The windings are arranged so that a vertical zone of at least 60 mm length in the centre part of the furnace can be maintained at the operating temperature and be uniform to within ± 5 °C.

Attached to the underside of the furnace is a cone shaped air flow stabilizer 500 mm long, 75 mm internal diameter at the top (furnace end) reducing to 9 mm internal diameter at the lower end.

The furnace temperature is measured by a thermocouple placed 10 mm from the wall of the furnace and at the mid-height of the specimen which in turn is placed at the centre of the uniform temperature zone. A second thermocouple is placed in the centre of the specimen, inserted from the top in a 2 mm hole drilled for this purpose.

In carrying out the test the furnace is heated and its temperature stabilized at 750 °C ± 10 °C for a minimum period of 10 min. The specimen in its holder is then lowered into the apparatus, this operation being performed in not more than 5 s. A record is then made for a further 20 min of the temperature of the two thermocouples using a continuous recorder; the occurrence and duration of any flaming in the furnace is also noted. During the period of the test the stabilized heating current is maintained unchanged.

Using the results of the test described above the combustibility of a material is assessed as follows.

The material will be deemed to be 'non-combustible' if, during the test, none of the three specimens either:

(a) caused the temperature reading from either of the two thermocouples to rise by 50 °C or more above the initial furnace temperature; or

(b) is observed to flame continuously for 10 s or more inside the furnace.

Otherwise, the material will be deemed to be 'combustible'.

It should be noted that according to this test a material is either combustible or non-combustible, there is no intermediate grading. Non-combustibility according to this test is a requirement in Clause A4(1) of Building Regulations for England and Wales and of Northern Ireland and in Clause A3(1) in the Building Standards in Scotland.

Method of assessing the heat emission from building materials. BS 476, Part II, 1982

This standard, newly published, uses a modified version of the non-combustibility test apparatus with a cylindrical test piece. The result is recorded in terms of temperature rise and mass loss.

External Fire Exposure Roof Tests BS 476: Part 3, 1958 and 1975

This test is intended to give information on the hazard that exists from a fire outside a building spreading to the roof of that building. It is not concerned with the behaviour of the roof when exposed to a fire inside the building.

The test has three components: a preliminary ignition test; a fire penetration test; and a surface spread of flame test. It is important to note that none of these tests bear any relation to the other tests described earlier in this section.

Figure 31 External fire exposure roof test apparatus.

The tests are applied to a specimen of a roof structure approximately 1500 mm square which must represent the actual roof construction including at least one specimen of any joints used in the materials and be complete with any lining which forms an integral part of the construction. The test specimen is mounted in the test apparatus, shown in Figure 31 and it can be placed in either a horizontal or sloping position (45° to horizontal) according to its construction and the test required.

For the preliminary ignition test a luminous gas flame 228 mm long from a 9 mm diameter orifice is applied for 1 min to the centre of the upper surface of the specimen, directed up the specimen with the nozzle resting on the specimen and at an angle of 5 ° to it.

Observations are made of the flaming which results. If flaming occurs it should be noted whether the duration exceeds 5 min after the withdrawal of the gas flame and whether the maximum distance of spread of flame in any direction, across and wholly within the region of burning, exceeds 380 mm. Any penetration is noted.

If these limits are exceeded or penetration occurs there is no point in proceeding with the major test.

For the fire penetration and flame spread test three specimens are tested and during the test each is exposed to radiant heat from four gas fire panels which are 305 mm square and so mounted as to form a radiant source whose overall dimension is 914 mm square.

The intensity of the radiation incident on the specimen is maintained at a uniform level of 14.6 kWm^{-2} (0.35 cal cm^{-2} s^{-1}). At intervals from the start of the test a luminous gas flame (as for preliminary test) is applied to the specimen for 1 min moving once up and once down the centre of the specimen. As the test proceeds observations are made of any flaming and afterwards the extent of flame spread is measured (to the nearest 25 mm).

The procedure under the 1958 version of the test was different. Separate tests were made for penetration and for flame spread. The specimens were smaller. The space beneath the specimen was held at a slightly reduced pressure to simulate the effect of wind. The results were presented differently too; the two versions are compared below.

Classification of roof coverings by BS 476 part 3:

1958							1975
AA,	AB,	AC				≡	P 60
BA,	BB,	BC				≡	P 30
AD,	BD,	CA,	CB,	CC,	CD	≡	P 15
unclassifiable						≡	P 5

in the 1958 system:

the first A referred to a penetration time   1 h
the first B referred to a penetration time   30 min
the first C referred to a penetration time   30 min
the first D signified penetration in the preliminary test

the second A signified zero flame spread
the second B signified flame spread of not more than 21 in
the second C signified flame spread of more than 21 in
the second D signified that the sample continued to burn 5 min
after the flame was withdrawn or that there was more than 15 in of flame spread in the preliminary test.

in the 1975 system: P indicates that the specimen passed the preliminary test. The number shows the time in minutes before penetration. No indication of flame spread is given by the classification although the record of the test must include the observations and measurements of flaming and flame spread.

The test results must also record the inclination of the roofing specimen, and any molten drips, mechanical failure or development of holes should be noted.

The Building Regulations in the British Isles all refer to the 1958 system of classification.

Other British Standard Tests

For some materials, for instance plastic sheets and textile fabrics, the tests described in the various parts of BS 476 are not appropriate and consequently other tests are specified or referred to by the relevant regulating authorities. These are listed very briefly below:

(a) BS 2782, 1970: Method 102C. Softening point of thermo-plastic moulding material (bending test)

As its name implies this test is only applicable to thermoplastic materials. It consists of applying a controlled and carefully specified amount of heat to a sample of the material and noting its deformation when a specified force is applied to it.

(b) BS 2782, 1970: Method 508A. Rate of burning, laboratory method

Applicable to all plastics, thermosetting and thermoplastic. It is a bench test designed to indicate the rate of heat release when a sample of the material is burnt under carefully controlled conditions.

(c) BS 2782, 1970: Method 508C. Flammability of polyvinyl chloride sheets

A test which indicates the characteristics of flame spread in a thin sheet of polyvinylchloride. The specimen used is a strip of the PVC material 550 mm × 35 mm.

(d) BS 2782, 1970: Method 508D. Flammability of plastics materials

This test is applied to all plastics materials (other than PVC) and the characteristics of flaming are assessed. A specimen size 150 mm square not exceeding 50 mm thick is used. The test is sometimes referred to as the Alcohol Cup Test.

(e) BS 3119, 1959. Method of test for flameproof materials.
BS 3120, 1959. Performance requirements for materials for flameproof clothing

Applicable to fabrics which are required to be inherently

non-flammable or durably flameproof, for instance, stage curtains and certain types of clothing.

(f) BS 4735, 1974. Burning characteristics of cellular plastics and cellular rubber

The full title of this standard is 'Burning characteristics of a specimen no larger than 150 mm × 15 mm × 13 mm of cellular plastics and cellular rubber material when subject to a small flame'. It is used mainly as a check on production consistency and is only a small scale bench test.

(g) BS 5111; Part 1, 1974. Methods of tests for determination of smoke generation characteristics of cellular plastics and cellular rubber materials

This test is not, as yet, used as the basis for any regulatory requirement.

It is to be emphasized that all of the tests listed above (in this section) are small scale bench tests using a small specimen and a small source of heat. They cannot therefore purport to indicate the behaviour of the material when installed in a building and subject to actual fire conditions.

Comparable Standard Tests[35]

Given below are tests which are standard in the various countries indicated and which are similar in purpose. However it must be clearly understood that although there may be similarity between the tests, the actual test conditions and acceptance criteria may differ and it should not be taken that a material or structure achieving a standard of performance in one country's test will necessarily achieve the same standard in the test of another country.

(1) Fire resistance of elements of structure

United Kingdom	BS 476: Part 8, 1972
USA	ANSI/ASTM E119
	ANSI/ASTM E152 (Doors)
	ANSI/ASTM E163 (Windows)
Federal German Republic	DIN 4102: Parts 2,3,5 and 6
France	Arrête of 5.1.1959.
Belgium	NBN 713–020
Denmark	DS 1051

Italy	Circular 91.(1961)
Netherlands	NEN 3884
International Standards Organisation (ISO)	ISO 834, 3008, 3009

(2) Behaviour of roof constructions

United Kingdom	BS 476: Part 3, 1958 and 1975
USA	ANSI/ASTM E108
Federal German Republic	DIN 4102:Part 7
France	Arrête of 10.9.1970
Belgium	—
Denmark	DS 1051, 1059.1, 1059.2
Italy	Circular 91.(1961)
Netherlands	NEN 3882
ISO	—

(3) Non-combustibility

United Kingdom	BS 476: Part 4, 1970
USA	ASTM E136
Federal German Republic	DIN 4102, Part 1
France	NF.P.92-501, NF.M. 03-005
Belgium	ISO 1182
Denmark	DS 1056
Italy	—
Netherlands	NEN 3881
ISO	ISO 1182

(4) Ignitability

United Kingdom	BS 476: Part 5, 1968
USA	—
Federal German Republic	DIN 4102: Part 1
France	—
Belgium	—
Denmark	DS 105.1, 1058.3
Italy	—
Netherlands	NEN 3883: Chap. 4
ISO	Under development

(5) Surface spread of flame

United Kingdom	BS 476: Part 7, 1971
USA	ANSI/ASTM E84
Federal German Republic	DIN 4102: Part 1
France	NF.P. 92–501, 92–503, 92–504, 92–506

Belgium	(uses French or British Test)
Denmark	DS 1058.3
Italy	—
Netherlands	NEN 3883: Chap. 4
ISO	Under development

(6) Heat release or contribution to flashover, fire propagation test

United Kingdom	BS 476: Part 6, 1968
USA	—
Federal German Republic	DIN. 4102: Part 1
France	NF.P. 92–501
Belgium	NEN 1076: Chap. C.
Denmark	DS 1058.2
Italy	—
Netherlands	NEN 3883: Chap. 4
ISO	Under development

(7) Smoke

United Kingdom	—
USA	ANSI/ASTM E662
Federal German Republic	DIN 53. 436, 53. 437
France	—
Belgium	—
Denmark	DS 1058.2
Italy	—
Netherlands	NEN 3883: Chap. 5
ISO	Under development

References

1. P.L. Hinkley, Some notes on the control of smoke in enclosed shopping centres, *Fire Res. Note No.* 875, Fire Research Station, Borehamwood, England, 1971.
2. P.H. Thomas, The role of flammable linings in fire spread, *Board Manufacture,* **12,** 96–101, 1969.
3. D.J. Rasbash, Efficiency of hand lamps in smoke, *Inst. Fire Engrs. Q.* **11,** 46, 1951.
4. H.L. Malhotra, Movement of smoke on escape routes; instrumentation and effect of smoke on visibility, *Fire Res. Notes Nos* 651, 652, and 653, Fire Reserch Station, Borehamwood, England, 1967.
5. T. Jin, Visibility through fire smoke, *Building Research Institute, Tokyo, Rep. No. 30, March* 1970; *Report No. 33, February* 1971.
6. E.G. Butcher, and A.C. Parnell, *Smoke Control in Fire Safety Design,* E. and F.N. Spon Ltd, London, 1979, 178pp.
7. H.M. Bunbury, *The Destructive Distillation of Wood,* Benn Bros, London, 1923.

8. W.D. Woolley, and M. Raftery, Toxic products of combustion of platics, *I.B.C.O.* **11**(2), 24–7, 1973.
9. E.G. Butcher, Plastics and fire. An increasing risk, *Fire Engrs J.*, **35**(98), 24, 1975.
10. D.J. Rasbash, Smoke and toxic products at fires, *Plastics Inst. Trans. J. Conf. Suppl. No. 2*, 55–62, 1967.
11. H.S. Carslaw, and J.C. Jaeger, *Conduction of Heat in Solids*, 2nd edn, Clarendon Press, Oxford.
12. *Building Research Establishment Digest. No. 108, August* 1969, (1975 edition): *Standard U-values.*
13. O. Pettersson, Structural fire engineering research today and tomorrow, *Acta Polytech. Scand. Civil Engineering and Building Construction Series No. 33, Stockholm,* 1965.
14. D.A. Elliott, Fire and steel construction. The protection of structural steelwork, *CONSTRADO, Publication 4./74, London,* 1974.
15. N. Davey, and L.A. Ashton, Investigations on building fires, PEV, fire tests on structural elements, *National Building Studies, Res. Pap. No. 12*, HMSO, London, 1953.
16. L.A. Ashton, and P.M.T. Smart, Sponsored fire-resistance tests on structural elements, *Joint Fire Research Organisation*, HMSO, London, 1960.
17. R.W. Fisher, and P.M.T. Smart, Results of fire resistance tests on elements of building construction, *Joint Fire Research Organisation*, HMSO, London, 1975.
18. R.E.H. Read, F.C. Adams, and G.M.E. Cooke, Guidelines for the construction of fire resisting structural elements, *Building Research Establishment*, HMSO, London, 1980.
19. J.H. McGuire, The estimation of fire resistance, *Fire Research Note No. 348*, Joint Fire Research Organisation, 1958.
20. M. Law, Structural fire protection in the process industry, *Building*, London, 1969, 217(6583); 29/86–29/89; (6587)33/65–33/68.
21. G.J. Langdon-Thomas, *Fire Safety in Buildings*, A. & C. Black Ltd, London, 1972, Appendix 9, p. 281.
22. T.T. Lie and W.W. Stanzak, *Engineering J. (USA)*, Third Quarter, 1973.
23. G.M.E. Cooke, Water filled structures, *Building with Steel*, No. 15.
24. G.V.L. Bond, Water cooled hollow columns, *Fire and Steel Construction*. CONSTRADO.
25. D.J. Rasbash, Improvements in and relating to the cooling of metal structures, *UK Patent Application,* 52375/67.
26. J.F. O'Rourke, The use of intumescent coatings for fire protection of structural steel, *Proc. 8th Symp. on Loss Prevention in the Process Industries, Philadelphia,* 11–15 November, 1973, Vol. 8, American Institute of Chemical Engineers, New York, 1974.
27. F.B. Liberti, Intumescent coatings composition, *Plastic Building Construction*, **1**(7), 13–14, 1975.
28. K. Odeen, Fire resistance of glued, laminated timber structures, *Paper 2, Proc. Symp. on Fire and Structural use of Timber in Buildings, Fire Research Station, Borehamwood, England, 27 October, 1967,* HMSO, London, 1970.
29. H.L. Malhotra, and B.F.W. Rogowski, Fire resistance of laminated timber columns, *Paper 3, Proc. Symp. on Fire and Structural use of Timber in Buildings, Fire Research Station, Borehamwood, England, 27 October 1967,* HMSO, London, 1970.

30. C.P. Butler, Notes on charring rates in wood, *Fire Res. Note No. 896*, Fire Research Station, Borehamwood, 1971.
31. F.W. Rogowski, Charring rate of timber in fire tests, *Paper 4, Proc. Symp. on Fire and Structural use of timber in buildings, Fire Research Station, Borehamwood, England, 27 October, 1967*, HMSO, London, 1970.
32. British Standards Institution, British standard code of practice for the structural use of timber; fire resistance of timber structures; Methods of calculating fire resistance of timber members, BS 5268: Part 4, Section 4.1, BSI London, 1978.
33. British Standards Institution, British standard code of practice for the structural use of timber (metric units), CP 112: Part 2, BSI, London, 1971.
34. F.W. Rogowski, The Fire Propagation Test: its development and application, *Fire Res. Tech. Pap. No. 25*, HMSO, London, 1970.
35. R.E.H. Read, International fire tests on building materials and structures, *Building Res. Establ. Inf. Pap., IP 21/80*.

5
Services

5.1 Coordination of building services

Planning

It is essential to consider the interaction of the mechanical, electrical, and fire protection services at an early stage in the building planning to ensure the provision of adequate plant spaces, access for installation and maintenance, economical services distribution both vertically and horizontally and conformity with any applicable regulations and insurance requirements.

To produce an efficient yet cost effective building from the client's point of view it is essential to provide the services engineer with sufficient information at a very early stage to enable him to produce accurate estimates of plant space requirements and thus give the client maximum lettable or useable space within the constraints of the proposed overall building outline. It is not sufficient to consider the environmental services, e.g. air conditioning and lighting, only at this stage and then hope that the appointed services contractor will be able to squeeze the fire protection and other emergency services into any odd spaces that may be left.

Full consideraton must be given from the very beginning to the fire protection and emergency services' requirements and decisions must be made in conjunction with the client and any specialist advisers including the Local Fire Authority and the Insurers as to the full extent of the fire and emergency services to be provided. This in turn will allow adequate space to be provided within the overall scheme for items such as fire pump houses, water storage tanks, emergency generator rooms, and gaseous extinguishing systems cylinder banks.

Emergency power

A very important early decision which must be made is the emergency services' power loading, especially if high capacity electrically driven fire water pumpsets, driven by motors of several hundred kilowatts, are included as part of the fire protection services. These in turn will affect power cable sizing, transformer and switchgear loading, and the space requirements for this equipment. If standby or emergency power generation equipment is to be provided it is essential, at an early stage, to agree which of the environmental and fire services are to be supplied from this unit, to enable adequate space to be provided for a plant of sufficient capacity.

Arrangements for bulky plant

Many plant items are bulky and difficult to handle, and by their design and complexity must be factory asembled and delivered to site as completed units. Provision must be made in the building design for the installation of this equipment and for its subsequent removal, on a number of occasions during the life of the building, for maintenance and or replacement. To enable this to be done it may be necessary to incorporate openings or hatchways in floor slabs and structural walls, and also provide overhead runway beams or other lifting attachments, all of which will involve both the structural and services engineers in a great deal of planning and coordination.

Compartmentation

Once the initial services' space requirements have been agreed it is essential to inform the services engineer of the details of the building compartmentation plan, to enable pipe, duct, and cable tray routes to be coordinated, to reduce to a minimum the number of penetrations of fire resisting elements of the structure. This includes not only compartment fire walls but also service riser shafts and structural floor slabs. Not only will this make fire stopping of the penetrations simpler, but it will also avoid the expensive site cutting of holes for odd services pipes and cables, very late in the contract.

Drainage and water damage

In addition to the provision of toilet block and rainwater drainage it is also necessary to consider, at an early stage, the provision of drainage for fire and emergency systems. Sprinkler installation control valve stations require large gulleys, designed for flow rates of several thousand litres per minute, to cope with testing. Fire water pump houses also require provision for drainage from pump glands, circulation and pressure relief valves, and diesel engine cooling systems, as well as pump test lines.

In many fire incidents the damage due to the actual fire may be very small, compared to the damage due to smoke and to the water used to extinguish the fire. To reduce damage from the latter cause consideration should be given to the provision of suitable floor drains, especially on floors above the ground floor, connected into the main building drainage system. This removes fire fighting water quickly and without damage to equipment and stock etc. on the floor below. To further reduce post-fire water damage from fractured service pipes some thought should be given to the valving of heating mains, and cold water servics, to enable sections to be speedily isolated following a fire incident.

Air handling services

In air conditioned buildings, without opening windows, consideration must be given early on in the design stage, to the question of heat and smoke venting. If the air conditioning system is to be used for this purpose the control and power supply circuits must be so arranged that power is always available, either from the mains supply or the emergency generator, so that the extract fans can be run for as long as necessary at full power during an emergency. This in turn will affect cable sizes and routes and, of course, the size of the emergency generator as mentioned previously.

Routine access

Access to services is especially important and where possible equipment requiring regular access for testing and maintenance should be grouped together behind one access panel. In turn access panels should not be located in positions where access, when the building is in use, will be difficult, e.g. in front of door openings, over plant and machinery.

Potential economies in development of service design

As detailed services design proceeds it is important to establish priorities, but at the same time it must be remembered that minor changes to the layout of one service can make major cost savings in another. This is particularly so in the case of automatic sprinkler systems in air conditioned areas containing large amounts of ductwork, where relatively small changes in ductwork size and location can effect considerable savings in the number of sprinkler heads required to protect the area.

Careful consideration of the relationship between lighting, ventilation grilles, and tile patterns can also effect savings, as a consequence of the reduction in the number of sprinkler heads required in areas with false ceilings. Reduction in false ceiling void depths to below 850 mm by careful coordination of the mechanical services can make major reductions in the cost of fire protection services, by eliminating the common insurance requirement to provide sprinkler protection within the void.

5.2 The selection of fire protection equipment and systems

Briefing

When considering the fire protection of a new building, the architect should study, at a very early stage, all the aspects of fire fighting equipment and systems as related to the design and usage of the building. In so doing, he should take into account the views and requirements of the following persons or bodies, as appropriate:

(a) the client and/or potential user;
(b) the local authority and their fire adviser (usually appointed by the Chief Fire Officer);
(c) the insurers and their technical representatives;
(d) any other bodies that may exercise jurisdiction over the design and use of the building.

He should take early steps to get to know the people concerned and to make known to them his own views and ideas.

Legislation

In order to be forearmed in discussions with these bodies, he will need to know any background statutory or local regulations, and any standards codes or rules, likely to affect his position and to control the technical aspects of the equipment. It is the function of this section to give a simple overall picture of the field, leaving a more specific description of the equipment and systems to Part 2.

Table 33   The selection of fire protection equipment and systems

---

Fire Detection

(a)   Human detection: manual call system of break-glass call points to central alarm.

(b)   Automatic detection system (with manual call points incorporated):
         heat-sensitive
         smoke-sensitive
         radiation-sensitive

Fire fighting

(a)   Manual:
         Equipment for beating out or otherwise suppressing fire, e.g. fire buckets, hoods on cooking
         ranges, fire blankets, etc.
         Portable fire extinguishers (up to 20 kg total weight)
         Wheeled fire extinguishers (above 20 kg total weight)
         Installed manual systems e.g. hose-reels.

(b)   Automatic systems:
         sprinkler systems
         water-spray systems
         foam systems (low-expansion)
         foam systems (medium-expansion)   Each of these is
         foam systems (high-expansion)   normally operated
         carbon-dioxide systems   automatically, with
         halon systems   manual operation
         dry powder systems   available also, with
         explosion suppression systems   certain types of system

---

Strategy

Fire protection equipment and systems may be subdivided as
shown in Table 32. These fall under three main headings: fire
detection and alarm, manual fire-fighting, and automatic
fire-fighting. The first decision for the architect to make is
whether he can depend solely on manual fire-fighting, or
whether he needs to install a fire-detection or a fire-fighting
system. This choice will be controlled by the nature of the
occupancy, the degree of fire cover in the neighbourhood, and
the views of the bodies mentioned above. Having decided this
issue, the following notes may be of help in making the choice
of equipment/system.

Alarm and detection equipment and systems

Manual fire alarm

This is the simplest system and is required by legislation in
many premises for life safety. The purpose is to provide a
simple means of raising the alarm for anybody who discovers a
fire. In very small premises it may be simply a hand bell; in

larger buildings there will be break-glass call-points throughout, but especially on the escape routes. The breaking of the glass in any call-point causes the alarm bells to ring.

Every person discovering a fire alone faces a dilemma: if he tackles the fire but fails, he will be criticized for not having raised the alarm. If he turns his back on the fire to raise the alarm, it may develop beyond control, but leave him with the conviction that he could have extinguished it. The manual fire alarm system makes it easy and quick for him to raise the alarm, so that he can turn his attention to such other matters as require it.

Furthermore, in many industrial situations the fire defence plan may require a number of different counter measures to be instituted immediately the existence of fire is known. For example, the closing of fuel-supply valves, stopping of ventilation fans, release of fire doors, ringing of local bells, calling works fire brigade and/or the public fire service. It would be optimistic to imagine that all these could be arranged simply by instructing staff accordingly. In any case they would have to perform the actions serially. An alarm system, on the other hand, can be wired for all these things to occur surely, simultaneously, and promptly, and for some or all of them to occur depending on the zone or zones affected, by a pre-programming arrangement.

Thus when people are present and awake, the manual fire alarm system has obvious value. It is however equally clear that when nobody is present, and while everybody is asleep such a system is of no value.

Automatic fire alarms

Although it is almost entirely the activities of people that cause fires, the danger presented to property is greatest when people are absent, and the danger to life is greatest when people are asleep. It is in these situations that automatic detection is most useful.

We may distinguish immediately between traditional and early warning means.

Traditional detectors (heat detectors). These detect a temperature rise or rate of change of temperature, and are characterised by tardy operation but high reliability against false alarms. Consequently their main use is as triggers for drastic measures, such as sprinklers.

Although heat detectors can be made a little more sensitive than sprinklers, not much improvement is possible because of the large temperature fluctuations in ambient temperature brought about by heating systems, for example, for which alarm is not required. As a result, the convected heat output of a fire at the time sprinklers or heat detectors operate is measured in hundreds of kilowatts for normal ceiling heights, rising to a megawatt when the ceiling height is 6 m.

Early warning detectors. These are able to detect fires (some types will respond only to certain types of fire) at a much earlier stage, but with higher risk of unwanted alarms. Consequently they are used for less drastic measures, such as drawing the attention of a night watchman, who can then make a human decision.

Increasingly, however, machine logic is being applied to process the indications of early warning detectors so as to fit them for various more drastic applications, particularly the release of CO_2 or Halon fire extinguishing gas.

Early detection not only reduces fire damage, but also greatly facilitates the extinction process, and this finds application wherever a small fire can cause much destruction. Examples of this are:

(a) Life safety in sleeping risks (death caused by smoke alone).
(b) Tainting of foodstuffs.
(c) Smoke, humidity or temperature damage to art treasures, precision machinery, and sophisticated electronics equipment as in computing suites.

Types of detector

Most early warning detectors are smoke detectors. These invariably operate on one of two principles:

(a) The ion chamber in which combustion particles from the fire interfere with the ion current.
(b) Optical or photoelectric detectors in which smoke scatters or (rarely) obscures a beam of light, this being detected by suitable photosensors.

Broadly speaking these detectors respond to almost every type of accidental fire, and are therefore applicable quite widely. Areas where they are not satisfactory are:

(a) Areas where smoke occurs without need for alarm such as welding shops, kitchens, foundries.
(b) Areas where steam is released or 100% relative humidity is experienced as in laundries.
(c) Outdoors.

Point type smoke detectors are invariably installed at ceiling level and frequently protect up to 100 square metres per detector, this figure being reduced by a factor of 4 or 5 where there is rapid dilution of fire smoke by, for example, high air change rates as experienced in computer suites.

Beam type detectors are now available for installation at near ceiling level, able to protect up to 100 metres by 14 metres, and capable of responding either to smoke or to turbulence from a fire below.

Radiation detectors respond to infrared or ultraviolet radiation travelling with the speed of light from flame. They can respond very quickly, without waiting for the transport of particles or gas from fire to detector which is necessary for both heat and smoke detectors.

The best ultraviolet detectors are solar-blind, but should be used only at limited range. The infrared detectors have very useful range and are improving in their tolerance of disturbing influences. Both types however are unable to respond unless there is flame, i.e. they cannot detect smouldering fires and consequently their use is restricted to special risks.

Outputs of alarm systems

The alarm system should be able to provide outputs matching in promptness and reliability the various requirements arising from the fire defence plan. The necessary machine logic is now cheap and highly reliable. Mention has already been made of local bells, switching-off auxiliaries, and remote calls to fire brigade or watch station. There is almost always a visual display. This is usually located at the point where fire fighters can be expected to enter the building, for the purpose of directing them to the likely area of fire origin. As the fire spreads to the second and perhaps further zones, additional lamps will illuminate at the display, and this sometimes leads to loss of identity of the first zone affected. The best displays show all the affected zones, but continue to indicate the first zone affected.

Normal facilities include re-ringing of bells each time the fire spreads to a new zone, a bell silence facility, means of re-ringing the bells, and perhaps an 'evacuate' control. A standby battery capable of running the system in the event of mains failure is essential, together with supervised means of maintaining the battery in a charged condition.

Value of detection systems

It can scarcely be overemphasized that by itself a detection system is useless; its value depends on the effectiveness of the supporting fire-fighting capability, and is a maximum when prompt attendance can be assured. Almost certainly the value of amateur first aid fire fighters has in the past been underestimated; when they are provided with early warning detection their value is even higher.

Whenever reliance is placed on non-professional fire-fighting efforts, opportunities should be provided for practising the use of portable extinguishers and hose reels on real fires. This will give confidence and expertise which will be handsomely repaid in the event.

Insurance premium rebates for automatic detection systems do not exceed 12½%, and this reflects past troubles with false alarms.

In recent years there have been energetic efforts to produce codes and standards for detectors and their applications. As they begin to take effect we can expect to see greatly improved performance.

A recent Home Office report indicates that in average buildings over many years there is little or no nett gain to be derived by the installation of detection systems. This may well be true for average buildings, but whenever the risk is higher than normal, or the value at risk either to life or to property is greater, then automatic early warning detection is justified.

Relevant British Standards, Codes, Rules, etc.

BS 5445/5 Heat detectors
BS 5446/1 Smoke detectors for life safety
BS 3116/4 Control and indicating equipment for automatic alarm systems
BS 5839/1 Code of practice for installation and servicing
BS 5364/1 Call-points
Rules of the FOC for automatic fire alarm installation

Fire-fighting equipment and systems

Manual

The range of manual equipment available for fire fighting is intended to be used by any available persons (preferably with regular training in fire fighting) to extinguish fires in their very early stages. It is essential that the equipment available 'matches' the types of fire likely to occur, and that there is adequate fire-fighting capacity available to deal with the likely extent of the outbreak or to hold it in check until the Fire Brigade arrives. Guidance on these points is given in Part 2.

Automatic systems

The automatic sprinkler system is the most widely installed automatic extinction system, and covers a wide range of industrial, commercial and residential risks. It is intended to operate 'on demand' when the hot gases arise from the fire and spread beneath the ceiling or roof of the affected part of the building. Thus only those sprinklers will respond which are directly immersed in hot gases of a temperature which will operate them.

In order to quantify the fire-fighting capacity of sprinkler systems so as to cover the wide range of risks against which they might be used, the insurance bodies have sub-divided these risks into three main categories and several sub-categories, and have specified the minimum design rate of water discharge per unit floor area to control fires in these categories. In adidtion, they have specified, for each category, the minimum areas over which the design rates must be capable of being maintained, in order to encompass the expected maximum fire area. Details of this classification are given in Part 2, based on the FOC Rules. The NFPA has a similar classification.

A sprinkler system may also include a water-spray system, as an adjunct to deal with a localized flammable liquid risk, e.g. an oil-cooled transformer, a heat-treatment bath, etc.

Water-spray systems may exist for cooling stored flammables, e.g. fuel storage tanks, LPG tanks etc., subjected to radiation from fire elsewhere or for dealing with larger flammable liquid risks, e.g. processing plant in chemical complexes. These installations are also covered in the Rules and Recommendations of the Fire Office's Committee, and by the requirement specifications of large organisations, e.g. ICI.

The next most widely used automatic system is the (low-expansion) foam system for dealing with flammable liquid fires in process plants and storage areas. These systems may be installed to meet FOC requirements, Institute of Petroleum requirements, Board of Trade (Marine) requirements, NFPA Standard No. 11, or to British Standard BS 5306 recommendations (in preparaton). In the United Kingdom, installations have to be approved by the Petroleum Officer, who is usually in cooperation with the Chief Fire Officer.

Medium expansion foam systems may also be used for flammable liquid risks, particularly where these involve a degree of 'volume filling' as well as the extinction of fire on a free flammable liquid surface. A typical example is a fire in a gas-turbine generating set where there is need to deal with both a spill fire and a fire 'in depth' up to a height of, say, five metres.

High-expansion foam systems may be used for dealing with both solid fuels and flammable liquid fuels, where there is need to fill a *volume* with foam. Examples are fires in underground basements and rooms where access is difficult or dangerous, fire in enclosed buildings where combustion may be occurring at several levels, e.g. in storages up to about 10 metres. While medium- and high-expansion foam systems are not widespread, their usage is slowly increasing.

Carbon dioxide systems are used generally for the inerting of spaces or volumes in which it is not desirable or safe to use water, e.g. where there is a predominant electrical hazard, possibly allied to a flammable liquid hazard. Local application of carbon dioxide to the potential trouble spots is normally followed by the total flooding of the whole volume involved. Because carbon dioxide in extinguishing concentrations will kill a human being in a very few minutes, these systems must only be used in areas which are gas tight, but can vent safely at high level. Since carbon dioxide is about 150% of the density of air, it should be injected low down in the protected volume, the air being displaced upwards. Automatic warning of imminent discharge should be given in sufficient time for personnel to escape and for the volume to be closed off. The system should be locked off while humans occupy the affected volume. Guidance for installation of carbon dioxide systems is contained in NFPA 12, and British and International standards are in preparation, as well as an insurance-based standard.

Halon systems are similar to carbon dioxide systems in their application, but because the extinguishing concentrations are generally less than the dangerous concentrations, they are potentially more safe for humans. Nevertheless, the question of safety is an important one, and it is highly undesirable for a human being to remain in a protected space once total flooding has occurred. The use of lock-offs is currently under debate. Advice on the installation of these systems is given in NFPA 12, and British and International standards are in preparation, as well as an insurance-based standard.

Dry extinguishing powders consist essentially of a range of small particles of the appropriate chemical powders, carefully graded for size and mixed with suitable flow additives to ensure freedom from caking and packing, and ready discharge from the fire-fighting equipment (extinguishers) or systems. Powders are available of the following types:

Class BC powders. For use on flammable liquid (class B) and gaseous (class C) fires.

Class BC (foam compatible) powders. As above, for use in conjunction with foams.

Class ABC powders. For use against solid fuel (class A) fires, as well as class B and C fires.

Class D powders. For use against fires in flammable metals, e.g. magnesium, titanium.

Powder discharge from small systems can be used to control localized fires, e.g. in dip tanks, garages, or on process equipment where frequent fires occur, e.g. in yarn carding equipment or metal burnishing equipment.

Powder discharge can also be used to extinguish fires in 'difficult' enclosures where foam would not be sufficient, e.g. in engine and boiler rooms where running fuel fires may occur which cannot be dealt with by foam. Powder is only effective while it is being discharged, and rapidly settles out leaving the fire zone unprotected. It does not form the equivalent of an 'inert' atmosphere. An exception to this is that ABC powders on solid fuels do form an 'inert' layer which will not readily re-ignite. The different classes of powder should *not* be mixed as each is special to its particular function, and mixing may be dangerous. A draft British Standard for powder systems is in preparation. They are also covered by NFPA 17.

Explosion suppression

Explosion suppression systems are used in special applications where the possibility of explosion exists and where the results could lead to a calamitous situation. For example, in a chemical process plant where a dangerously flammable chemical has to be heated above its self-ignition point in order to react. Such systems consist essentially of an inhibiting gas, such as Halon 1301, which can be injected into the reaction vessel as soon as a sudden rise in temperature or presure gives warning of the explosion. The pressure or temperature sensitive device would respond immediately to a sudden change and trigger off discharge of the inhibitor.

6
Fire Insurance

The completed building will almost certainly need to be insured and if this is to be done economically then some basic requirements and rules which have been laid down by insurance interests will need to be studied.

6.1 Building for fire loss prevention and reduction

When considering drawings and specifications for new buildings, alterations or extensions, there are a number of features which insurers will examine closely.

(a) Construction

The prime aim, particularly in relation to FOC grades of construction, is to limit the amount of combustible material. In addition to the pure structural elements, attention will also be paid to items such as linings, roof lights, and internal partitions. Fire protection to structural steelwork may also be considered depending on the type of building, its size, value, and intended use.

(b) Compartmentation

In spite of modern open plan tendencies, fire insurers are still very keen on compartmentation, both for segregation of hazard and limitation of value exposed. Compartmentation will be examined in both a vertical plane and, if a storeyed building, in a horizontal plane between floors. In the latter case attention will be given to the degree to which stairs and lifts are enclosed. Openings in walls which the insurers are using as a fire separation (fire break walls) will need to be protected by fire doors or shutters. Ducting passing through fire break walls or floors will require fire dampers.

(c) Ventilation

Initial reaction to fire/smoke ventilation from the fire insurance market was one of undisguised horror. Gradually however, attitudes have changed to the extent that for certain types of risk Insurers would expect to see the provision of ventilation. Apart from whether or not to install ventilation, discussion may also take place regarding automatic or manual operation. If automatic is chosen and the building is sprinklered, insurers will wish to make sure that the operating temperature of the ventilation is at least as high as the sprinkler head, and preferably higher.

Fixed fire protection

The fact that the discount offered by insurers for automatic sprinklers may be as much as four or five times as great as that offered for automatic fire detection, speaks for itself. In both cases, however, FOC rules exist, designed to ensure that when required the system operates to maximum efficiency.

In the case of fixed foam, dry powder or gas flooding systems however there are no insurance rules. In these cases, the discussion will usually range over the type of media to be used and the extent to which it is used (e.g. partial or total flooding), rather than the more specific details such as quantities and pipe sizes. Discounts are not normally given for this type of fixed protection.

Consultation

All too often insurers still find themselves presented with a *fait accompli*, which they either do not like or for which they could have made suggestions which would have resulted in a reduced premium, had they been consulted earlier.

It is always advisable to consult, or recommend a client to consult, the insurer at the planning stage of any new building, extension or alteration.

6.2 Detailed information about insurance

The insurance market in the UK is large and varied but in other countries (e.g. USA) it appears to be dominated by one or two large companies or conglomerates.

(1) UK insurers

In the UK the insurance offices may be divided into three categories: Lloyds, tariff, and independents.

(i) Lloyds

Lloyds is probably the best known name in insurance, originally a City of London coffee house where merchants gathered, at a time when mercantile risks were becoming too large for one man or a small group to carry alone.

Still a City Institution, Lloyds will accept risks only through the agency of a Lloyds broker. Business is written by under-writers acting on behalf of syndicates of members who accept liability as individuals, without limit. Any number of syndicates may share a risk.

(ii) Tariff offices

These offices, numbering approximately 35 current full members, belong to the Fire Offices Committee. They include most, but not all, of the major UK groups.

They agree among themselves to abide by certain rules, governing the conduct of business in matters such as policy conditions, some rates and technical matters (e.g. sprinkler rules) with the object of creating a stable market.

The Monopolies Commission investigated and reported on these agreements in 1972, recommending a number of changes. However, successive governments have taken no action and meanwhile the FOC have modified or abandoned some of their agreements. The end of the system has been annually and reliably forecast for some years.

(iii) Independent offices

These offices form the remaining major sector. Collectively their capacity is smaller than the tariff offices, but they include several major groups and are capable of underwriting large schedules. Often they will follow a tariff lead, offering some discount on tariff terms, justified by lower operating costs. They also tend to follow the FOC lead in technical matters.

(iv) Captive Insurers

A modern development alongside the conventional market, captives are set up for the purpose of writing the business of one company or group, of which they are usually a subsidiary. One of the incentives for their establishment is the benefit to the parent of being in a low tax territory.

The principle insurer will often provide the technical or other facilities normally available with more traditional arrangements.

(2) Overseas insurers

In very general terms the system operating in other countries may seem similar to that applying in the UK. There will be groups of companies which agree together on a uniform way of writing business and there will be other companies which will operate independently of any such agreement.

However, it must be recognized that when insurance is affected in an overseas territory the policy conditions and cover may differ widely from UK practice and vary from country to country.

(i) Europe

Work has been going on for some years to try and achieve some standardization within the EEC but so far, to little effect.

(ii) USA

There are a number of major insurance companies and some of these operate in combines. Their influence both inside US and in other countries, including UK, is very considerable. In technical matters US practice varies considerably but where major risks are concerned they tend to combine low rates with a strong emphasis on fire engineering and to accept partial protection to a greater degree than UK insurers. This is sometimes known as the HPR (highly protected risks concept). US and UK approaches are often incompatible.

(iii) Others

Almost every country will have its own insurance organizations but in many cases these will operate by seeking support in the major insurance markets. (eg UK or US). In technical matters they will almost certainly follow the lead of the larger countries and in general terms their influence on insurance matters is small.

6.3 Intermediaries

The satisfactory arrangement of insurance for a client is, or can be, very complicated and for this reason the insurance will probably be arranged by a specialist intermediary. These intermediaries, collectively known as agents fall into three categories.

(i) Brokers

Brokers are insurance specialists who must now be registered if they use the description 'broker'. Some are major international companies with a large experienced staff able to match the insurer in expertise. At the other end of the scale are small brokers, perhaps with one or two principals and a small staff, typically dealing with domestic and small commercial and industrial business. *The basic function of a broker is to use his expertise to place clients business in the best market.*

Technically, most are agents of the insurer, earning commission, but some now act for a client on a fee-paying basis, especially in large cases. It may be necessary to employ a Lloyds broker if access to Lloyds is required.

(ii). Insurance Consultants

Those who work to provide a specialist insurance service, but are not registered as brokers. In other respects they function in much the same way as brokers, earning either commission or fees.

(iii) Agents

Most agents are professional men or businesses who are in a non-insurance sphere but who are in a position to influence the placing of insurance business.

Solicitors, bank managers, accountants often hold agencies and building societies, estate agents, motor garages are usually agents for one or more insurance company.

Agents do not usually have more than a limited knowledge of the insurance field, although large organizations, e.g. banks and building societies often have specialist insurance departments at their regional or head offices.

6.4 Type of cover

In general the architect is unlikely to be asked to decide details of the insurance cover required but it may be useful here to list very briefly the kind of cover which is commonly included in a Fire Insurance Policy together with other items which impinge on an architect's operations.

(i) Standard fire cover

(a) Material damage

This cover is designed to meet the physical losses suffered by the insured to his property, usually buildings and/or their contents, but often extended to property in the open and to property of others for which the insured has liability. There may also be extensions to cover the property of the insured at the premises of others. The cover granted by the basic policy is for fire and explosion of boilers used for domestic purposes, that is space heating, water supply to washrooms and the like. There is one major variation to this in that Lloyds policies give unlimited explosion cover. For a fire to have occurred in the fire insurance sense, there must have been actual ignition; something on fire which ought not to be on fire; and it must have been fortuitous insofar as the insured is concerned. Damage caused by the inevitable consequences of the fire, such as smoke and extinguishing water, are also included.

(b) Consequential loss (CL)

This covers the indirect losses resulting from an insured peril and cover is granted for gross profit loss during an indemnity period.

(c) Additional perils

These are items which are traditionally included in a fire policy. Normally they are storm, tempest, flood and burst pipes, impact, aircraft, explosion, earthquake, riot, civil commotion and malicious damage, with subsidence and heave now generally available.

(d) Conditions

Insurance policies will always be subject to conditions which are categorized as standard conditions and special conditions.

An example of a standard condition could be a clause which gave the insurer the right to reinstate the damage rather than pay the cost and a special condition of interest to the construction industry would be the Local Authorities (Reinstatement) Clause which provides that where a loss occurs because of Local

135

Authority or legislative requirements, it is necessary to build in a more costly form than the original, the additional cost will be met.

(ii) Other associated types of cover available

(a) Sprinkler leakage

Gives cover for loss sustained by the accidental discharge of sprinklers.

(b) First loss

Most policies are based on cover for the full value of the insured property but exceptionally cover may be based on a first loss basis, that is the sum assured is set at a figure lower than the full value, the insured meeting any loss above this figure. First loss cover is proportionally more expensive.

(c) Contractor's all risks (CAR)

A form of cover designed to meet the potential liabilities, contractural or legal, of builders and contractors arising from their operations. The cover may be taken out by the contractor or his employer.

Cover will be provided for work completed but not handed over and for damage to neighbouring property resulting from negligence on the part of the contractor.

(d) Variations

There is now a great variety of covers available and it is possible by negotiation to persuade an insurer to vary normal conditions.

However, it should be borne in mind that insurers prefer standard cover for ease of administration and low cost and they prefer standard wording because case law has established the meaning of most of them beyond doubt.

6.5 Assessment of risk

The *underwriter* or insurer, when presented with a proposal for insurance will need to be provided with information about the risk and for a large proposal he will probably call on a *fire surveyor* who will furnish him with a *fire survey report*.

The fire survey report may vary in detail according to the company but typically it will give information on:

(a) construction of the building(s);
(b) occupation, relating particularly to trade hazards;
(c) power supplies;
(d) water supplies;
(e) heating arrangements;
(f) fire protection arrangements;
(g) exposure from adjoining/adjacent buildings;
(h) availability of public fire brigades;
(i) housekeeping/standard of management;
(j) previous fire history (if any).

(For a new building still in the design stage some of this information may not be available.) The fire survey report may suggest a rate and give an estimate of the maximum probable loss. Plans may be required, either from the designer or prepared by the fire surveyor. Insurance plans are normally 1:500 and use the generally accepted insurance symbols (Appendix 1).

The fire surveyor may make suggestions for improving the risk. If these are ultimately put to the proposer or building designer they may be either:

(a) conditional to the insurance being accepted;
(b) advantageous from a rating/premium point of view;
(c) purely a matter of good practice.

The fire surveyor makes his report to the underwriter but he will always be prepared to offer advice to the designer on all matters relating to fire protection and fire prevention.

6.6 Rating

The premium charged for most fire insurance is usually based on a rate percent of the sum insured. The rate itself, which may vary considerably from building to building will be based on a basic rate with various loadings and/or discounts applied.

(i) Basic rate

This will vary considerably depending on the risk from, say, 0.075% for office accommodation to, perhaps, 0.75% for very hazardous risks.

(ii) Loadings

Features which are considered to increase the hazard will be penalised in the form of loading to the basic rate. Examples of such features are:

(a) combustible construction;
(b) heating (both process and space heating);
(c) machinery (high hazard trades);
(d) chemical or industrial processes of high hazard;
(e) storage of combustible materials.

(iii) Discounts

Varying by as much as 5% to 60% or more may be obtained for good features. Examples are:

(a) superior construction (e.g. sub-division of multistorey buildings between floors);
(b) fixed/portable fire protection (e.g. sprinklers, automatic fire alarm systems, hosereels, extinguishers, etc.);
(c) hazard reducing features for trade machinery (e.g. waste extraction system to external cyclone from wood working machinery);
(d) long term agreements where insured agrees to renew the insurance for a predetermined number of years.

6.7 Rules and recommendations

(i) In the UK

(a) Fire Offices Committee.

This committee has prepared rules and regulations on behalf of the Tariff office. The tariffs and the general rules prepared by the FOC are confidential to the insurers but some information is available to the public. The list given below may be useful:

Tariffs ⎫ confidential and not available to the
General rules ⎭ public
Construction rules—Standards I/V,
Grades 1/2
Sprinkler rules (currently 29th edition)
Rules for automatic fire alarm systems
Fire door and shutter rules

Scales of allowances for fire extinguishing appliances
Recommendations for good practice

(b) Fire insurers' research and testing organization

This is a research and testing organization supported by the FOC which carries out standard tests, *ad hoc* tests, and research projects. Anyone requiring information about a material or construction can sponsor work at this laboratory and their services may be important in determining whether the material or construction will satisfy the various rules.

(c) Fire Protection Association

Sponsored by the Fire Insurance Market, but also supported by subscriptions from industry and the professions, it produces a series of data sheets, booklets, fire safety sheets, information sheets and design guides (see Appendix 2). The Fire Prevention Design Guides, *Fire and the architect* have been produced in collaboration with the RIBA.

The FPA also organizes training courses and seminars on fire related subjects. Attendance at these is in general open to anyone who has an interest in the subject.

(ii) In the USA and Canada

(a) National Fire Protection Association

Situated at Boston USA, the Association publishes annually the National Fire Codes which are a compilation of NFPA Codes, Standards, Recommended Practices and Manuals.

This publication is widely used in US by insurers and by the Building Control Authorities. It is also becoming used outside the US.

(b) Factory Mutual Insurance of US

Have published loss prevention sheets and recommendations which are extensive and run to several volumes. They cover the subjects of construction, sprinklers, water supplies, extinguishing equipment, electrical, industrial heating, hazard and storage, with also an in depth loss analysis.

There is considerable cross referencing between this publication and the National Fire Codes, and it operates a materials approval system.

(iii) Other countries

Fire Protection Associations

Many overseas countries will have their own Fire Protection Associations and these act to provide information to the building designer about the requirements imposed in that country for insurance purposes.

6.8 Statutory regulations and fire insurance

Building regulations

It is important to remember that Building Regulations are concerned with health and safety and deal with structural precautions necessary for the safety of personnel. The insurer on the other hand is concerned with the safety of the building and its contents.

For this reason it will often happen that the insurers requirements differ from those of the Building Regulations and in many instances the insurance requirements are more stringent than those specified by Building Regulations.

Fire Precautions Act 1971

The provisions of this Act have not had any marked effect on the insurance market but again there may be occasions when the requirements of this Act and those of insurance are at variance (for example, the provision for escape purposes of a door in a wall which insurers require to have several hours of fire resistance).

Health and Safety at Work etc. Act 1974

This Act has been described in other sections of the book and has serious insurance aspects as it puts the duty of care by 'self-regulation' on employers and employees, to maintain reasonable standards of safety in places of work.

Guidance is frequently given by the Health and Safety Executive on reasonable standards and sites and buildings identified as of special risk will now be controlled by the Health and Safety at Work etc. Act special premises regulations. These place the sole duty of approval on the Health and Safety Executive and their standards may be different because of the risks involved, than those normally covered by Building Regulations or Fire Precautions Act (see detailed description in other chapters).

Other miscellaneous acts

Examples of these are: The Explosives Act, The Petroleum Act, The Highly Flammable Liquids and Liquified Petroleum Gases Regulations 1972, etc.

It is generally fair to say that where the provisions of statutes such as these are being adhered to the insurers will not require any more stringent precautions to be taken.

6.9 British Standards and Codes of Practice

In many respects the requirements of insurers and of specific British Standards (e.g. fire alarm systems) are very similar. Where appropriate the insurance interests are consulted in the drafting of new standards and codes of practice and they are represented on the various committees.

However, there is some mistrust of some of the aspects of BS 476 which specifies fire tests on building materials and structures. Indeed it is generally recognized that because real fires are all different the use of a standard test can never represent the true behaviour of a material or construction when exposed to an actual fire. Nevertheless while the insurers accept some of the BS 476 tests for their specifications (for instance BS 476:Part 8, 1972, Tests for fire resistance of elements of building construction, and BS 476:Part 4, 1970, Non-combustibility test for materials), in other respects it prefers to rely on the specification of the materials used in some of their standards of construction.

The problem of using a standard test to indicate behaviour in real fires is a continuing one and research using large scale test rigs is in progress.

6.10 Sources of information and advice on fire protection

Name of organization	Location
UK	
Fire Offices Committee	London
Fire Insurers Research and Testing Organization	Borehamwood
Fire Research Station, Building Research Station	Borehamwood
Fire Protection Association	London
Royal Institute of British Architects	London
Overseas	
National Fire Protection Association	Boston, USA
Factory Mutual	USA
Underwriters Laboratory	USA
Fire Protection Associations	in all major countries

Appendix 1
Fire Insurance Plan Drawing Symbols

1 Walls

(a) brickwork, stone or concrete not less than 225 mm (9 in) thick without cavity

(b) brickwork, stone or concrete other than as in (a)

(c) non-combustible material on non-combustible frame other than as in (a) or (b)

(d) material or frame not conforming with (c)

(e) metal column, protected

(f) metal column, unprotected

(g) brick or concrete column

Note: A wall of mixed construction shall be shown by the symbol for the construction having the least fire resistance.

2 Wall openings

Openings in walls must be shown if they exist in any storey.

(a) unprotected doorway or opening other than a window in a wall as defined in 1(a)

(b) window in a wall as defined in 1(a)

(c) window or other opening overlooking the roof of an adjoining building (exposure hazard), the window marks to appear inside the higher building

(d) openings as in 2(a), 2(b) or 2(c), protected by single fireproof door or shutter

(e) openings as in 2(a), 2(b) or 2(c), protected by double fireproof doors or shutters

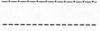

3 Roofs

Symbols (a) to (f) below shall be marked in the right-hand bottom corner of drawing of building.

Symbols (j) and (k) below shall be marked in right-hand top corner of drawing of building.

(a) concrete, with or without a covering of weather-proofing material   CONC

(b) entirely non-combustible materials, other than concrete   NC

(c) external surface of slates, tiles, asphalt, asbestos, or metal, or a roof of felt on a non-combustible deck, other than as in 3(a) or 3(b)   S

(d) wood, including felt on wood   W

(e) metal, coated on both sides with bitumen   B

(f) materials other than those specified above   X

(g) roof profiles, e.g., span or hipped roof (the absence of a roof line denotes a flat roof)

(h) glass lantern or rooflight in non-combustible frame

(i) glass, plastics or glass-fibre reinforced lantern or rooflight, frameless or in combustible frame

(j) non-combustible roof linings   NCL

(k) combustible roof linings   CL

4 Floor openings

To indicate that a staircase or lift is enclosed, the walls shall be drawn to the appropriate symbol in Section 1 on walls.

Floors which are pierced shall be indicated.

(a) staircase having stairs and landings of brick, stone, concrete or metal

(b) staircase having stairs and/or landings of wood

(c) lift or hoist

(d) other floor openings – well-holes, etc.

143

5 Miscellaneous

(a) Structures

    (i) height of buildings shall be indicated by the figure in the left-hand bottom corner of the building, which denotes the number of storeys. Prefix B for basement

    (ii) fire-resisting construction shall be indicated in the left-hand top corner by the letters FRC

(b) Storage tanks

    (i) on ground level in the open, according to shape (contents shall be indicated)

    (ii) elevated, according to shape (contents shall be indicated)

    (iii) where a bund or catchpit is provided this shall be shown by an additional thin line around symbol (i) or (ii)

(c) Fuel dispensing pumps

    (i) petrol

    (ii) diesel

    (iii) kerosene

(d) Building containing cartway

(e) Adjoining or adjacent buildings not included in the premises shall be shaded round the edge

(f) A bridge giving access from one building to another shall be drawn in appropriate construction under Section 1 – WALLS with indication of floors served; e.g., open timber gangway giving access from second floor of one building to third floor of another

(g) Boundary walls and fences

    (i) brick, stone or concrete

    (ii) metal, asbestos or wire

    (iii) timber

(h) Materials in the open – indicate material

6 Fire protection arrangements

(a) Fixed

    (i) the area covered by automatic sprinklers

   (ii) the area covered by automatic fire alarms

  (iii) surface of building covered by drencher protection

(b) Water supplies

    (i) hydrant, single, double

   (ii) open water, with access point

  (iii) static water supply, surface tank, with capacity in gallons

Appendix 2
Information Available from FPA

Compendium of fire safety data comprising:

Binder 1   *Management of fire risks*

MR 1   Management responsibility for fire prevention
MR 2   How to establish a planning programme
MR 3   Fire facts and figures
MR 4   Fire safety patrols
MR 5   Security against fire-raisers
MR 6   Fire precautions during stoppages of work in factories
MR 7   Procedure in event of fire
MR 8   Protecting against the aftermath of fire
MR 9   First-day induction training
MR 10   Industrial fire safety training
MR 11   FPA guide to how factory buildings can be adapted to control fire spread

Organization of fire safety

OR 1   Fire protection law
OR 2   Fire brigades
OR 3   The Health and Safety Commission
OR 4   Government Departments
OR 5   Fire Research

Nature and behaviour of fire

NB 1   The physics and chemistry of fire
NB 2   Ignition, growth and development of fire
NB 3   The physiological effects of fire

Binder 2   *Industrial and process fire safety*

FS 6011   Flammable liquids and gases: explosion hazards
FS 6012   Flammable liquids and gases: explosion control
FS 6013   Flammable liquids and gases: ventilation
FS 6014   Flammable liquids and gases: electrical equipment
FS 6015   Explosible dusts, flammable liquids and gases: explosion suppression
FS 6016   Hydraulic oil systems: fire safety
FS 6017   FPA guide to safety with piped services

FS 6018	FPA guide to safety precautions in heat treatment plants
FS 6019	Heat treatment baths
FS 6020	Electro-plating
FS 6021	Explosible dusts: the hazards
FS 6022	Explosible dusts: control of explosions
FS 6023	Explosible dusts: the elimination of ignition sources
FS 6024	Explosible dusts: extraction
FS 6025	Electric soldering irons
FS 6026	FPA guide to safe practice with flammable liquids
FS 6027	Bund walls for flammable liquids storage tanks
FS 6028	Safety containers for flammable liquids
FS 6029	Non-sparking tools
FS 6030	Cleaning contaminated electronic equipment
FS 6031	Shrink-wrapping
FS 6032	Vapour degreasing
FS 6033	Crushing and grinding
FS 6034	Reciprocating compressors
FS 6035	Electro-discharge machining
FS 6036	Electrostatic wet paint spraying

Binder 3	*Housekeeping and general fire precautions*
GP 1	Fire safety with outside contractors
GP 2	Cutting and welding
GP 3	Hot work permits
GP 4	Blowlamps and torches
GP 5	Safe practice in production areas
GP 6	Safe practice in storage areas
GP 7	Outdoor storage
GP 8	Planning guide to space heating
GP 9	Planning guide to fire dangers from smoking
GP 10	Waste incinerators
GP 11	Oil soaked floors
GP 12	FPA guide to fire doors and shutters
GP 13	Foundry pattern stores
GP 14	Flame retardant treatment for textiles

| Binder 4 | A list of the 96 information sheets on hazardous materials are contained in this binder. |

Binder 5	*Fire protection equipment and systems*
PE 1	Automatic fire detection and alarm systems
PE 2	Fire points
PE 3	Fire blankets
PE 4	Portable fire extinguishers
PE 5	First-aid fire fighting: training
PE 6	Fixed fire—extinguishing equipment: the choice of system
PE 7	Fixed fire—extinguishing equipment: hose reels
PE 8	Fixed fire—extinguishing equipment: hydrant systems
PE 9	Safety during sprinkler shut-down

Binder 6	*Buildings and fire design guide*
FPDG 1	Fire prevention design guide: fire and the law
FPDG 2	Fire prevention design guide: site requirements—space separation

147

FPDG 3   Fire prevention design guide: control of fire and smoke within a building
FPDG 4   Fire prevention design guide: planning means of escape
FPDG 5   Fire prevention design guide: fire-fighting facilities for the fire brigade
FPDG 6   Fire prevention design guide: equipment for detection and warning of fire and fighting fire
FPDG 7   Fire prevention design guide: fire hazard assessment
FPDG 8   Fire prevention design guide: fire insurance
FPDG 9   Fire prevention design guide: building services
FPDG 10   Fire prevention design guide: cavities and voids in building construction
FPDG 11   Fire prevention design guide: suspended ceilings
FPDG 12   Fire prevention design guide: construction of roofs
FPDG 13   Fire prevention design guide: flame retardant treatments for wood and its derivatives
FPDG 14   Fire prevention design guide: fire doors and shutters

Building products

B 1   Wood wool building products
B 2   Asbestos insulating boards and asbestos wallboards
B 3   Rock fibre building insulation products
B 4   Gypsum plasterboard
B 5   Vermiculite-silicate building products
B 6   Sprayed vermiculite cement
B 7   Gypsum plasters
B 8   Sprayed mineral fibre
B 9   Glass reinforced cement
B 10   Asbestos based partition board
B 11   Fibre reinforced calcium silicate insulating boards
B 12   Fibre reinforced Portland cement

Appendix 3
Table of Calorific Values of Common and Industrial Materials

Materials	Calorific value		
	Btu lb^{-1}	cal g^{-1} or k cal kg^{-1}	Wood equivalent lb wood/lb material or kg wood/kg material
Solids			
(a) *Solid Fuels*			
Coal			
Anthracite	13 300	7 390	1.66
Bituminous	14 000	7 780	1.75
Sub-bituminous	10 000	5 555	1.25
Coke (average)	12 500	6 944	1.56
Woods (average hard and softwood)	8 000	4 444	1.00
Peats (average)	9 500	5 278	1.19
Charcoal	12 900	7 167	1.61
(b) *Common solids*			
Asphalt	17 400	9 667	2.18
Bitumen	15 200	8 444	1.90
Carbon	14 600	8 111	1.83
Cotton (dry and combed)	7 200	4 000	0.90
Dynamite	2 300	1 278	0.29
Flax	6 500	3 611	0.81
Furs and skins (average)	8 500	4 722	1.06
Glucose	6 700	3 722	0.84
Glycerin	7 700	4 278	0.96
Graphite (plumbago)	14 200	7 890	1.78
Guncotton	1 900	1 055	0.24
Gunpowder	13 500	7 500	1.69
Hair (animal)	9 500	5 280	1.19
Leather	8 000	4 440	1.00
Lignite	6 500	3 610	0.81
Tallow	17 100	9 500	2.14
Ozokerite (wax)	19 700	10 900	2.46
Paper (average)	7 000	3 890	0.88
Paraffin wax	18 600	10 300	2.33

Materials	Calorific value		
	Btu lb^{-1}	cal g^{-1} or k cal kg^{-1}	Wood equivalent lb wood/lb material or kg wood/kg material
Pitch	15 000	8 330	1.88
Rubber	17 000	9 440	2.13
Silk (raw)	9 200	5 110	1.15
Starch	7 500	4 170	0.94
Straw	6 000	3 330	0.75
Tallows	17 100	9 500	2.14
Tan bark	9 500	5 280	1.19
Tar (bituminous)	16 000	8 890	2.00
Waxes	17 000	9 440	2.13
Wool			
Raw	9 800	5 440	1.23
Scoured	8 900	4 940	1.11
Woods			
Average for soft and			
hardwoods	8 000	4 440	1.00
12% moisture			
(c) *Foodstuffs*			
Barley	6 400	3 555	0.80
Bread	4 500	2 500	0.56
Corn meal	6 400	3 555	0.80
Flour	6 400	3 555	0.80
Hominy	6 400	3 555	0.80
Macaroni	6 400	3·555	0.80
Oatmeal	7 200	4 000	0.90
Rice	6 300	3 500	0.79
Soya bean flour	7 300	4 055	0.91
Wheat			
Whole	6 500	3 610	0.81
Bran	5 000	2 780	0.63
Butter	13 400	7 440	1.68
Cheese (cheddar)	8 200	4 555	1.03
Prunes (dried)	6 600	3 670	0.83
Bacon	11 300	6 280	1.41
Beef (average)	4 000	2 220	0.50
Sardines in oil	5 700	3 170	0.71
Gelatin	6 600	3 670	0.83
Margarine	13 400	7 440	1.68
Nuts			
Almonds	11 600	6 440	1.45
Brazils	12 500	6 940	1.56
Chestnuts	4 400	2 440	0.55
Coconut (dry)	12 000	6 670	1.50
Peanuts	10 000	5 555	1.25
Walnuts	12 700	7 055	1.59
Chocolate			
Unsweetened	11 000	6 110	1.38
Sweetened	9 100	5 055	1.14
Cocoa	8 900	4 940	1.11
Sugar	7 000	3 890	0.88

	Calorific value		
Materials	**Btu lb^{-1}**	**cal g^{-1} or k cal kg^{-1}**	**Wood equivalent lb wood/lb material or kg wood/kg material**
(d) *Industrial chemicals*			
Acetahalide	13 500	7 500	1.69
Acids			
Benzoic	11 700	6 500	1.46
Citric	4 500	2 500	0.56
Lactic	6 300	3 500	0.79
Oxalic	1 200	667	0.15
Palmitic	17 000	9 440	2.13
Picric	4 900	2 720	0.61
Stearic	17 100	9 500	2.14
Tartaric	3 300	1 830	0.41
Miscellaneous			
Cetyl alcohol	18 600	10 330	2.33
Anthracene	17 200	9 555	2.15
Bagasse (53% moisture)	4 000	2 220	0.50
Benzoin	9 100	5 055	1.14
Caffeine	8 600	4 780	1.08
Camphene	19 000	10 555	2.38
Camphor	16 200	9 000	2.03
Casein	10 500	5 830	1.31
Cellulose	7 500	4 170	0.94
Cellulose acetate	8 100	4 500	1.01
Dextrin	7 800	4 330	0.98
Magnesium	10 900	6 055	1.36
Naphthalene	17 300	9 610	2.16
Octane	20 600	11 440	2.58
Phenol (carbolic acid)	14 100	7 830	1.76
Plastics			
Nylon	10 000	5 555	1.25
Polyester	10 000	5 555	1.25
Polystyrene	19 000	10 555	2.38
Polyruethane	16 000	8 890	2.00
Polyvinylchloride	9 500	5 280	1.19
Polyethylene (polythene)	22 000	12 220	2.75
Polypropylene	22 000	12 220	2.75
Acrilic	11 200	6 200	1.40
Stearin	16 900	9 390	2.11
Liquids			
Acetaldehyde	11 400	6 330	1.43
Acetone	13 500	7 500	1.69
Acids			
Acetic	6 300	3 500	0.79
Carbolic	14 000	7 780	1.75
Formic	2 500	1 390	0.31
Oleic	16 900	9 390	2.11
Alcohols			
Allyl	16 200	9 000	2.03
Amyl	13 700	7 610	1.71

Materials	Calorific value		
	Btu lb^{-1}	cal g^{-1} or k cal kg^{-1}	Wood equivalent lb wood/lb material or kg wood/kg material
Butyl	15 500	8 610	1.94
Denatured	11 700	6 500	1.46
Ethyl	12 900	7 170	1.61
Methyl (wood)	9 600	5 330	1.20
Propyl	14 500	8 055	1.81
Aldol	11 200	6 220	1.40
Amyl acetate	14 400	8 000	1.80
Amylene	20 600	11 440	2.58
Anilene	15 700	8 720	1.96
Benzene (benzol)	18 000	10 000	2.25
Butane	21 400	11 890	2.68
Carbon disulphide	10 100	5 610	1.26
Chloroform	1 300	722	0.16
Decane	20 400	11 330	2.55
Diethyl ether (ether)	16 500	9 170	2.06
Ethyl acetate	10 900	6 055	1.36
Ethyl bromide	5 700	3 170	0.71
Ethyl iodide	4 200	2 330	0.53
Foodstuffs (misc.)			
Honey	5 900	3 280	0.74
Syrup	5 000	2 780	0.63
Marmalade	6 000	3 330	0.75
Molasses	5 200	2 890	0.65
Olive oil	16 700	9 280	2.09
Glycerol	7 700	4 280	0.96
Hexane	20 400	11 330	2.55
Methane	24 000	13 330	3.00
Nicotine	15 800	8 780	1.98
Nitro-benzene	10 900	6 055	1.36
Nitro-glycerin	3 400	1 890	0.43
Oils and waxes			
Vegetable, nut and animal oils	17 100	9 500	2.14
Castor	16 000	8 890	2.00
Coal tar	18 400	10 220	2.30
Fuel oil	18 900	10 500	2.36
Gas oil	19 500	10 830	2.44
Mineral lubricants	17 100	9 500	2.14
Paraffin	18 000–20 000	10 000–11 110	2.25–2.50
Sperm	18 000	10 000	2.25
Toluene	18 300	10 170	2.29
Xylene	18 400	10 220	2.30
Gases			
Acetylene	21 600	12 000	2.70
Allylene	21 200	11 780	2.65
Butane	21 400	11 890	2.68
Butylene	20 900	11 610	2.61
Cyanogen	9 000	5 000	1.13
Dimethyl ether (methyl)	13 600	7 555	1.70

Materials	Calorific value		
	Btu lb^{-1}	cal g^{-1} or k cal kg^{-1}	Wood equivalent lb wood/lb material or kg wood/kg material
Ethane	22 300	12 389	2.79
Ethylene	21 700	12 055	2.71
Formaldehyde	8 000	4 440	1.00
Hydrogen	61 000	33 890	7.63
Methane	24 000	13 330	3.00
Methyl chloride	5 850	3 250	0.73
Pentane	20 900	11 610	2.61
Propane	21 500	11 940	2.69
Propylene	21 000	11 670	2.63

Part 2

Part 2

CHAPTER SEVEN

Inception and feasibility

7.1
Fire safety aspects of site selection

SITE FACTORS

(a) Those which might cause or contribute to a fire
(b) Those which might affect the design of fire safety measures
(c) Those which might affect fire fighting operations.

Any site analysis should include these factors.

The illustrations show how three different sites could present some of these factors, which would obviously have to be analysed in much greater detail. For example, the coal mine of the green field site might cause subsidence so that special measures would be needed to cope with building settlement which might pose problems in maintaining continuity of fire-resisting construction (6) — but the mine might also be able to provide equipment or trained manpower to help deal with a fire on the new site. etc.

Green Field Site

(a) Heath/wood-land
    Power line
(b) Mining subsidence
    River/canal:
(c) +water for firefighting
(a),(b) flooding
    Trunk road/railways:
(a) Transport accidents
    involving hazardous
    material encroaching on
    site
(c) Emergency services
    availability
(a),(b) Gradients & falls
(b),(c) Lack of 'infrastructure'

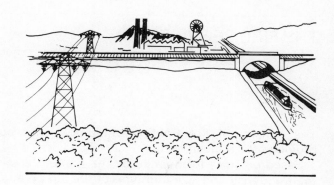

Suburban Site

    Adjoining users:
(a),(b) Threats from –
(c) Threats to –
(a) Transport hazards
(a),(b) Falls & gradients
(c) Road congestion effect on
    emergency service
    attendance

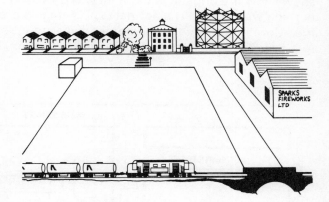

Urban Site

(c) Restricted Access
(a),(c) Adjoining users:
(b) Restricted exits for people
(b) Tighter statutory controls
    where buildings are close
(b),(c) Road congestion effect on
    emergency services
    attendance

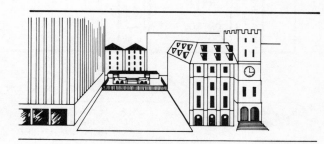

THE FIRE SERVICE

Fire cover

The density of fire fighting equipment and personnel provided for a given area.

Based on rules formulated by the home office in which the frequency and size and type of fires to be expected in an area have a strong influence

Access

The diagram below (reproduced by courtesy of *Fire*) shows how fire brigade equipment was deployed around a burning warehouse. The normal tactics are to surround the fire. More details on the recommended amount of access to a new building's perimeter is given in section 8.1.

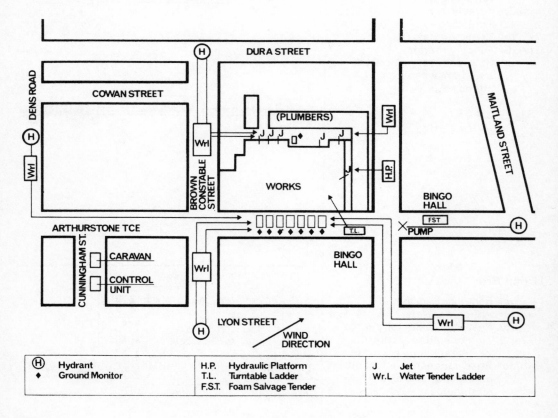

Ⓗ	Hydrant	H.P.	Hydraulic Platform	J	Jet
◆	Ground Monitor	T.L.	Turntable Ladder	Wr.L	Water Tender Ladder
		F.S.T.	Foam Salvage Tender		

Fire 'engines'—known by the general term 'appliance' or by specific titles such as:

> Pump
> Water tender
> Turntable ladder (TTL)
> Hydraulic platform (HP)
> Foam tender
> Hose laying vehicle
> Salvage tender
> Control vehicle

vary widely from one fire authority to another. The minimum requirements for access roads are given in section 8.1.

Water

Water

As one hose jet (called a 'branch') may require 6,000 gallons/hour (27,276 litres/hour) very substantial water supplies may be needed — at the incident above the peak flow rate could have been 100,000 gallons/hour (454,600 litres/hour)

As well as mains hydrants open water can be most useful in fire fighting

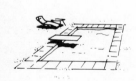

Swimming pools

Ornamental pools

Rivers   Canals

Lakes

The fire authority has a duty to see that reasonable provision is made for water for fire fighting purposes.

By using a series of pumps and long hose runs water can be relayed over long distances (1 mile plus) but it is slow and no new building should rely on such a system

Interested parties

Organisations having an interest in aspects of fire safety at the earliest stage of planning (obviously with any one project only a few of these bodies are likely to be involved)

District Council

Planning
Public Health (Environmental Health)
Licensing — Petroleum
                Entertainments
                Liquor (occasionally)

County Council

Planning
Highways and traffic engineering
Fire

Water Authority

Health and Safety Inspectorate:

Fire authority — Chief fire officer's check list

Site size and building size
General complexity of development
Relationship to other features of the area
Type of structure
Type of occupancy
Will there be any hazardous materials or processes, e.g. chemicals, fuels, radioactivity?
How does the new risk compare with existing ones in the area?
Is there going to be any effect on the existing road and traffic pattern?
Will water supplies be affected in the vicinity by the demands of the development?
Where is there space to muster emergency vehicles during an incident? There could be 50 attending a large development

Adequate drainage to remove fire fighting water
Suitability of brigade's appliances.

Consideration of these factors may, in extreme cases, lead the chief fire officer to recommend his authority to build a new fire station. The 'risk category' of the area around the development could be reclassified and new appliances or equipment have to be acquired.

The fire service college has been developing a system that allows problems of this sort to be considered at the design stage. A model is made of the development and surrounding area. A moving gantry carries a TV camera which views the model at scale eye-level through an optical probe, and produces a detailed realistic picture on a closed circuit monitor.

The illustrations show the simulation of a fire incident in a town centre used by the college in the training of senior officers.

7.2
Fire protection
objectives

Inception and feasibility

The determination of *life safety* and *property protection* objectives should be a part of the development in the brief

LIFE SAFETY

(1) Identify the people at risk and rank them by vulnerability e.g. in a maternity unit

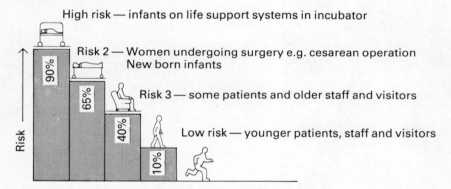

High risk — infants on life support systems in incubator

Risk 2 — Women undergoing surgery e.g. cesarean operation
New born infants

Risk 3 — some patients and older staff and visitors

Low risk — younger patients, staff and visitors

90%   65%   40%   10%

Risk

Only three or four levels need be identified

Allow for effects of surroundings as well as personal attributes

E.g.
Crowds — panic reaction or congestion more likely
Unfamiliarity with surroundings
Darkness — adjustment to low light takes longer in older people
Reduced sensitivity to designs of danger — sleep, drugs, noise, smell, heat.
Isolation from signs of danger —
Distance (large building)
Heavy construction
Layout (functional requirement)

(2) Identify the potential hazards to life

Causes or sources of fire	Fire behaviour

Highly combustible materials
    Stored
    Made
    Used
    Incorporated in plant or
       fittings
	Rapid fire spread
	    Closely spaced fuel material
	    Vertical element in fuel
	       disposition
	    No physical barriers
	    Heat not dispersed to atmosphere
	    Delayed discovery

Process Risks
e.g. Heat treatments
    Use of materials heated
       near flash point, e.g.
       deep fat frying
    Formation of combustible
       dust, e.g. flour milling
    Paint spray flammable solvent
	Rapid smoke/toxic gas spread
	    'Smokey' fuel
	    Burning rate restricted by air
	       supply
	    No physical barriers
	    No significant venting
	       to atmosphere

Equipment
    Boilers, heaters
    Motors,
    Moving parts subject to
       overheating
    Electrical equipment
    Open-flame devices, e.g.
       welding torch	

HUMAN BEHAVIOUR

Causing fires	Exacerbating fires

Careless disposal of
   matches or cigarettes, etc.
Arson and vandalism
Mistakes in use of potential
   fire-risk plant or material
Failure to maintain potential
   fire-risk equipment
	Failure to maintain protective
	   systems, e.g. leaving doors open
	Failure to recognize that
	   a fire is burning
	Doing the wrong thing when
	   fire emergency occurs

(3) Study arrangements of activities and spaces to see how (1) and (2) might affect one another

Assess or grade alternative layouts according to level of fire risk occupants are exposed to.

(4) Consider passive and active measures to reduce risk — recognizing that full potential of any measure is rarely achieved in practice

(5) Identify basic escape/exit requirement for each different activity/major space/occupant type

(6) Check preferred arrangement against the relevant statutory requirements

All this has to fit in to the other facets of the design problem:

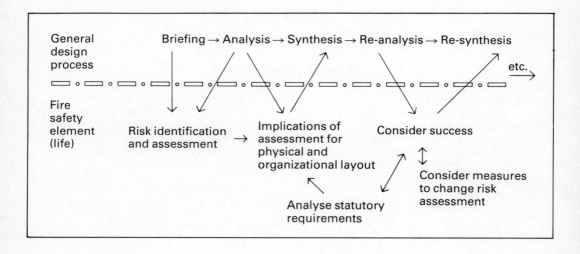

PROPERTY LOSS

(1) Identify the high value parts

The fabric of the building
The contents of the building
    e.g. Works of art
         Records or 'software'
         Manufactured product
         Raw material
         Expensive or hard-to-replace plant
The service provided from the building
    as for a power station, hospital, company H.Q.
    etc
(High value is not necessarily ≡ high capital cost)

(2) Determine acceptable level of loss

Agree the objectives of the property protection measures in each part, e.g. accept a small chance of catastrophic loss but take steps to guard against frequent minor loss

(3) Form of protection

Determine the extent to which protection will be physical or through insurance
(There may not always be this alternative)

(4) Risk Reduction by design

Study arrangement of activities processes and spaces to minimize the risks and assess the results

(5) Protection systems

Consider active or passive measures to further reduce risks where need be or changes in the brief to eliminate a risk altogether

METHODOLOGY OF RISK ANALYSIS

Although every problem is different and the analysis of risk is, despite statistics and probability theory etc., subjective to a considerable extent, various systematic approaches to the subject have been developed. Reproduced below is a 'decision tree' developed at the US general service administration which can be used as a check list in the course of the design process.

Starting at the top — the tree proposes alternative ways (not necessarily mutually exclusive) of meeting pre-determined fire safety objectives.

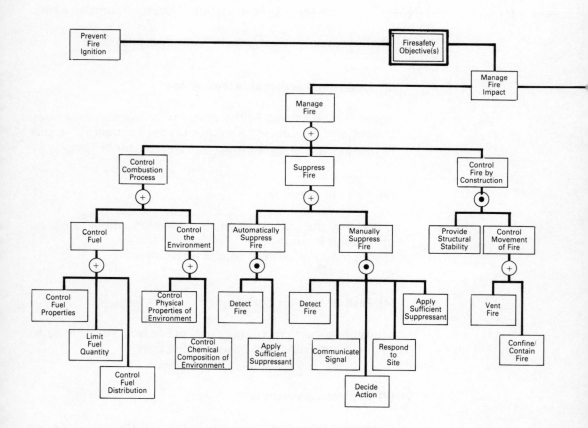

Ultimately the hope is that numerical probabilities can be attributed to the success of the action proposed by each 'box' on the tree so that it will be then possible to determine mathematically the best approach to any given problem.

However, little or nothing is known about many of the boxes in numerical terms at present. The tree is useful as an *aide-memoir* to logical and consistent thought and analysis although the desired objectivity is far distant.

DECISION TREE

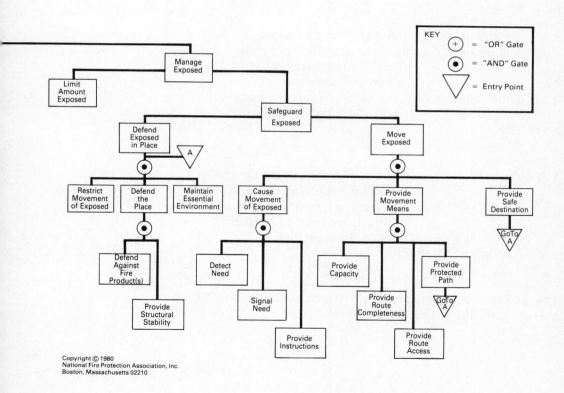

7.3
Structural fire
precautions

Inception and feasibility

PURPOSE GROUPS

For purposes of regulation, buildings or parts of buildings are classified according to use or intended use into 'Purpose Groups', eight of which are defined in Building Regulations.

Purpose Group

    I Small Residential. (not flats or maisonettes)
   II Institutional. (hospital, home, school, or similar establishment where people sleep in the premises)
  III Other Residential. (any residential accommodation not in Groups I or II)
  IV Office.
   V Shop.
  VI Factory.
 VII Other Places of Assembly. (Place, public or private, used for social, recreational, educational, business or other activity not comprised within Groups I to VI.)
VIII Storage and General.

The above are for England and Wales, a more detailed system is in use in Scotland.

The interrelationship of volume, floor area, height, type of occupancy and the fire resistance required for the structure by building regulations, is an important determinant in the early development of the form of the scheme.

On the following pages the relationships codified in the building regulations for England and Wales 1976 are shown diagramatically

Regulation E5: Fire resistance of 'structural elements'

The regulations dictate —
> maximum volume of compartment or of a building without compartmentation: and/or
> Maximum area per floor within a compartment (there could be several floors of this area in one compartment)

On the basis of —
> (in Scotland) the number of storeys
> (in England and Wales) height

But as fire resistance required of the structure increases with volume area and height too. Both aspects must be studied together.

SMALL RESIDENTIAL	REGULATION E5: FIRE RESISTANCE OF 'STRUCTURAL ELEMENTS'
Purpose Group **I** Multi-Storey Building	Any area any vol. — ½ hour — 1 hour 3 storey (max) any height Reduced to ½ hour if basement area does not exceed 50m² 250m² per floor max any vol. — 1 hour modified — 1 hour 4 storey (max) any height Any area any vol. — 1 hour — 1½ hours Ground level Any height Any number of storeys
Single Storey Building	Any area — ½ hour

SMALL RESIDENTIAL	REGULATION E4: MAXIMUM COMPARTMENT SIZE
Purpose Group **I**	
Multi-Storey Building	If 3 or more storeys and basement area exceeds 100m² floor immediately over basement to be a compartment floor
Single Storey Building	NO REQUIREMENT

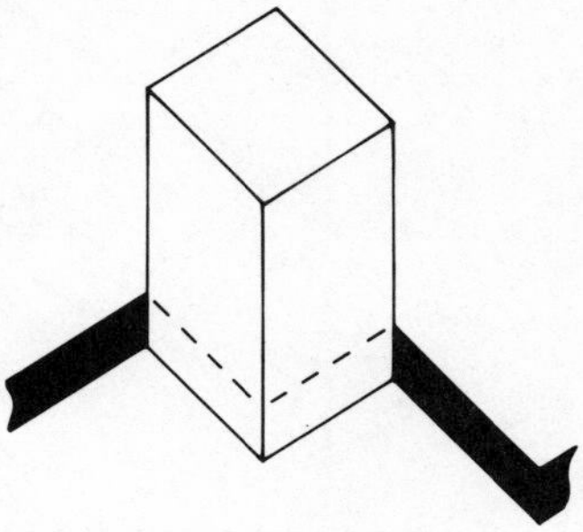

INSTITUTIONAL	REGULATION E5: FIRE RESISTANCE OF 'STRUCTURAL ELEMENTS'
Purpose Group **II**	
Single storey	3000m² max floor area ½ hour
Multi-storey	2000m² max. area/floor any volume — 28m max. building height — 1 hour — Ground level — 1½ hrs — 2000m² max. area/floor any volume — Over 28m height — 1½ hours — 2 hours

Any wall or floor between a Purpose Group II area and an area in another Purpose Group (except P.G. III) should have at least one hour's fire resistance.

INSTITUTIONAL	REGULATION E4: MAXIMUM COMPARTMENT SIZE
Purpose Group **II**	
Single storey	3000m² max. floor area any volume — Any height
Multi-storey	2000m² max. area/floor — any vol. — Any height — All floors in Purpose Group II buildings to be compartment floors

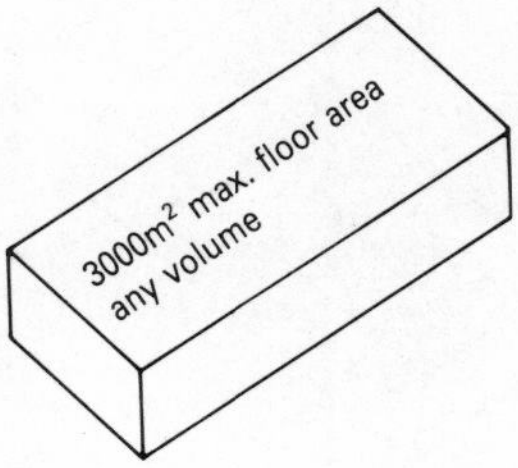

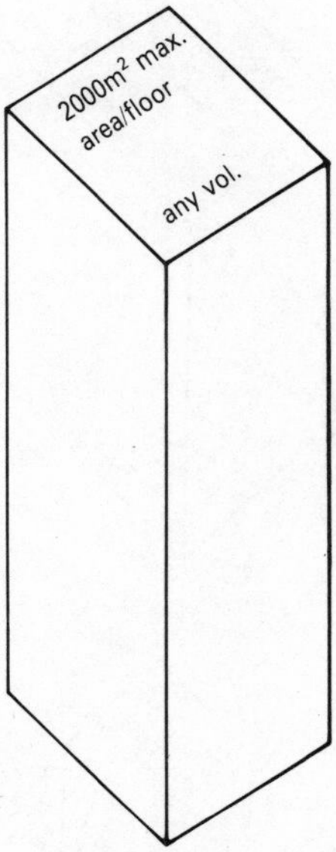

OTHER RESIDENTIAL	REGULATION E5: FIRE RESISTANCE OF 'STRUCTURAL ELEMENTS'
Purpose Group III	
Single storey building	
Multi-storey building	

Any wall or floor between a Purpose Group III area and an area in another Purpose Group (except PG II) should have at least one hour's fire resistance.

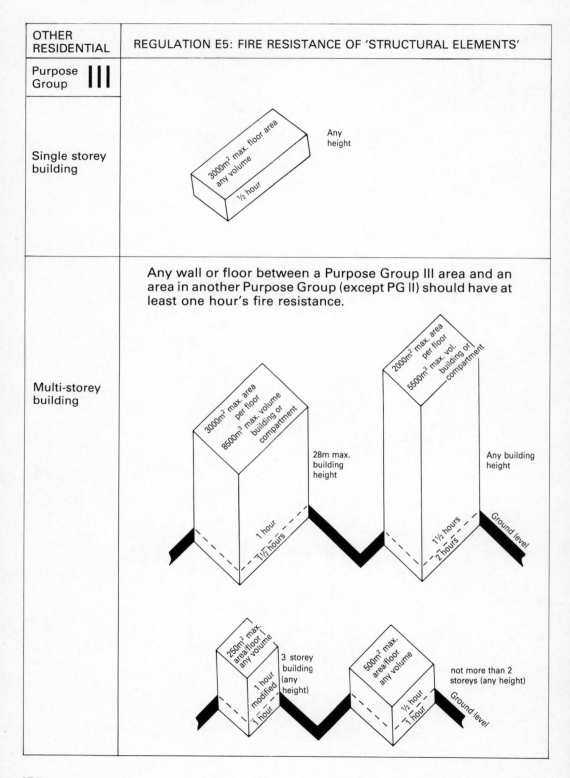

OTHER RESIDENTIAL	REGULATION E4: MAXIMUM COMPARTMENT SIZES
Purpose Group III	
Single storey building	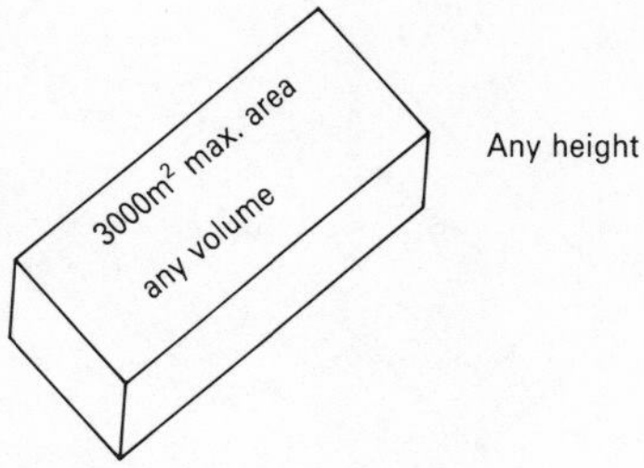 3000m² max. area any volume — Any height
Multi-storey building	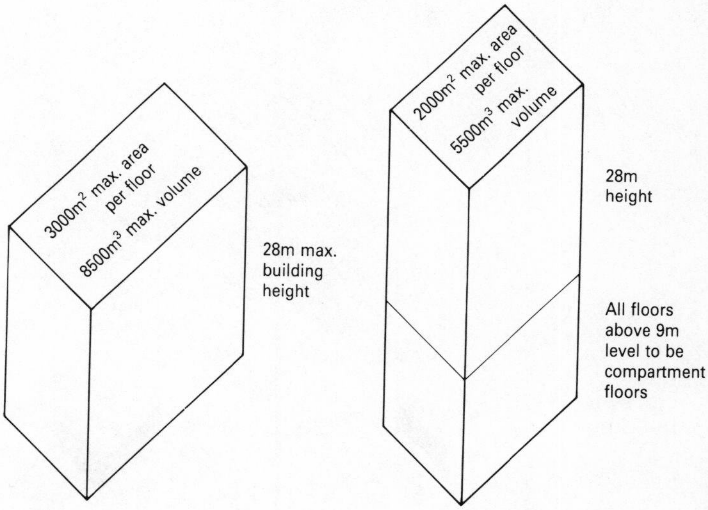 3000m² max. area per floor — 8500m³ max. volume — 28m max. building height
	2000m² max. area per floor — 5500m³ max. volume — 28m height — All floors above 9m level to be compartment floors

Any floor over a basement should be a compartment floor if the basement exceeds 100m².

OFFICE	REGULATION E5: FIRE RESISTANCE OF 'STRUCTURAL ELEMENTS'
Purpose Group **IV**	

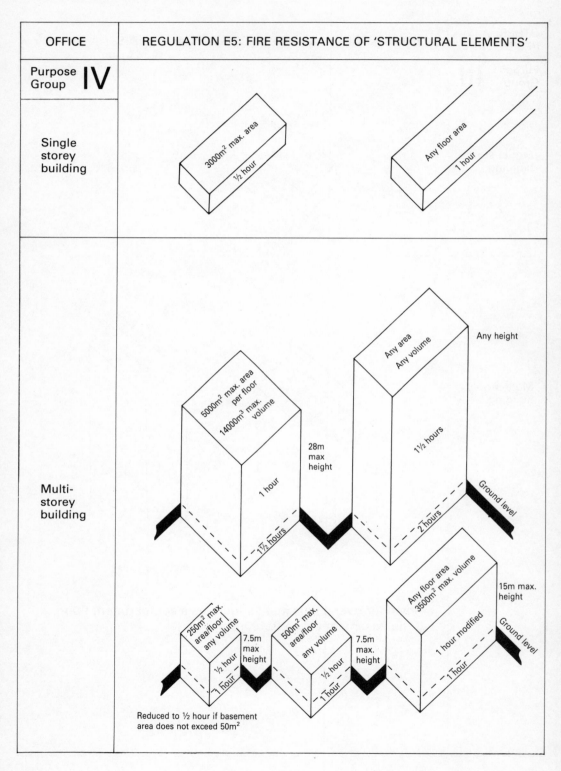

Single storey building

3000m² max. area — ½ hour

Any floor area — 1 hour

Multi-storey building

5000m² max. area per floor
14000m³ max. volume
1 hour
1½ hours

28m max height

Any area
Any volume
1½ hours
2 hours
Any height
Ground level

250m² max. area/floor
any volume
½ hour
1 hour
7.5m max height

500m² max. area/floor
any volume
½ hour
1 hour
7.5m max height

Any floor area
3500m² max. volume
1 hour modified
1 hour
15m max. height
Ground level

Reduced to ½ hour if basement area does not exceed 50m²

OFFICE	REGULATION E4: MAXIMUM COMPARTMENT SIZE
Purpose Group **IV**	
Single storey building	NO REQUIREMENT
Multi-storey building	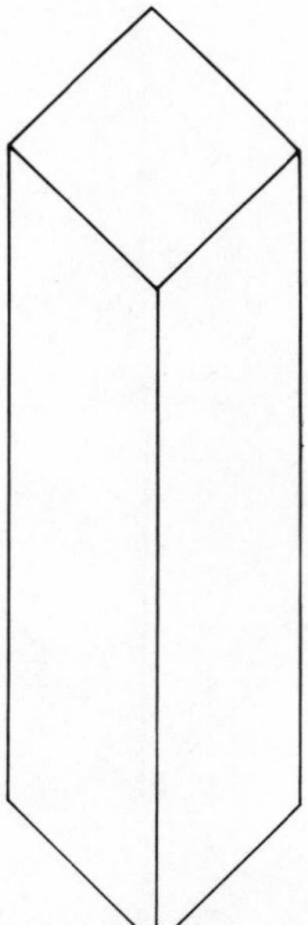 Over 28m building height All floors over 9m above ground to be compartment floors

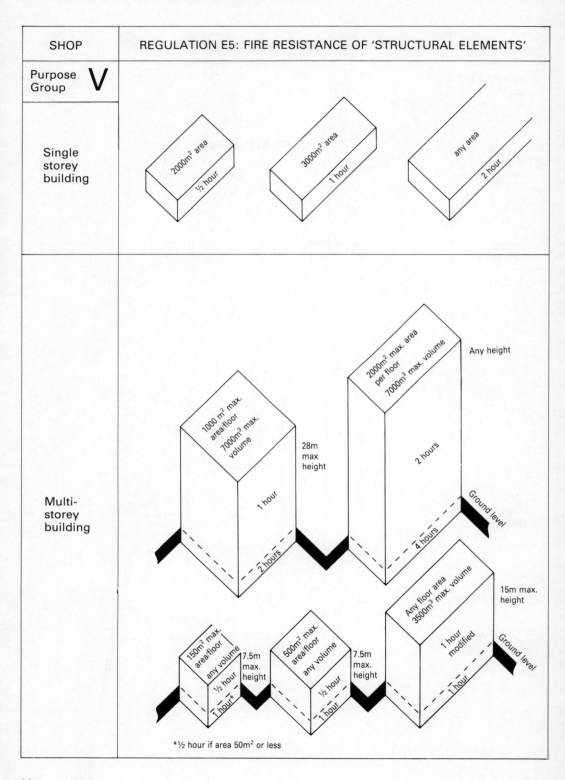

SHOP	REGULATION E5: FIRE RESISTANCE OF 'STRUCTURAL ELEMENTS'
Purpose Group **V**	
Single storey building	
Multi-storey building	

2000m² area ½ hour

3000m² area 1 hour

any area 2 hour

1000 m² max. area/floor 7000m³ max. volume — 1 hour — 2 hours — 28m max height

2000m² max. area per floor 7000m³ max. volume — 2 hours — 4 hours — Any height — Ground level

150m² max. area/floor any volume ½ hour 1 hour* — 7.5m max. height

500m² max. area/floor any volume ½ hour 1 hour — 7.5m max. height

Any floor area 3500m³ max. volume 1 hour modified 1 hour — 15m max. height — Ground level

*½ hour if area 50m² or less

SHOP	REGULATION E4: MAXIMUM COMPARTMENT SIZES
Purpose Group **V**	
Single storey building	NO REQUIREMENT
Multi-storey building	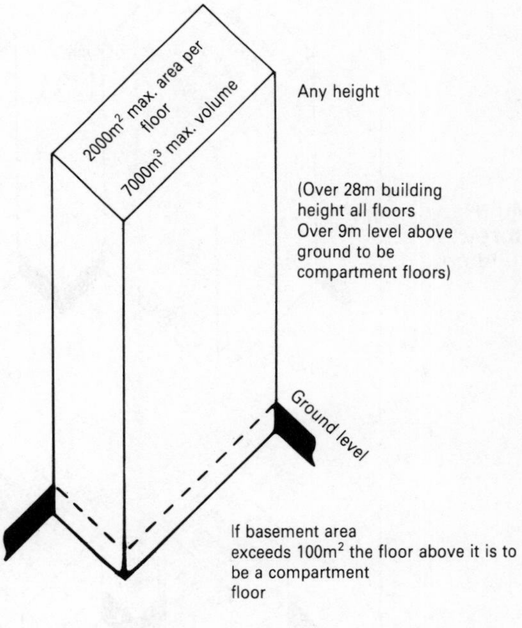

2000m² max. area per floor

7000m³ max. volume

Any height

(Over 28m building height all floors
Over 9m level above ground to be compartment floors)

Ground level

If basement area exceeds 100m² the floor above it is to be a compartment floor

181

FACTORY	REGULATION E5: FIRE RESISTANCE OF 'STRUCTURAL ELEMENTS'
Purpose Group **VI**	

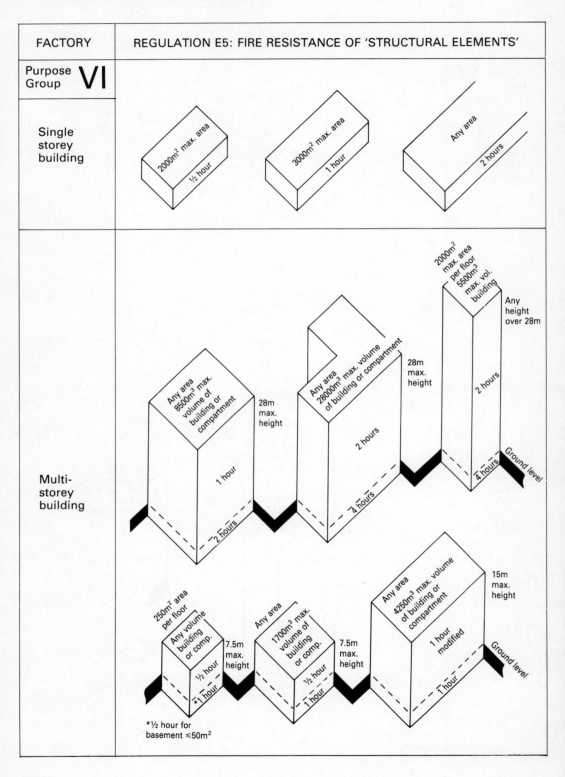

Single storey building

2000m² max. area — ½ hour

3000m² max. area — 1 hour

Any area — 2 hours

Multi-storey building

Any area 8500m³ max. volume of building or compartment — 28m max. height — 1 hour — 2 hours

Any area 28000m³ max. volume of building or compartment — 28m max. height — 2 hours — 4 hours

2000m² max. area per floor 5500m³ max. vol. building — Any height over 28m — 2 hours — 4 hours — Ground level

250m² area per floor — Any volume building or comp. — 7.5m max. height — ½ hour — *1 hour

Any area 1700m³ max. volume of building or comp. — 7.5m max. height — ½ hour — 1 hour

Any area 4250m³ max. volume of building or compartment — 15m max. height — 1 hour modified — 1 hour — Ground level

*½ hour for basement ≤50m²

FACTORY	REGULATION E4: MAXIMUM COMPARTMENT SIZE
Purpose Group **VI**	
Single storey building	NO REQUIREMENT
Multi-storey building	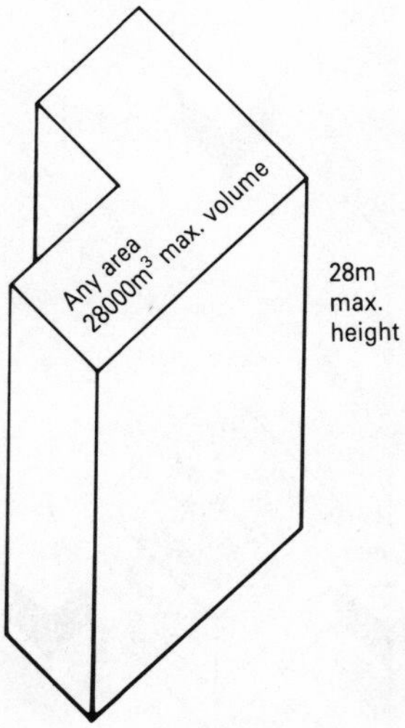

Any area 28000m³ max. volume

28m max. height

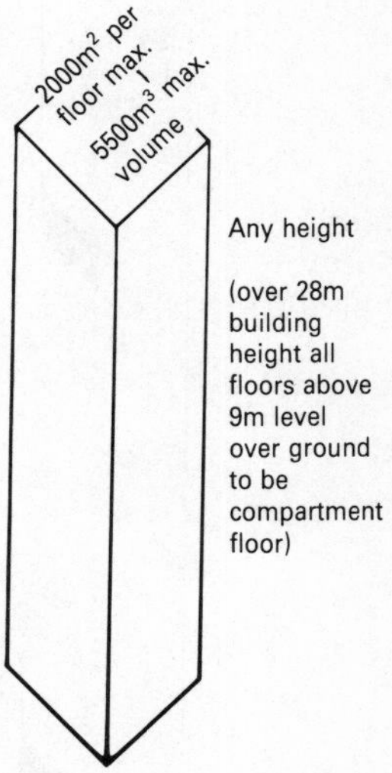

2000m² per floor max. 5500m³ max. volume

Any height

(over 28m building height all floors above 9m level over ground to be compartment floor)

ASSEMBLY	REGULATION E5: STRUCTURAL FIRE RESISTANCE
Purpose Group **VII**	

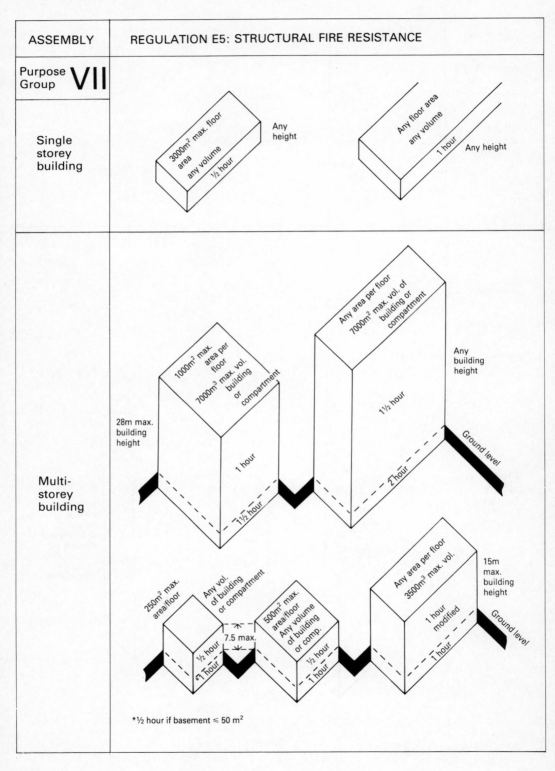

Single storey building

- 3000m² max. floor area, any volume — ½ hour — Any height
- Any floor area, any volume — 1 hour — Any height

Multi-storey building

- 1000m² max. area per floor, 7000m³ max. vol. building or compartment; 28m max. building height; 1 hour; 1½ hour; ½ hour
- Any area per floor, 7000m² max. vol. of building or compartment; Any building height; 1½ hour; 2 hour; Ground level
- 250m² max. area/floor; Any vol. of building or compartment; 7.5 max.; ½ hour; *1 hour
- 500m² max. area/floor; Any volume of building or comp.; ½ hour; 1 hour
- Any area per floor, 3500m³ max. vol.; 15m max. building height; 1 hour modified; 1 hour; Ground level

*½ hour if basement ⩽ 50 m²

184

ASSEMBLY	REGULATION E4: MAXIMUM COMPARTMENT SIZES
Purpose Group **VII**	
Single storey building	NOT CONTROLLED
Multi-storey building	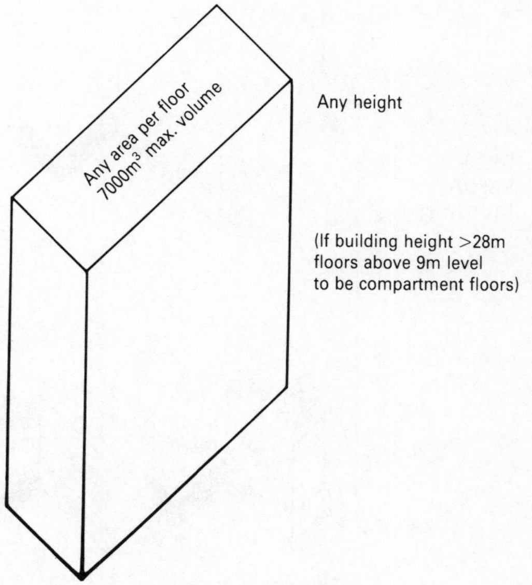 Any area per floor 7000m³ max. volume Any height (If building height >28m floors above 9m level to be compartment floors)
Notes: For definition of height in E5 check E5(1)(b)	

185

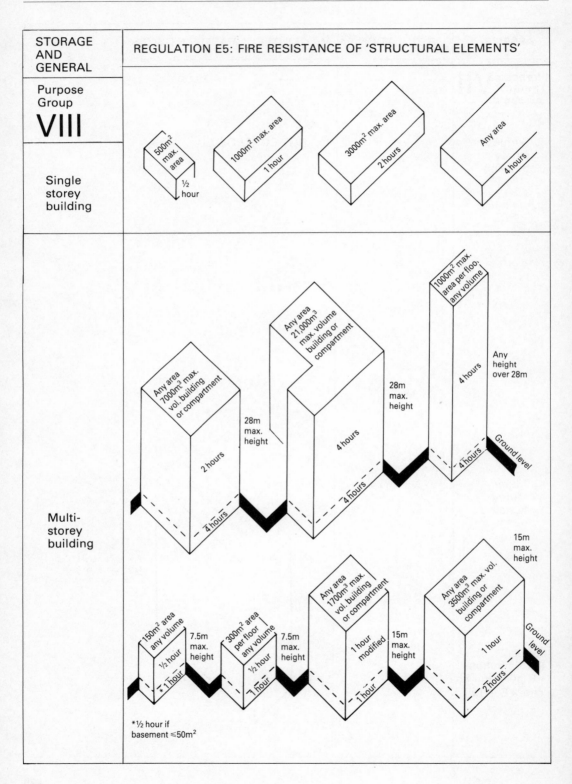

STORAGE AND GENERAL

Purpose Group

VIII

Single storey building

Multi-storey building

REGULATION E5: FIRE RESISTANCE OF 'STRUCTURAL ELEMENTS'

500m² max. area ½ hour

1000m² max. area 1 hour

3000m² max. area 2 hours

Any area 4 hours

Any area 7000m³ max. vol. building or compartment
2 hours
28m max. height
½ hour

Any area 21,000m³ max. volume building or compartment
28m max. height
4 hours
4 hours

1000m² max. area per floor, any volume
4 hours
28m max. height
Any height over 28m
4 hours
Ground level

150m² area any volume
½ hour
* 1 hour
7.5m max. height

300m² area per floor any volume
½ hour
1 hour
7.5m max. height

Any area 1700m³ max. vol. building or compartment
1 hour modified
1 hour
15m max. height

Any area 3500m³ max. vol. building or compartment
1 hour
2 hours
15m max. height
Ground level

* ½ hour if basement ≤50m²

STORAGE AND GENERAL	REGULATION E4: MAXIMUM COMPARTMENT SIZE
Purpose Group **VIII**	
Single storey building	**NO REQUIREMENTS**
Multi-storey building	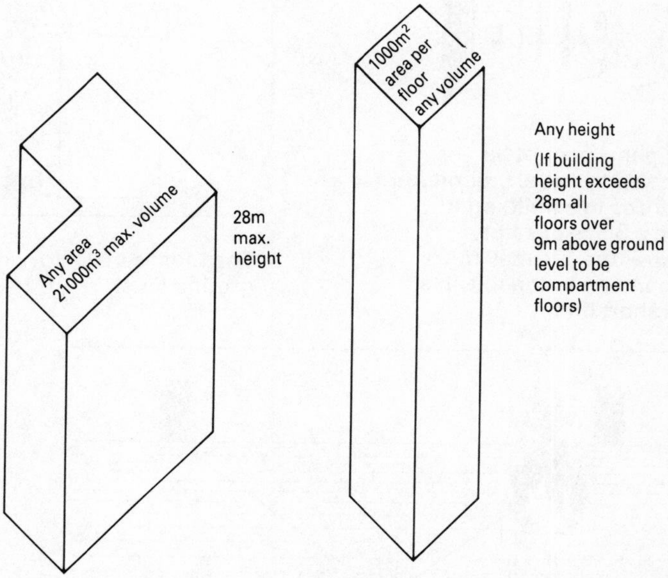

Any area 21000m³ max. volume

28m max. height

1000m² area per floor any volume

Any height

(If building height exceeds 28m all floors over 9m above ground level to be compartment floors)

Inception and Feasibility

7.4
Designing for escape

BASIC PRINCIPLES

Escape considerations are rarely major determinants of form in new buildings, especially with green-field sites. The exceptions are likely to be those buildings where evacuation is not a matter of simply walking briskly out. Hospitals, residential homes for the elderly or handicapped may present such problems. For different (partly historical) reasons associated with crowd behaviour, escape requirements for theatres and the like can also have a big effect on overall design. Facets of these problems are dealt with in **section 8.2** in more detail.

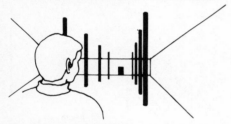

Occupants cannot be expected to travel unlimited distances in a building to reach a place of safety because the fire may make the building untenable in a very short time.

The most satisfactory place of safety is the open air at ground level.

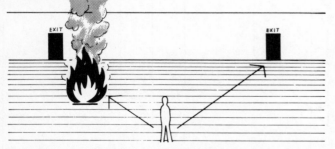

Where occupants do not have immediate access to a place of safety they should be provided with alternative routes to reduce the chance of their being trapped. They cannot rely on external rescue.

LEGISLATION

Requirements for means of escape can be made under several different statutes depending largely on the use to which the building is put. In Scotland the situation is less complicated than in England and Wales because the building regulations deal with means of escape for most types of building and the only major legislation outside these regulations is the fire precautions act. The GLC have excellently-produced codes of practice for use within their jurisdiction.

For more detailed information on the range of legislation see **section 8.2**.

Inception and feasibility # Appointment of consultants

FIRE ENGINEERING CONSULTANTS

A very wide range of engineering skills can be involved in the design of building services and in the fire protection field some of these are highly specialized. It is unlikely that one consultancy will be able to provide the full range of design skill.

A consultant should be selected able to advise on the selection of active and passive fire protection systems and their potential value in life and property protection. Experience in projects where specialist systems have been installed will enable the consultant to protect the client's interests in technical matters outside the architect's normal competence.

STRUCTURAL REQUIREMENTS

Architect and client to identify the need for consultant having special knowledge of fire related matters, such as:

To assess fire-resisting performance required of a structure where special conditions suggest that regulations are not relevant.

To design a structure to a specific fire resistance standard using more or less conventional techniques and to 'prove' the design to the authorities as need be.

To advise on the interaction of structure with other elements of construction in a fire to ensure adequate performance of the whole.

To advise on selection of contractors if specialist work on structure is involved.

To commission fire tests on elements of the structure.

To inspect specialist site work to ensure that fire protection is installed as designed.

To act as expert witness to support application for a departure from standard solutions to structural fire protection problems.

FIRE PROTECTION SYSTEMS REQUIREMENTS

Plumbing—	hosereels and dry risers	Architect or M & E consultant (depends on the overall size and complexity of the scheme)
	wet risers	M & E engineer or specialist contractor
	sprinklers and water spray or drencher	Specialist designer (often installers and/or manufacturers too)
Electrical—	Automation detection	M & E consultant, specialist installer (the larger manufacturers give design service)
	Fire Alarm	M & E consultant or installer (depending on size)
	Emergency power	M & E consultant
	Emergency lighting	M & E consultant, specialist installer
Other—	CO_2 flooding	M & E consultant in conjunction with specialist (usually design/instal/manufacture company)
	Halon flooding	M & E consultant in conjunction with specialist (usually design/instal/manufacture company)
	Halon local application	M & E consultant or manufacturer/installer
	Foam or Dry Power fixed installations	M & E consultant in conjunction with specialist manufacturer/installer
	Smoke venting	H & V consultant and/or manufacturer
	Smoke control pressurization system	H & V consultant
Portable fire fighting equipment		Architect, client's fire staff (large client organisations), insurance surveyor, fire brigade

7.6
Fire safety considerations in the project programme

Inception and feasibility

TIME FOR DESIGN

(1) Standard solutions

Versus

Innovation

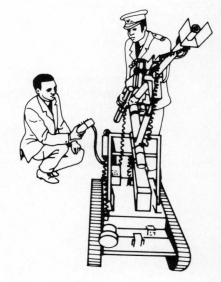

Think about:
Development time
Getting approvals — or relaxations or
going to appeal

(2) In any case:

Plan the work of consultants and specialists — who needs
to know what, when?

**(3) The philosophy of the design — is the product a 'loose
fit' solution or a closely determined one?**

Will there have to be flexibility (e.g. to allow extension of a
sprinker system)? How much 'value' is in the fabric cf. the
contents?

192

TIME FOR CONSTRUCTION

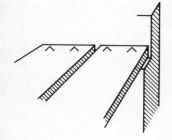

(1) Prefabrication, dry jointing techniques may be chosen for speed

Are they liable to cause problems where the continuity of fire-resisting construction has to be preserved?
Will installation of cavity barriers or fire-stopping negate speed advantage?

(2) Coordination of specialist sub-contractors and suppliers in contract programme

(3) Fire safety during construction

The sequence or timing of certain operations may be influenced by fire considerations, e.g. provision of useable stairways, or separation of area under construction from one completed for phased handover, or provision of water supply for fire fighting at early stage.

(4) Commissioning of fire systems

Some systems — e.g. pressurization, audible alarms, can only be commissioned when building is substantially complete.

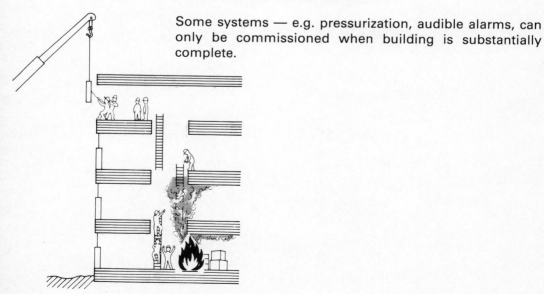

CHAPTER EIGHT

Outline
design

Outline design

8.1
Site planning

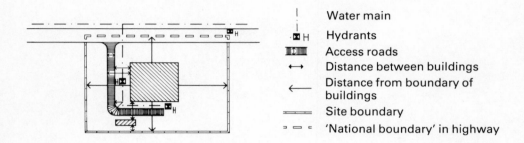

ǀ	Water main
H	Hydrants
	Access roads
↔	Distance between buildings
←	Distance from boundary of buildings
═══	Site boundary
⌐ ▭ ⌐	'National boundary' in highway

DISTANCE OF BUILDING FROM BOUNDARY AND OTHER BUILDINGS ON SITE

Determined under building regulations by:

Elevational treatment (unprotected area)

Purpose group or occupancy

Compartmentation behind the relevant elevation

Height of the relevant elevation

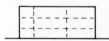

HYDRANTS

Statutory hydrants in public highways are the responsibility of the fire authority. They may decide to provide additional hydrants to cover a new development and any new roads that are to become public highway will almost certainly have hydrants installed in them.

Therefore it is essential that the water section of the fire brigade is notified of development plans at site planning stage.

Private hydrants within a site may be recommended by the fire authority to a developer. Their installation and upkeep is the responsibility of the developer/owner but they should obviously be compatable with fire brigade equipment.

Hydrants should conform to BS 750 : 1964 *Underground hydrants.*

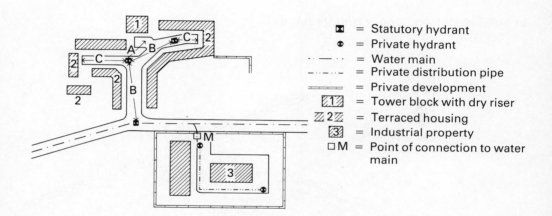

⊠	=	Statutory hydrant
⊕	=	Private hydrant
—·—··	=	Water main
—·—·—	=	Private distribution pipe
=====	=	Private development
⌁1⌁	=	Tower block with dry riser
⌁2⌁	=	Terraced housing
⌁3⌁	=	Industrial property
☐M	=	Point of connection to water main

Although each authority may have its own rules the following guidance can be used for initial planning of hydrants for a new development:

(a) Maximum distance from hydrant to hardstanding used by pump which is feeding a dry riser — **18m**.

(b) Maximum distance between hydrants in a residential road — **120m**.

(c) Maximum distance between hydrant and dead end of road — **90m**.

(d) Not less than 6 m from building or risk so that they may be useable during a fire.

NOTE:

(a) A private supply pipe should not be less than 75 mm internal diamater, 100 mm is preferable. Private systems of any size should be calculated and this may show larger pipes to be needed.

(b) The water authority will determine whether hydrants are sealed or metered. Fire authorities usually prefer the sealed type.

ACCESS ROAD DESIGN

Generally the larger a building is the more important it becomes to have access all around it. In Scotland the building regulations contain requirements for hard-standing beside some types of building. Thus:

Scotland

In buildings of occupancy groups A4, B, C, D, or E

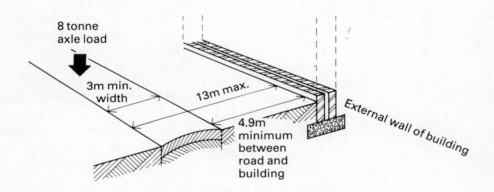

minimum length of access road, measured parallel to the wall of the building = the greater of:

    2.4 m for every 90m² of floor area in buildings of more than 2800 m³

or 3.0 m for every 90m² of floor area.

England and Wales

Proposed amendments of the building regulations for England and Wales would make the following requirements:

(1) Buildings without wet or dry risers

Building volume

<7100m³

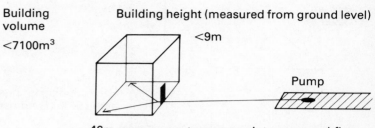

Building height (measured from ground level)

<9m

Pump

46m max. pump to every point on ground floor

<7100m³

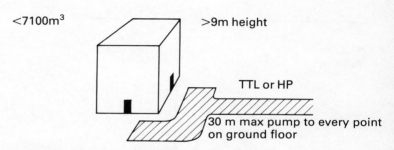

>9m height

TTL or HP

30 m max pump to every point on ground floor

Hardstanding for TTL/HP along at least 16% of total perimeter (there should be access to the interior in each section of wall)

Volume
>7100m³
<28,500m³

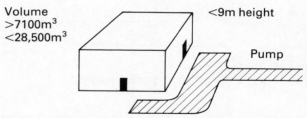

<9m height

Pump

Hardstanding for pump along at least 16% of total perimeter

Volume
>7100m³
<28,500m³

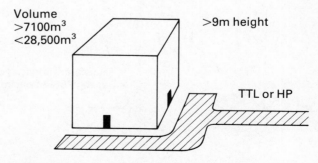

>9m height

TTL or HP

Hardstanding for TTL/HP along 50% perimeter

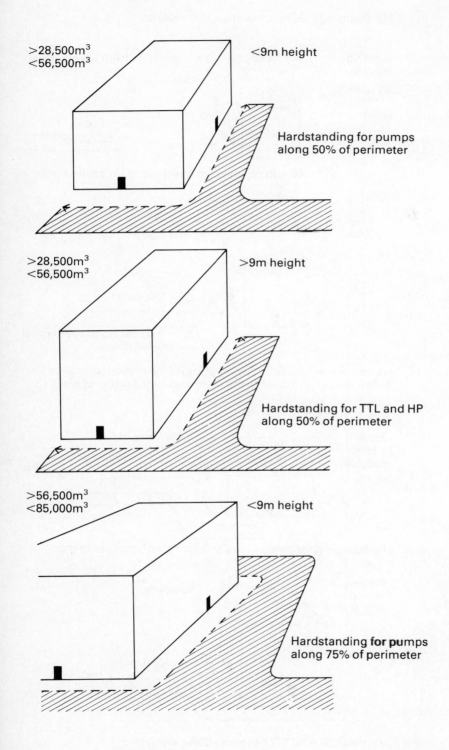

>28,500m³
<56,500m³

<9m height

Hardstanding for pumps
along 50% of perimeter

>28,500m³
<56,500m³

>9m height

Hardstanding for TTL and HP
along 50% of perimeter

>56,500m³
<85,000m³

<9m height

Hardstanding **for pu**mps
along 75% of perimeter

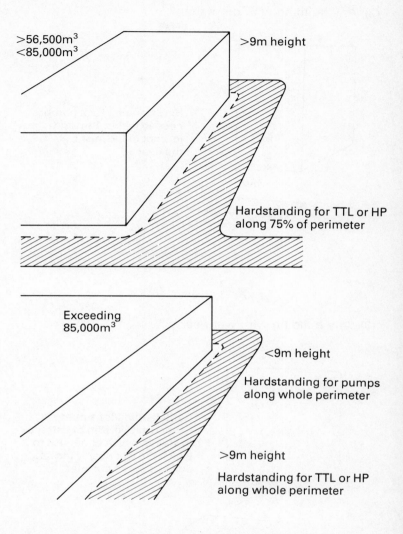

>56,500m³
<85,000m³

>9m height

Hardstanding for TTL or HP
along 75% of perimeter

Exceeding
85,000m³

<9m height

Hardstanding for pumps
along whole perimeter

>9m height

Hardstanding for TTL or HP
along whole perimeter

Other reference: Home Office fire prevention note 1
(1970), *Access for fire appliances*,
HMSO. (Now under revision)

(2) Any building with dry riser

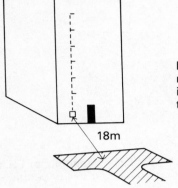

Hardstanding for a pump is
needed within 18m and
in sight of the inlet to
the riser

18m

(3) Any building with wet riser

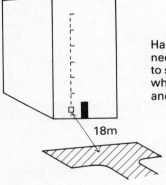

Hardstanding for a pump is
needed within 18m of entrance
to stair in which or nearest to
which the wet riser is located
and in sight of the inlet

18m

Flats and maisonettes of over two storeys

(Recommendations of BS CP 3, chapter IV, Part 1, 1971)

(1) Blocks with dry risers:
Dry risers are recommended for all blocks with storeys
above 18m

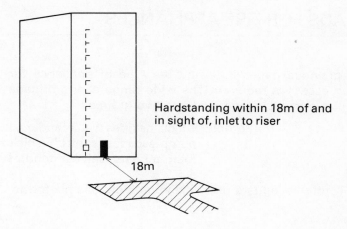

Hardstanding within 18m of and
in sight of, inlet to riser

18m

(2) Blocks with wet risers: Recommended for buildings over 60m high

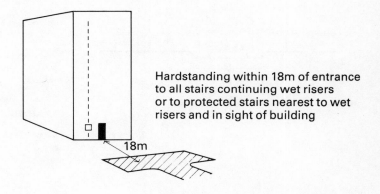

Hardstanding within 18m of entrance
to all stairs continuing wet risers
or to protected stairs nearest to wet
risers and in sight of building

18m

(3) Blocks without rising mains wet or dry

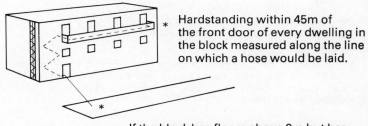

Hardstanding within 45m of
the front door of every dwelling in
the block measured along the line
on which a hose would be laid.

If the block has floors above 9m but has
no dry or wet riser there should be access
roads for TTL or HP along the
elevations in which there is access to
the interior.

203

ROADS FOR FIRE APPLIANCES

The previous pages indicated the type of appliance for which access is required. The wide range of fire brigade vehicles may be categorised into two groups:

Pumps: which includes water tenders, pump-escapes, control vehicles, foam tenders, salvage tenders, etc.

Turntable ladders (ttl): including hydraulic platforms

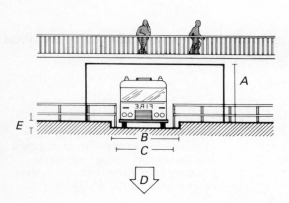

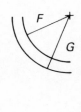

			PUMP	TTL
A	=	Minimum clearance height (m)	3.7	4.0
B	=	Minimum width of roadway (m)	3.7	3.7
C	=	Minimum width of gateway (m)	3.1	3.1
D	=	Vehicle weight (tonnes)	10.25	20.0
E	=	Max. kerb crossover height (mm)	100	100
F	=	Minimum bend radius (m)	16.8	21.5
G	=	Minimum sweep radius (m)	18.5	24.5
H	=	Max. gradient	1 in 10	1 in 10*

* The camber or gradient of hardstanding where ladder or platform is deployed must be considerably less than this for stability. Also space for Appliance Jacks is needed in deployed position. Check with appropriate Fire Brigade.

ACCESS — OTHER POINTS

Foam inlets

Oil fired heating plant and oil tank rooms may be provided with means for injecting fire fighting foam into the room from fire brigade equipment outside

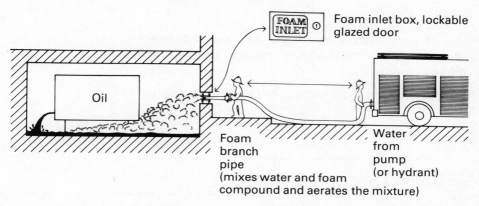

Foam inlet box, lockable glazed door

Foam branch pipe (mixes water and foam compound and aerates the mixture)

Water from pump (or hydrant)

The same considerations for pump access apply here as for a dry riser, i.e. 18 m max. pump to inlet with uninterrupted view.

Ladder access

Aluminium extending ladders are replacing the wheeled escape ladders. In planning the landscape and paths etc. around a building the following points should be observed to allow a ladder to be set to a window up to 11m above ground:

Will trees etc. interfere?

As the ladder has to be carried the distance from vehicle access road should be 20m maximum. A hard footpath is desirable

Foot of ladder needs a clear area 2m × 2m Foot of ladder will be about ⅓ window height out from the wall

$3x$

x

See also section 9.2 on windows as means of escape.

Outline design

A means of escape consists of one or several different parts depending on the building design: cellular/open plan; single/multistorey.

(And which point in the building is taken as a starting point)

COMPONENTS

The most common parts are:

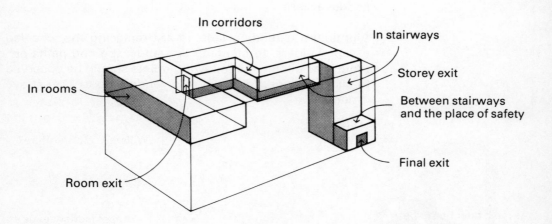

In corridors

In stairways

In rooms

Storey exit

Between stairways and the place of safety

Final exit

Room exit

ASSUMPTIONS

The detailed design of means of escape in each part is based on the principle mentioned in section 7.4 the following assumptions:

In a small room (up to about 30m²) one exit is sufficient because occupants will be aware of the danger before it prevents escape.

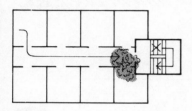

A route that could be blocked by fire, leaving no alternative, should be short:

(a) so that people are not too remote from a fire to be aware of the danger only when it is too late.
(b) so that the occupants have a chance of making a quick dash through the danger area;
(c) so that few people are at risk.

Smoke and fumes are capable of contaminating large voids very quickly and the prevention of early smoke spreading especially into stairs and sections of route where escape is only possible in one direction, is very important.

Fires are extremely unlikely to start in protected stairs and corridors if properly maintained, but the possibility of smoke spread into stairs makes total reliance on one stair unwise in many multistorey buildings.

The escape route should not involve any gymnastics or the use of any mechanical aids such as pulleys or lowering devices.

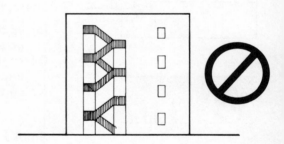

There should be full standing headroom and changes of level should be negotiated by ordinary stairs or ramps.

It should not normally be necessary to employ an external staircase to provide adequate means of escape from a new building.

(In any case building regulations require stairs over 6m high to be protected from the weather i.e. enclosed.)

The standard of physical ability is set by the least able, in any case a very conservative view of capability must be taken because (*inter alia*):

(a) stress may greatly reduce it;
(b) individuals will not necessarily have the information to enable them to take the right decision (Where is the fire? Where am I? Is this the quickest way out?).
(c) congestion may reduce it, especially if there is no overall discipline or control.

LEGISLATION FOR MEANS OF ESCAPE

The legislative picture is a very confused one. Different parts of the country having different methods and controlling statutes, and different building types being subject to various authorities, some with overlapping powers, others with anomalous 'loopholes', give clearly written standards and a deal of inflexible 'by the book' control.

THE MAIN LEGISLATIVE CONTROLS OUTSIDE THE INNER LONDON AREA:

BUILDING OR OCCUPANCY	LEGISLATION
RESIDENTIAL — PRIVATE	
Houses of one or two storeys	none
Houses of more than two storeys	Building Regs.
Houses in multiple occupation	Housing Act 1961 §16(Building Regs. in Scotland)
Flats and Maisonettes of over two storeys	Building Regs. (by reference to BSCP 3, Chapter IV, part 1 in England and Wales
Sleeping accommodation in lettable dwellings, etc. that is over 20 feet above ground and in above first floor level	Public Health Act 1936 § 60 (Building Regs in Scotland)
RESIDENTAL — INSTITUTIONS, ETC.	
Hotels, Motels, Boarding Houses	Fire Precautions Act 1971 (*and* Building Regs in Scotland)
Homes for elderly	National Assistance Act 1948 (Building Regs in Scotland)
Homes for children	Children and Young Persons Act 1969 (Building Regs in Scotland)
Schools (residential part)	Public Health Act 1936 § 60 (Building Regs in Scotland)
Hospitals and Nursing Homes private establishments	Nursing Homes Act 1975 (Building Regs in Scotland)
Public establishments	none
OFFICE	Building Regs — except single stair buildings over four storeys in England and Wales — by ref to BSCP 3, chapter IV part 3 in England and Wales. *And* Fire Precautions Act 1971. NB Some countries have their own acts for tall buildings.
SHOP	Building Regs — except those with less than 250m²/floor sales area or not more than three storeys in England and Wales — by reference to CP3, chapter IV part 2 in England and Wales. *And* Fire Precautions Act 1971. NB County acts concerning tall buildings

BUILDING OR OCCUPANCY	LEGISLATION
FACTORY	Fire Precautions Act 1971 (*and* Building Regs in Scotland) Fire Certificates (Special Premises) Regulations 1970 Highly Flammable Liquids and LPG Regs. 1972 Petroleum (consolidation) Act 1928
STORAGE (depending on what materials or goods are stored)	Petroleum (Consolidation) Act 1928 (*and* Building Regs in Scotland) Highly Flammable Liquids and LPG Regs 1972 NB There are some county acts which make special provisions that can concern large storage buildings
EDUCATIONAL non-maintained schools	Education Act 1944 and Standards for School Premises Regulations 1972 and by reference to DES Building Bulletin 7 (5th edn) in England and Wales and Building Regulations in Scotland
maintained schools	Education Act 1944 etc. Crown Exemption from Building Regulations in England, Wales and Scotland
Further Education Colleges and Universities	none in England and Wales Building Regulations in Scotland unless Crown Exemption applies
ASSEMBLY	*all are subject to Building Regs in Scotland*
Theatre	Theatres Act 1968 Private Places of Entertainment (Licensing) Act 1967
Cinema	Cinematograph Acts 1909 and 1952 Private Places of Entertainment (Licensing) Act 1967
Bingo hall, casino	Gaming Act 1968
Dance hall, concert hall	Public Health Acts (Amendment) Act 1890 — only refers to some counties in England and Wales Local Entertainments Licensing Acts for singing or dancing or musical performance
Exhibition hall	Public Health Act 1936 § 59 in England and Wales Public Health Acts (Amendment) Act 1890 — where adopted Local Acts
Public house and any premises licensed for liquor sales	Licensing Act 1964
Museum, Art gallery	Public Health Act 1936 § 59 in England and Wales

Inner London

The Inner London area is covered by the London building acts and constructional bye-laws and the standards for means of escape are set out in a GLC code of practice.

Additional requirements may be made under section 20 of the London building acts for high or voluminous buildings

SCOPE OF GLC CODE OF PRACTICE FOR MEANS OF ESCAPE IN CASE OF FIRE

ASPECT OF PLANNING
SUBJECT TO CONTROL

	Work places	Places where people resort: (a) entertainment or assembly	Places where people resort: (b) shops, restaurants, pubs and the like	Places where people sleep: (a) single family dwellings incl. flats	(b) hotels, boarding houses, hostels, etc.	Garages, car parks and vehicle servicing areas	Ancillary service accommodation
Provision of fire resisting enclosure	•	•	•	•	•	•	•
Travel/direct distance	•	•	•		•	•	•
Number of exits	•	•	•	•	•	•	
Position of exits		•	•		•	•	•
Width of escape route	•	•	•		•	•	
Width of protected stairs	•	•	•		•	•	
High fire risk access in relation to escape routes or exit location	•	•	•		•		
Arrangements for stairs from basements	•		•		•	•	
Provision of smoke doors	•				•		
Wall and ceiling linings		•	•				
Limitation of the height above or below street level of floors		•					
Seating layout		•					
Slope of floors to seating areas or auditoria		•					
Provisions for lifts	•		•		•		
Provisions for artificial and safety lighting	•	•	•		•	•	
Provisions for ventilation of:							
stair lobbies		•					
high fire risk areas							•
stage area		•					
Special provisions or exceptions for:							
small premises		•	•		•		
single stair buildings	•						•
kitchens			•		•		
garages				•		•	
bedroom corridors					•		

REFERENCES

Building Regulations:	BSCP3, Chapter IV, Parts 1, 2, and 3
Fire Precautions Act:	Home Office Guides to the Fire Precautions Act No. 1. Hotels and Boarding Houses No. 2. Factories No. 3. Offices Shops and Railway Premises (HMSO)
Housing Act §16:	GLC Code of Practice for means of escape from houses in multiple occupation (only effective in GLC area but used as a guide elsewhere) 2nd edition 1979
Standards for School Premises Regulations:	DES Building Bulletin 7 (5th edition)
Theatre Licensing:	GLC Technical Regulations for Places of Public Entertainment (only effective in GLC area but used as a guide elsewhere) Local Authorities may have their own documents

There is no other generally-available official guidance on the means of escape provisions of legislation.

MEANS OF ESCAPE DESIGN INFORMATION

Travel distance:

From any point in the building to a place of relative safety

Travel distance depends on	$\dfrac{\text{Speed of movement}}{\text{Time before fire prevents movement}}$

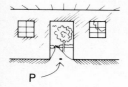

Places of relative safety ('P' on the diagrams):

External door to a place from which one can move freely away from the building

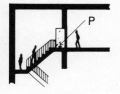

Storey exit into a protected stairway (or to the lobby of a lobby-approach stairway)

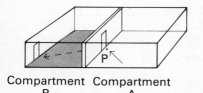

Door in a compartment wall or separating wall leading to an alternative exit

Compartment   Compartment
     B   A

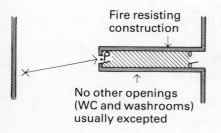

Fire resisting construction

Door to a protected corridor leading directly to a protected stair or a final exit

No other openings (WC and washrooms) usually excepted

Speed of travel

Fast Walk = 2.3 m/s
Slow Walk = 1 m/s

Two people carrying
 a third = 0.3 m/s  Limited range
  say – 15 m

Crowd movement
e.g. congested
 corridor = 0.2 m/s

Shuffle — very
handicapped = 0.05 m/s

Pushing a bed
or stretcher- = 1 m/s average if
trolley   momentum not
   lost at corners

Time available for escape: The $64,000 question!

The early chapters have shown that this is highly variable and can be very limited.

Scottish Building Regulations allow occupants about 2½ mins to vacate an area threatened by fire.

Experiments at Hackney Hospital by DHSS and Fire Research Station suggested that 10 minutes would be *needed* to clear a hospital ward at very least, and 20–25 mins would be more realistic with limited help available.

Therefore:

(a) Either assume a figure for time available and design around it; or
(b) Assume a figure for the time needed and design around that.

Method (a) may require severe travel distance restrictions and rely on adequately staffed and organized evacuation.

Method (b) may emphasize structural fire precautions and active fire protection systems to hold a fire 'at bay'.

214

Capacity of escape routes

Crowds of people do not move in the same way as water flows down a pipe.

Movement slows as crowd density increases until a total blockage is caused when the pressure of bodies shoulder to shoulder wedges an 'arch' of people temporarily between the sides of the corridor or gangway.

The graph shows that for practical purposes the capacity of an escape route should be calculated on the basis of a flow rate of 1.5 people/second/metre width

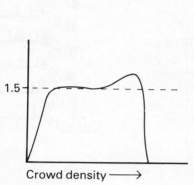

This is on level floors.

On stairs going down the rate is about 1.15 people/second/metre width and stairs going up the rate is about 1.1 people/second/metre width (assuming that no one is trying to move against the flow).

Reference: BRE Information Paper 15. 6/77, April 1977.

Note: In Scotland stair and exit widths are controlled by building regulations.

Evacuation methods

From the information on numbers of occupants, mobility, the likelihood of congestion etc., a general picture of the kind of evacuation to be catered for should now be available.

e.g. (a) Crowds leaving a cinema — A simultaneous surge of people in a tight press.
(b) A hospital ward evacuation — Rapid two-way traffic superimposed on very slow one-way movement.
(c) An office evacuation — Possibly dense but more orderly crowd than in (a); people know each other and this effects their behaviour.
(d) A cold store — Relatively few occupants, some may be driving vehicles and may choose to drive out of the building.

215

(e) A school — Children in groups and under discipline but perhaps more susceptible to panic or dangerous action if not controlled.

Simultaneous

If every occupant of a large multi-storey building is to be evacuated simultaneously the stairs will have to be uneconomically wide, or some delays will occur, or extra stairs will be needed to serve the lower floors.

The same problem applies to parts of the exit routes from a large single storey building.

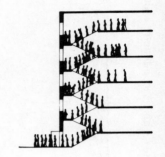

Staged

Alternatively only the occupants in immediate danger (say the fire floor and the floor above) are evacuated initially with progressive extensions to the evacuated area if the fire risk persists

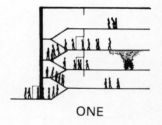

ONE

To be successful this obviously requires good planning, control and communications (which precludes its use in public buildings unless the public are very much in a minority),
and stairs must be protected from fire and smoke contamination;
and the structure must withstand fire throughout the evacuated period.

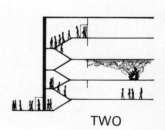

TWO

Horizontal

Obviously in single storey buildings only horizontal movement is involved in reaching safety.

Where there is poor mobility stairs can be barrier to movement. In hospitals, old peoples homes and the like, where there is this problem, and evacuation is likely to take longer than usual the architect has a choice

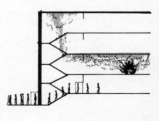

THREE

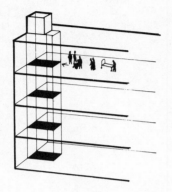

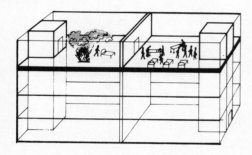

(a) Build low and arrange multiple points of access to the outside so that evacuation is horizontal direct and simple
but
This needs site space, and leads to extended internal circulation and higher building costs/m^2.

(b) Build to a more economic height and trust to the protection of normal means of escape
With ample emergency help from extra staff, police, firemen etc.
but
What would really happen in a fire? Could a fire door be left open? The average old peoples home may have only two members of staff at night.

(c) Build to a more economic height and plan a system of refuge areas on each floor.

The simplest arrangement might be to bisect each floor with a compartment wall so that:

(i) The number of people requiring immediate help is halved;
(ii) Those at risk are moved sideways to relative safety;
(iii) There is more time and space to organize vertical stage of evacuation if necessary.

Travel distance

More detailed information is given in section 9.2 of legislative requirements. The following list is suitable for use at a preliminary design stage, or where there is no controlling legislation

Principal occupancy	EXIT no alternative route	EXIT EXIT >45° alternative routes	NOTES
Residential institutions	15m	32m	
Old peoples homes	9m	18m	
Hospital wards	15m	32m	
Flats/masionettes, hotels and any other residential	15m	32m	1
Offices	18m	45m	2
Shops	15m	32m	1
Factories	18m	45m	1,4
Assembly — From seat to exit of auditorium		18m ordinary seating / 15m continental seating	
Storage/warehouse	18m	45m	
Vehicle park		32m	2
Plant	60m	105m	3

Notes:
1. Some of these are designed under the fire precautions act.
2. This may be 45m in car parks with no basement and 5% natural vents.
3. Within the plant room itself max. TD = 15m.
4. Distance varies with risk attached to the process carried out or materials involved, etc.

Checks to make against sketch plans:

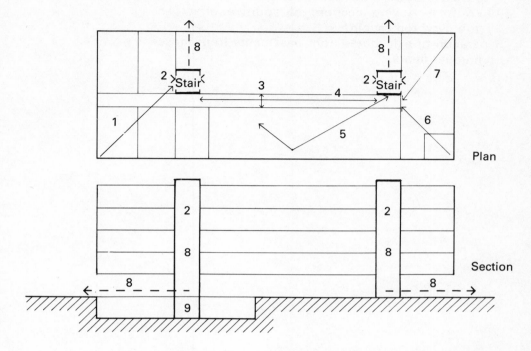

Plan

Section

1. Travel distance (allowing for partitions, etc) where there is no alternative route — to protected stair enclosure (or exit in the case of ground floor).
2. * Stairs: (a) Number of;
   (b) Width of;
   (c) Fire resistance required for means of escape (as opposed to structural protection required by, say, building regulations).
3. Corridor width or width of escape route through open plan areas it should not decrease towards the exit except that door frames may project into corridors provided the clear opening of the doorway is adequate.
4. Distance between stairs — some codes, e.g. BS CP3, Chapter IV Part 1 and DES Building bulletin 7 specify maximum distances.
5. Travel distance, where alternative is available, to nearest stair (or exit if ground floor).
6. Travel distance from inner room to door out of outer room.
7. Travel distance within large rooms (limited in fire precautions act guidance documents).

* On ground floor read 'exits' for 'stairs'.

8. (a) Travel distance in protected route to final exit (not usually subject to legislative control).
   (b) Width — taking account of additive effect as 'tributary' routes join.
9. Separation of exit routes from basements from those from upper floors.

Travel distance measurement

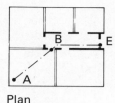

Plan

Route with no alternative

'E' Is the exit either to open air or into a protected stair.

'A' Is the point furthest from 'E' (excluding unoccupied spaces like cupboards or ducts but including infrequently occupied spaces such as plant rooms).

'B' Is the point of entry to a protected corridor on the route from 'A' to 'E' (most codes call for such 'dead end' corridors to be protected).

A—E Must not exceed the maximum travel distance for routes having no alternative.

A—B Is limited in most codes.

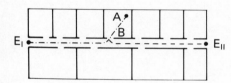

Route with alternative

'E_I' and 'E_{II}' are exits (stair or open air)

'A' is the furthest point from E_I that is served by E_I as an exit.

A–E_I Must not exceed the maximum travel distance for routes having an alternative.

A–E_{II} Is not directly controlled.

i.e. Every point must be within the travel distance limit of either E_I or E_{II} but they do not have to be within the distance from both E_I and E_{II}.

A–B If the rooms are large a limit is sometimes put on A–B or an alternative exit is required from the room (FP Act guidance note 1.

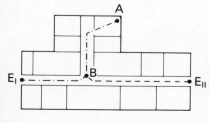

Route partly in dead end and partly with alternative.

E_I and E_{II} are exits

B Is the point where the dead end joins the other corridor

A Is the furthest point from B in the dead end section

221

A–B Must not exceed the maximum travel distance for routes having no alternative.

E_I–A or E_{II}–A (whichever is the less) must not exceed the maximum travel distance for routes having an alternative.

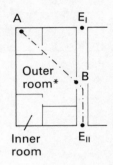

Route from inner room
E_I and E_{II} are exists
B Is the doorway from the outer room
A Is the point in an inner room furthest from B

A–B Must not exceed the limit for travel from inner rooms to outer room exit.

A–E_I or A–E_{II} (whichever is the less) must not exceed the distance for travel in routes having an alternative.

If the outer room has two exits A–B is taken for the nearer exit for each inner room.

* The outer room should not be an area of high fire risk.

222

Lifts

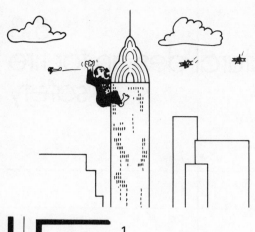

In very tall buildings great reliance is placed on lifts for normal vertical circulation.

But there are good reasons why ordinary lifts should not be regarded as suitable for escape from fire.

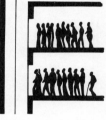

(1) Delay —

In a situation where seconds count time spent on or near the fire level waiting for a lift to arrive, is time wasted.

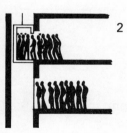

(2) Capacity —

When a lift does arrive it is unlikely to be able to take more than a fraction of those waiting — further delay for the rest — panic.

(3) Failure —

Fire may damage lift mechanism or power supply, stopping it between floors and trapping occupants.

(4) Stack effect — A failure of the protection of the shaft against smoke will allow the shaft to act as a flue drawing the toxic and incapacitating fumes upwards poisoning or cooking any occupants of the lifts.

(5) Controls —

Some types of lift call-button (the capacitive variety) may be actuated by the heat of the fire so that the lift stops at the fire floor, exposing occupants to the worst conditions.

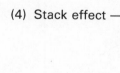

Outline design

8.3
Structural design for fire safety

OBJECTIVES

(1) To define the fire resistance requirements of all parts of the structure.
(2) To consider alternative structural solutions.
(3) To consider the interaction of the structure with other elements of construction in a fire.

FIRE RESISTANCE REQUIREMENTS

Legislative = building regulations

Fire resistance for a given occupancy   depends on   Building height, volume and area of compartments or building

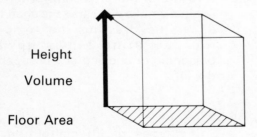

Height

Volume

Floor Area

see section 7.3 for details.

Over and above the legislative requirements there may be other considerations.

Life safety

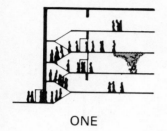

ONE

If staged evacuation is planned parts of the building may be occupied for longer than usual after a fire has started and the legislative requirement may not constitute adequate endurance.

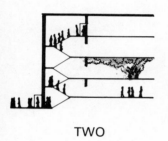

TWO

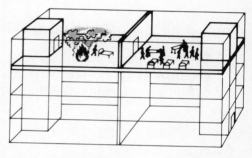

The same may be true if the scheme plans to use a refuge system.

If the building design is such that fire fighting could only be done from within it — as in tall or voluminous buildings, for example — increased structural fire resistance may be needed to safeguard fire fighters.

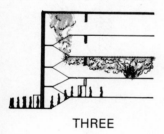

THREE

Property protection

Legislation (to date) is not concerned with property protection and so if there is a priority to prevent fire damage to the structure a greater degree of protection or inherent fire resistance is possibly needed.

METHODS OF ACHIEVING STRUCTURAL FIRE RESISTANCE STANDARDS

Where structural members will not have the inherent fire resistance necessary there are four basic methods for protecting them.

Insulation:

(a) Dry sheet material to enclose the member

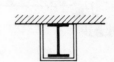

(b) Wet applied coating forming a hard protective layer

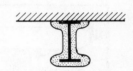

Thickness varies from 0.5mm for intumescent paint to 30mm or more for mineral/cement spray or more if one includes composite steel-reinforced concrete.

Oversizing:

This has two effects — one is that the member's temperature rises more slowly — the other is that the member is more lightly stressed and should therefore go on working to a higher temperature.

This is also the principle in the 'sacrificial loss' approach to timber structures. The outer surfaces char so that the loadbearing cross-section becomes smaller and the stress increases until failure. By beefing up the original section one can buy time before the critical stress is reached.

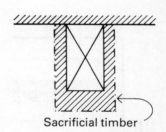

Sacrificial timber

Dissipation:

A member's temperature rises in a fire because it is losing heat to its surroundings far more slowly than the fire is supplying heat to it. While insulation slows the rate at which heat (thermal energy) 'reaches' the structural member, the dissipation techniques provide heat sinks to carry away some of the heat that reaches the member.

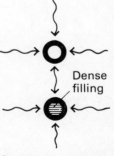

Dense filling

Increase mass per unit surface area

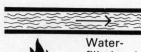

Water-
filled and
cooled

Structural hollow
section

(a) Increase thermal capacity by increasing ratio of mass to surface area, e.g. by filling a hollow steel member with concrete, or by choosing a heavier section.

(b) Active cooling system by using water-filled hollow sections in which convection or pumps set up flow to carry heat away from the section subjected to the fire.

[See Part 1 for more details]

Outline design

Design of services

SERVICES AS ROUTES FOR FIRE SPREAD

Legislative controls on layout:

Building regulations aim to prevent rapid fire spread, by-passing fire resisting elements, from one compartment or building to another. Openings in these elements for the passage of services have to be fire stopped and air ducts fitted with dampers.

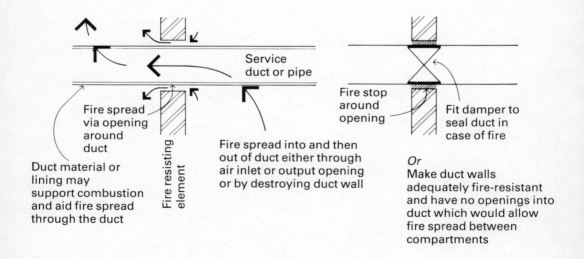

Service duct or pipe

Fire spread via opening around duct

Duct material or lining may support combustion and aid fire spread through the duct

Fire resisting element

Fire spread into and then out of duct either through air inlet or output opening or by destroying duct wall

Fire stop around opening

Fit damper to seal duct in case of fire

Or
Make duct walls adequately fire-resistant and have no openings into duct which would allow fire spread between compartments

Services — being concealed usually — run in cavities. Building regulations limit the extent of cavities (experience in multiple-fatality fires, where undetected and rapid fire/smoke spread in cavities contributed significantly to the loss, provided the impetus for this). Extensive cavities have to be subdivided by fire-resisting cavity barriers and any services passing through the barriers have to be suitably fire stopped/dampered. This is costly, has possible maintenance/alteration complications and if many openings have to be made in a barrier the changes are that it will not retain its fire-resisting integrity.

Plan of service void with cavity barrier crossing service ducts

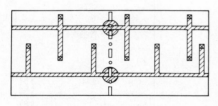

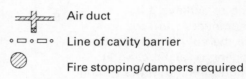

Air duct

Line of cavity barrier

Fire stopping/dampers required

Good liaison needed between architect and engineer to minimize the number of intersections of services with barrier.

Regulations do not limit the extent of the space within ducts, flues, chutes, pipes, conduits, or protected shafts, provided they do not constitute a by-pass route for fire.

Legislation concerned with means of escape (fire precautions act, national assistance act, theatres act, etc.) Make requirements for protected areas which involve integrity of fire resisting elements:

Protected corridors — usually dead-end corridors — are often affected

Either the ceilings (▫ ▫ ▫) or the wall over the fire-resisting walls (ooooo) can be made the line of fire resistance (provided with ▫ ▫ ▫ that there is not a need for cavity barriers by virture of an extensive ceiling cavity)

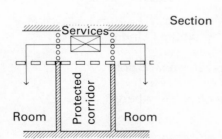

Section

Fire stopping and/or dampers will be needed wherever the line of fire-resistance is crossed.

Coordination

It is essential that services engineers should know where lines of fire resistance are to be so that they may design accordingly

e.g.
If the floor requires fire resistance there is no point in using a fire resisting suspended ceiling to achieve it if the engineers want to make the void into a plenum supplying or exhausting air through opening in the ceiling.

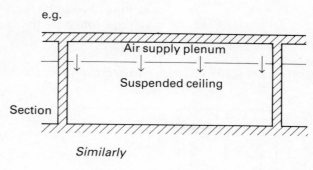

e.g.

Similarly

The engineer sees a need to ventilate an electricity distribution cupboard but this negates the corridor protection (especially if the rising feeder provides a route for fire spread in the way shown here).

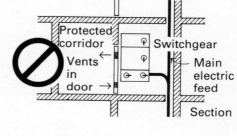

Technical and practical problems

Fire and more particularly smoke and toxic fumes can be spread throughout a building by the mechanical air handling system

Therefore there must be arrangements for closing the system down or changing its mode of operation but deciding how or when to do this may be difficult —

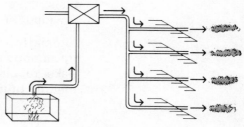

e.g. On operation of manual switch — by whom? Under what conditions? etc.
On operation of fire alarm — false alarms? Empty building?
On signal from in-duct smoke detectors — where? False alarms?

A complete shut-down may have other unforeseen effects on smoke movement. Perhaps keep the extraction side running (later sections look at smoke control by mechanical means).

Fire dampers are usually heat-activated (either fuseable link releasing mechanical shutters or intumescent honeycomb swelling to seal opening) and are therefore not necessarily effective against smoke spread in ducts. Cool smoke and gas may pass indefinitely.

Smoke detection in the rapid air movement in ducts requires special equipment.

If the air is coming from smokey rooms, e.g. kitchens or a bar, it can be difficult to distinguish between 'ambient' smoke and fire smoke in the duct, and false alarms may result.

As well as plastic and cellulosic duct materials metal service runs can spread fire, even though they do not burn, by conducting heat to some combustible material close to or in contact with the metal.

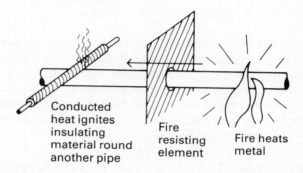

Conducted heat ignites insulating material round another pipe

Fire resisting element

Fire heats metal

The identification of problem areas in these respects, at the drawing board stage, can be tricky.

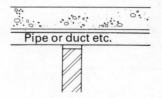

Pipe or duct etc.

While this looks quite good in section ....

It is a much more obvious gap if seen in elevation

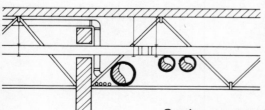

One needs to know how the work will be done on site.

Drawings by the different consultants tend to ignore the full complexity by showing only their own bit of the whole assemblage.

Getting parts of this wall built at all may be a major struggle — fire stopping the openings, a near impossibility.

231

SERVICES AS POTENTIAL SOURCES OF FIRE

Chapter 1, Table 5 gives statistics on sources of ignition of
fires in occupied buildings

64% of these fires
were ignited by some
constituent part of the
buildings' services in 1974

64%

In evaluating means of escape proposals enforcing
authorities often identify energy-using equipment
(electrical, oil, gas etc.) as requiring special attention —
which usually means enclosure with fire-resisting
construction.

The relationship of such equipment to escape routes is
thus important but it is equally important to have an
understanding of the true level and nature of the risk.
Where new plant or novel combinations of plant or
processes are involved the skill of the services or process
engineer should be drawn on to build up a picture of
possible risks and estimate the probabilities.

The fault tree is one way to organize such estimation
exercises.

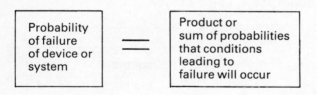

| Probability of failure of device or system | = | Product or sum of probabilities that conditions leading to failure will occur |

e.g.

P. flat tyre ⊏ P. I forgot to pump it up
P. I have a puncture
P. The valve fails

Symbols

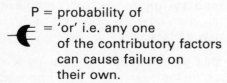

P = probability of
= 'or' i.e. any one
of the contributory factors
can cause failure on
their own.

If need be each contributory factor can be broken down too.

e.g.

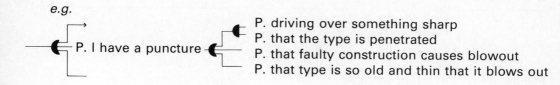

P. I have a puncture

P. driving over something sharp
P. that the type is penetrated
P. that faulty construction causes blowout
P. that type is so old and thin that it blows out

Key to logic symbols:

"or" i.e. any one of the contributory events can on its own bring about the consequential event

"and" i.e. all the contributory events have to occur at one time to bring about the consequential event

The end result of such analysis is a figure for the probability of the equipment or system causing a fire and a 'tree' diagram like this

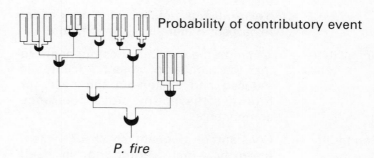

Probability of contributory event

P. fire

On a simpler every day level where such analysis would be hopelessly cumbersome ask these questions

How could this equipment cause a fire?
What are the likely consequences [Direct injury, fire spread]?
Is maintenance/housekeeping likely to be better or worse than usual?
Is misuse or abuse of the equipment more or less likely than usual?

CONSEQUENCES OF A FAILURE OF SERVICES

Failure of fire protection services

May be due to failure within the service or failure of some other service on which it depends (water or electricity supply for example).

Do not ignore the possibility of human failure where system operation depends on human action.

It is impossible to achieve 100% reliability but it is usual to try to make fire protection systems more reliable than most ordinary equipment using the following techniques:

Redundancy — If an important component fails another takes over automatically.

Fail safe — In failing the system operates so as to reduce the fire risk, e.g. process control shuts a process down or an electromagnet holding a fire door open, releases it if there is a power failure.

Simplicity — Minimize the number of components so that the number of potential failures is reduced and design-out the need for highly stressed or close tolerance components.

Monitoring — Constant or frequent check of system integrity which should not in itself reduce the life of components significantly.

Maintenance — In statistical terms the 'down-time' has an appreciable effect on overall reliability. Maintenance is both preventive and restitutive provision of specialists for maintenance may be necessary.

Suitability for purpose — System design and construction/installation is such that it is not damaged or degraded unreasonably by use, abuse or environmental conditions.

The following diagram gives an indication of the established failure rates for some common components.

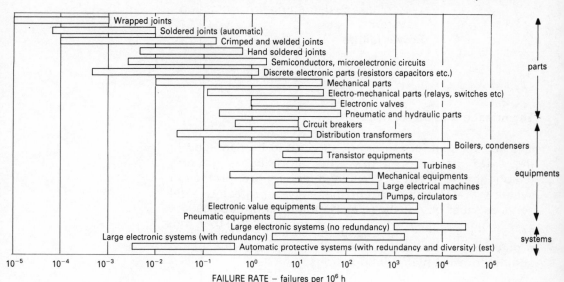

FAILURE RATE – failures per 10^6 h

Architects are not likely to have any detailed use for such information and in the field of electronics overall reliability has probably improved somewhat since these figures were collected. It is however interesting to note the general order of magnitude of failure rate.

The failure rate is expressed in number of failures during a million hours of operation.

Note that the best automatic protection systems may only fail once in 100,000,000 hours and that large electronic systems may fail every week!

Failure of other service

When considering the adequacy of fire protection services it is necessary to assess the risks that could arise if other services fail.

They may (a): Cause fires;
(b): Neutralize fire protection measures.

Examples of (a): Processes out of control
Overheating caused by electrical faults
Leaks in containers of flammable gas or liquid
Bearings overheating or sparking

Examples of (b): Lighting failure making escape routes
                  unusable
                  Water leakage damaging fire protection
                  system
                  Power failure

The effect of fire on services

It is not unusual for important services to be damaged in the early stages of a fire. Lifts stop, lights go out, telephones fail, etc. As outlined above fire protection systems are to some extent themselves protected. Vital services must obviously be extremely well protected.

These vital services must be identified and any scheme of protection examined and 'tested' on the drawing board against foreseeable fault conditions.

FIRE PROTECTION SERVICES

Basic space-requirements for the main components of some fire protection systems

(a) Rising mains

To Fire Authority Specification:

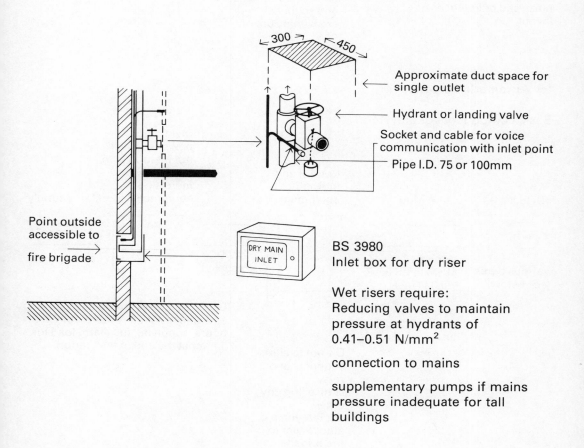

Approximate duct space for single outlet

Hydrant or landing valve

Socket and cable for voice communication with inlet point

Pipe I.D. 75 or 100mm

Point outside accessible to fire brigade

BS 3980
Inlet box for dry riser

Wet risers require:
Reducing valves to maintain pressure at hydrants of 0.41–0.51 N/mm^2

connection to mains

supplementary pumps if mains pressure inadequate for tall buildings

(b) Alarms

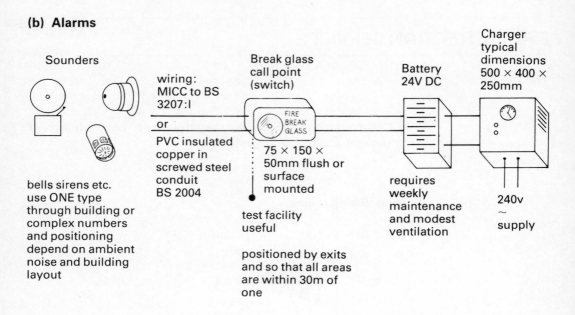

Sounders

wiring:
MICC to BS
3207:I

or

PVC insulated
copper in
screwed steel
conduit
BS 2004

bells sirens etc.
use ONE type
through building or
complex numbers
and positioning
depend on ambient
noise and building
layout

Break glass
call point
(switch)

FIRE
BREAK
GLASS

75 × 150 ×
50mm flush or
surface
mounted

test facility
useful

positioned by exits
and so that all areas
are within 30m of
one

Battery
24V DC

requires
weekly
maintenance
and modest
ventilation

Charger
typical
dimensions
500 × 400 ×
250mm

240v
~
supply

(c) Automatic Detection

Basic components of a system:

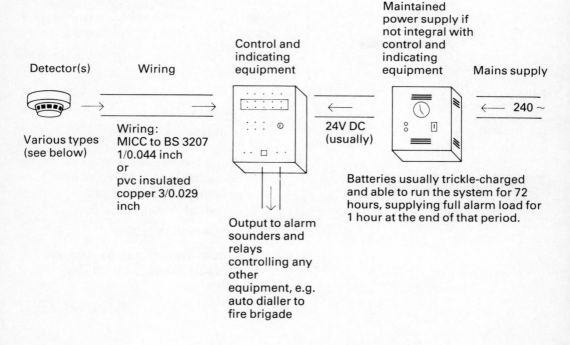

Detector(s)

Wiring

Control and
indicating
equipment

Maintained
power supply if
not integral with
control and
indicating
equipment

Mains supply

Various types
(see below)

Wiring:
MICC to BS 3207
1/0.044 inch
or
pvc insulated
copper 3/0.029
inch

24V DC
(usually)

← 240 ~

Output to alarm
sounders and
relays
controlling any
other
equipment, e.g.
auto dialler to
fire brigade

Batteries usually trickle-charged
and able to run the system for 72
hours, supplying full alarm load for
1 hour at the end of that period.

Zones

Unless the protected area is very small detector systems are usually split into zones to help pin-point the fire. The detectors in each zone are connected to the control and indicating equipment so that when a detector is triggered the control and indicating panel shows which zone the detector is in.

The location of zones depends on:

The number of detectors the control and indicating equipment can handle in one zone.

The use of the parts of the building — there may be times when it is useful to devote a zone to a single room.

Size, shape, number of floors and arrangement of compartmentation.

Money — cost increases with number of zones.

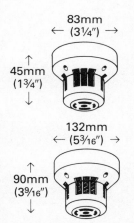

83mm
← (3¼″) →

↑
45mm
(1¾″)
↓

132mm
← (5³⁄₁₆″) →

↑
90mm
(3⁹⁄₁₆″)
↓

(Typical dimensions)

Point detectors

Heat sensitive —
   trigger when element heated to a particular temperature and/or when a particular rate of rise in temperature is exceeded

'Smoke' sensitive —
   ionisation type (illustrated) —
   trigger when minute change is induced in an electrical circuit by the intrusion of very small particles into an ionisation field produced by a small radioactive source.

Obscuration type —
   trigger when smoke enters a light beam inside the unit and causes a change in the output of a photocell or photoresistor

Backscattering type —
   trigger when smoke enters a light beam inside, scattering light onto a photo cell (etc) which is not normally illuminated

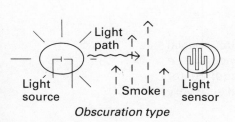

Light source   Light path   Smoke   Light sensor

Obscuration type

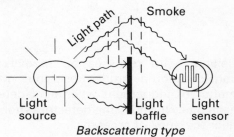

Light path   Smoke

Light source   Light baffle   Light sensor

Backscattering type

Coverage:

The floor area that one point detector can project is between 10 and 100 m² but depends on mounting height, air movement pattern, type of fire risk, etc.

Heat detectors:

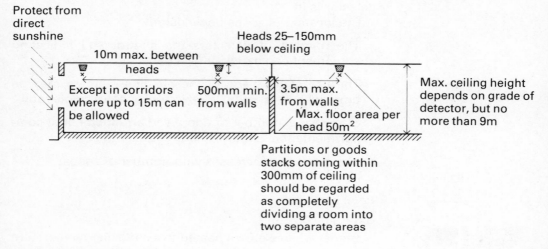

Protect from direct sunshine

10m max. between heads

Except in corridors where up to 15m can be allowed

500mm min. from walls

Heads 25–150mm below ceiling

3.5m max. from walls

Max. floor area per head 50m²

Max. ceiling height depends on grade of detector, but no more than 9m

Partitions or goods stacks coming within 300mm of ceiling should be regarded as completely dividing a room into two separate areas

Smoke detectors:

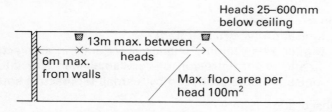

Heads 25–600mm below ceiling

13m max. between heads

6m max. from walls

Max. floor area per head 100m²

Recesses, vaults etc.:

Ceilings with recesses or downstands require special consideration as smoke reservoirs may be formed. It is a matter of judgement whether a detector is required for each one. Normally the detectors should be fitted at or very near the apex of recesses.

Other types of detector

(1) Linear —   Special cable is run through the protected space (often a machine cabinet or storage racking). When heated at any point on its length the insulation between the cables conductors breaks down and shorts. The short causes control circuitry to trigger the fire alarm or other measures.

A similar principle employing plastic tube containing compressed air has the advantage for areas with inflammable atmospheres, that there is not risk of sparking. Heat ruptures the tube and the sudden pressure drop is detected.

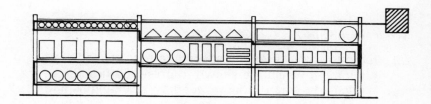

(2) Beam —   Infrared or ultraviolet ray is projected across the top of the protected space to a photocell. Mirrors can be used to increase the 'area' covered by the beam. Smoke or hot air turbulence cause refraction of the beam and reduce the photocell output to trigger alarm. Experimental systems in cable ducts have used laser beams.

Coverage of up to 1000 m^2 is possible but only in calm atmospheres and not where there are processes releasing steam clouds or hot air, etc.

Infrared systems can be affected by sunlight.

Mirror   Emitter
                                          detector

(3) Flame
Detectors — These are area detectors sensitive to infrared or ultraviolet radiation from a flame, Non-fire sources of this radiation are eliminated by circuitry which looks for the characteristic fluctuation associated with the slow flicker rate of flames.

The detector scans 360° and can therefore cover a large area (10,000 m²).

Smouldering combustion will not be detected.

Fixed extinguishing systems: General considerations

What are they for?

(a) Extinguishing fires in specific areas or items of equipment which are known to present a fire risk — particularly where a large quantity of extinguishing agent has to be brought to bear quickly, or where manual fire fighting is likely to be hazardous or unsuccessful for some reason.

e.g.
A machine pit where, say an oil leak may start a fire in an inaccessible area

A fixed array can deliver extinguishing agent — even inside the machine casing.

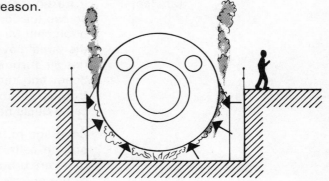

(b) Extinguishing fires that threaten specific items of high value where quick fire fighting by other means cannot be assured

e.g.
A library's precious book store, which may be unoccupied for long periods.

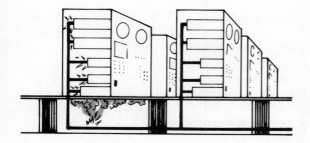

or
electronic equipment, where
cabinets delay discovery and
hinder manual fire fighting
and quantities of wiring are
concealed under floors, etc.

(c)   Some fire fighting techniques are more effective and
        less hazardous to personnel using fixed installations:

        e.g. Total flooding — where the atmosphere is made
        unbreathable; or deluging with water or high
        expansion — when conditions are both unpleasant
        and disorientating if not immediately incapacitating.

(d)   Certain installations attract substantial insurance
        premium discounts — notably sprinkler systems — so
        that they are economically attractive as property
        protection devices.

What do they do?

They apply extinguishing agent either directly onto the fire
or into the space in which the fire has occurred.

   Activation may be manual or automatic or, where there
are safety interlocks to prevent discharge into an occupied
space, by a combination. There are ultra-fast-acting
systems for explosion suppression which react to the
rising pressure as the explosion begins and injects an
inhibiting agent before the explosion reaction 'takes off'.

Extinguishing agents

Agent	Applied Form	Effect	Suitable for fires in
Water	Sprinklers	Cooling, smothering	Solids
	Spray	Cooling, smothering	Solids and some liquids
	Foam	Cooling, smothering	Solids and some liquids
CO_2	Gas/solid	Smothering (cooling)	Solids liquids gases (but not for inerting flammable atmospheres)
Halon	Gas, gas/liquid	Inhibiting, smothering	Liquids, gases, solids
Powder	Powder suspension	Inhibiting, smothering	Liquids, solids

Fixed extinguishing systems using gas or vaporizing liquids

The two most significant mechanisms for extinguishing fire with these systems are:

Inerting

The extinguishant takes the place of atmospheric oxygen and smothers combustion.

Carbon dioxide (CO_2) is the most common agent.
Nitrogen gas (N_2) is occasionally used.

Inhibiting

The extinguishant (or products of its decomposition) interfere with the combustion chemistry to interrupt the chain reaction involved.

Halons — A chemical family of which the two members that are currently used for fire fighting are:
BCF or Halon 1211
(Bromochlorodifluoromethane);
BTM or Halon 1301 (Difluorobromomethane).

All these substances are gases at room temperature but are stored as liquids either under pressure or refrigeration. They do therefore have a limited cooling effect when discharged.

Methods of application

Local:
The stream is concentrated on an identified fire risk within a room;
Sometimes it is piped directly into the cabinet of the equipment to be protected.

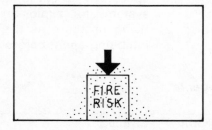

Total flooding:
An extinguishing concentration is produced throughout the protected room(s).

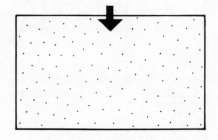

CO₂ systems

A concentration of 25–30% of CO_2 in air (by volume) is needed to be effective.

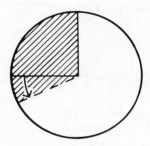

But if combustion is deep seated
or if there is likely to be much leakage from the protected space more CO_2 will be needed.

The following table gives a very rough guide for total flooding

Fire in	Weight CO₂ (lbs) per 10 cu ft of room
Bulk Paper Storage	1.25
Textile Storage	1.7
Small electrical machines	1.0
Cable ducts of less than 2000 cu ft	1.0
Ordinary electrical wiring hazards	0.8
Flammable liquids (fuel oil paraffin petrol)	
in room < 140 cu ft	0.8
in room 140–500 cu ft	0.67
in room 500–1600 cu ft	0.63
in room 1600–4500 cu ft	0.56
in room 4500–50,000 cu ft	0.5
in room > 50,000 cu ft	0.45

Highly flammable liquids — increase the figure for flammable liquids

Propane	by	10%
Carbon monoxide		140%
Acetylene		150%
Hydrogen		210%

Guidance on flow rates etc. for local application systems is available in National Fire Protection Association (of USA) code No. 12 Appendix pp. 75–80.

The main floor space requirement of the system is for CO_2 storage.

(a) *High pressure storage*

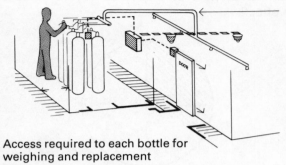

Design of discharge pipes for two phase flow requires specialist knowledge

Actuation system:

Automatic detection plus manual alarm with safety locks to prevent discharge while the room is occupied.

Cylinders opened electromechanically.

Automatic closure of door and window/ventilator openings may be incorporated.

Access required to each bottle for weighing and replacement

Bottle sizes 50, 80 or 100lbs.

(b) Low pressure storage

Where tonnage quantitites are needed it may be cheaper to store the CO_2 as a liquid at low temperture (-17 °C) and moderate pressure 300 PS1.

The refrigeration tank and controls can be supplied as a packaged unit. As filling and replenishing is by road tanker, hard standing for the vehicle should be provided as near to the tank as possible.

Prolonged failure of refrigeration will lead to the blowing off of CO_2 gas. The siting and design of the unit should allow for the safe dispersal of the gas bearing in mind that it is heavier than air.

Halon systems	BTM	BCF
Minimum effective concentration in air	5%	6%
Weight of halon to produce effective concentration in a 10,000 cu ft space	200lbs	260lbs
Cost per unit weight	£2x	£x
Concentration producing anaesthetic effect after short exposure	7%	4½%

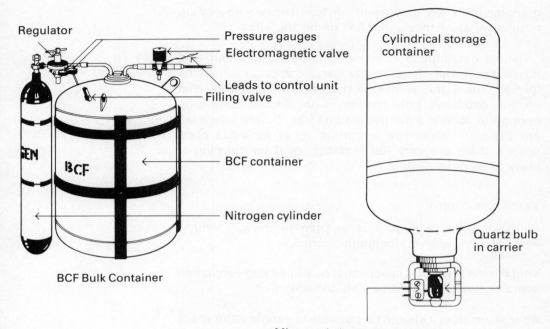

Regulator

Pressure gauges

Electromagnetic valve

Leads to control unit

Filling valve

BCF container

Nitrogen cylinder

Cylindrical storage container

Quartz bulb in carrier

BCF Bulk Container

Micro-switch operates when bulb shatters to shut down extractor fans or sound audible alarm

BTM Automatic Extinguishing System for fume cupboards, equipment cabinets etc.

Storage — In liquid form under pressure.

BTM having boiling point of −50 °C is self-expelling but in practice is under compressed nitrogen at 360–600 PSI.

BCF has a higher boiling point and is expelled by nitrogen from a separate pressure bottle, Its semi-liquid (two phase) jet tends to have a longer throw than gaseous BTM

Toxicity

BTM may be judged as slightly superior to BCF in that the minimum effective extinguishing concentration is less than the minimum toxic concentration whereas the reverse is true of BCF.

The long term effect of exposure to BCF and BTM is a subject of debate. US codes require safety interlocks to prevent discharge into occupied spaces. The manufacturers say the loss of consciousness is equivalent to medical anaesthesia and has no lasting effect.

Halons decompose at elevated temperatures and acid gases and other dangerously toxic compounds can be formed. The highly acrid smell makes it most unlikely that anyone could willingly remain in an affected area long enough to absorb a dangerous quantity. Safety interlocks are therefore especially important if, as in some plant spaces, there are very hot surfaces, or if the burning is likely to be deep seated.

Ventilation control

Air–halon mixture is more dense than air and will tend to leak out via low level openings or cracks.

Vents to the protected space must be sealed and ventilation supplies turned off when halon is discharged.

After an incident it should be possible to ventilate the space quickly to allow re-occupation without affecting other areas.

 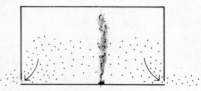

Other fixed extinguishing systems

Dry powders

There are several different powders but the mechanism of extinguishing is to a greater or lesser extent a combination of chemical inhibiting and physical inerting, in all cases. As the chemical effect increases with powder surface area, a finely divided powder should be superior, but practical problems of 'caking' in storage, clogged delivery pipes and poor penetration into the fire, put a limit on particle size. One type overcomes this problem by splitting into fine particles only in the heat of the fire (decrepitation).

Weight for weight effectiveness of different powders after Rasbash	Weights or equivalent effectiveness
Sodium Bicarbonate (NaH CO_3)	x
Potassium salts (Bicarbonate or Sulphate)	$0.7x$
Potassium Bicarbonate-Urea Based (Decrepitating)	$0.4x$
For Further Comparison	
Halon BTM	x

200 lbs Sodium Bicarbonate is needed to flood a 10,000 cu ft room.

Powder is expelled under gas pressure and behaves like a fluid in the discharge pipework except at changes of direction if these are too sharp. Blockages can occur.

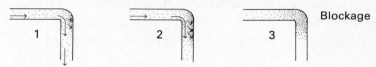

Like silt in a river powder can come out of suspension.

Toxicity

Sodium bicarbonate (also known as baking soda) is not chemically toxic but like all the dry powders is unpleasant to inhale and will cause respiratory problems if any quantity gets into the lungs.

There should therefore be no people in a space when total flooding takes place. Localized application is normally acceptable.

Other points

Mechanical parts, especially small ones such as electrical relays and contacts, will be affected by powder and cleaning up can be a lengthy and expensive process. A dry powder system would be ruled out in some cases by this consideration — e.g. a room which contains electromechanical switchgear.

Mechanical ventilation systems, ductwork and filters, should be protected against 'inhaling' dry powder and this protection must be maintained until cleaning up is complete.

High expansion foam

Fire fighting foam is basically water, with an additive, into which bubbles have been entrained. Its effect is twofold:

(a) It smothers by cutting off the fire's oxygen supply and giving off steam

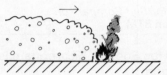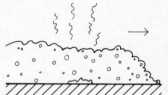

(b) It cools the surrounding area and shields it from radiation from the flames. (Foam is a vehicle for the water, holding it in the critical area instead of it flowing away.)

'Expansion' = ratio of volume of foam to volume of water in foam.

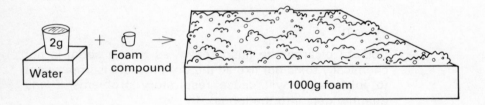

e.g. A 500 expansion produces 1000 gallons of foam from 2 gallons of water.

Foam compounds

There are several types of compound serving different purposes. The architect need not be much concerned with the selection.

Snags

Water damage — Can be as bad as with direct use of water
— worse if the foam is not removed quickly.
Corrosion   — The ordinary corrosive effect of water is exacerbated with some foam compounds.

250

Electrically
conductive —   To disperse high expansion foam people
have usually to wade into it, complete
electrical isolation can be difficult to
achieve.

Visibility/dispersal/
smouldering —   It can be difficult to decide when the fire
is extinguished, smouldering can persist
within the foam. There can be
unpleasant surprises for those moving
through it working dispersant sprays.

Room
section

Persistant   Zero
smouldering   visibility

Foam production

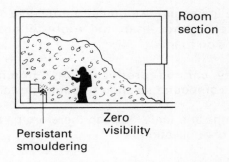

High Expansion Foam

Mesh
screw

H₂O

Mixing

Pump →

Foam
compound
tank

Fan

Expanded
foam

Foam
will breakdown
if ducted at a
speed of more
than 4m/minute

This foam can not be projected so the generator must
either be in or above the protected space or be connected
to it via short ducts.

Rates of application vary with the anticipated type of fire.

Burning liquid — 0.16 litres foam/m² floor area/second.
Burning solid — 0.06 m³ foam/m² floor area/minute/unit
of fire load expressed as kg of
wood equivalent per m² floor area.

251

If the fire is likely to reach the ceiling before foam coverage of the floor is complete the normal application rate should be increased to 2.5 m³ foam/m² floor area/minute, minimum.

Note   These rates are empirical. Various factors affecting the formation and breakdown rates may require higher rates (see NFPA codes vol. 7 1973–4 code 11A).

Low and medium expansion foam

These foams are used only to provide a shallow covering blanket (rather than for room-filling, as with high expansion foam).

They can be produced by pumping a premixed water/compound solution through special nozzles.

Pumps and tanks etc. can therefore be remote from the point of application.

The foam can be projected and aimed by monitors which may be fixed or directed manually or by remote control.

Special outlets have been designed which pop up from a flush floor mounting in similar way to some built-in lawn watering devices. (This type was developed for aircraft hangars.)

There are several different types of foam compound each having different properties (cost, storage life, extinguishing capability, susceptibility to breakdown by particular flammable liquids, etc.) The selection of a particular compound and the equipment to apply it is a specialist matter on which a fire engineer or the fire service should be consulted.

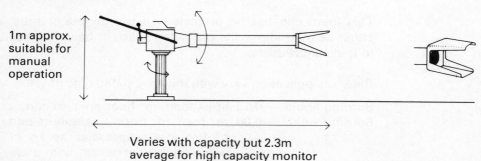

1m approx. suitable for manual operation

Varies with capacity but 2.3m average for high capacity monitor

Emergency power supplies

The choice of system depends largely on the load which in turn is determined by decisions about what emergency power is needed for. Agreement must be reached on this with the client before a system can be designed.

Fire protection services are obvious candidates for emergency supply. Automatic detection systems and alarms are almost always installed with back-up battery power which is both a British Standard and an insurance (FOC) requirement.

Supply arrangements

Emergency power may be provided locally, e.g. from batteries within a luminaire or from a central point via the normal circuitry or using separate emergency circuits. There are many variations —

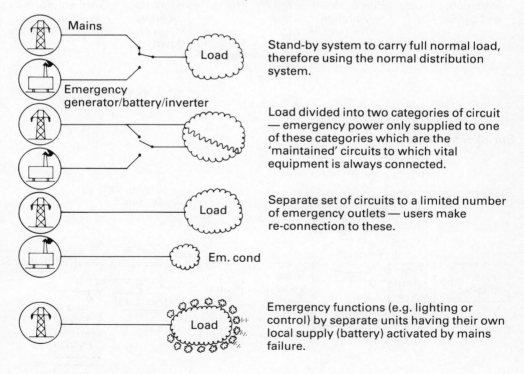

Stand-by system to carry full normal load, therefore using the normal distribution system.

Load divided into two categories of circuit — emergency power only supplied to one of these categories which are the 'maintained' circuits to which vital equipment is always connected.

Separate set of circuits to a limited number of emergency outlets — users make re-connection to these.

Emergency functions (e.g. lighting or control) by separate units having their own local supply (battery) activated by mains failure.

253

Generator sets

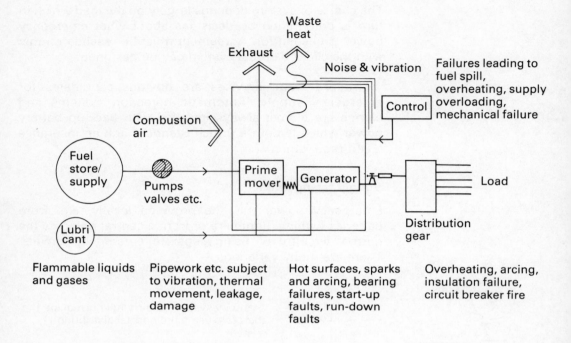

Sprinker systems

System components

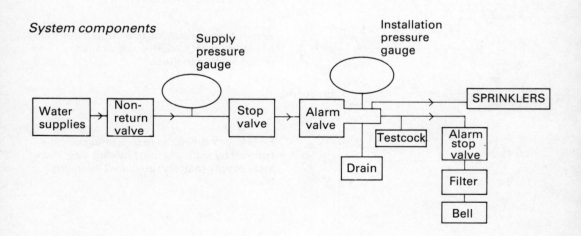

As sprinklers are almost always installed for insurance purposes the FOC Rules (29th edition) are all-important.

Building Regulations for England and Wales allow the size of compartments to be increased in steps if a sprinkler system is installed which complies with the relevant recommendations of CP 402.201:1952 (Reg. E4(1)).

Types of system:

(An excellent description of the essentials of sprinkler systems is to be found in Building Research Station CP 79/75)

wet system — the whole system is water filled at all times;

dry system — system beyond alarm valve is air-filled until a sprinkler head opens. (This gives frost protection);

alternating — the system may be wet or dry (usually wet in summer and dry when there is a risk of frost);

re-cycling — or re-setting the system is wet but the sprinkler heads are capable of closing if the fire is extinguished (this reduces water damage);

pre-action — a normally dry system in which water may be admitted to the sprinkler array on a signal from some other fire detector, e.g. smoke detector.

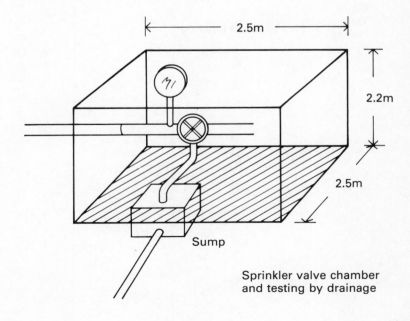

Sprinkler valve chamber and testing by drainage

Basic space requirements

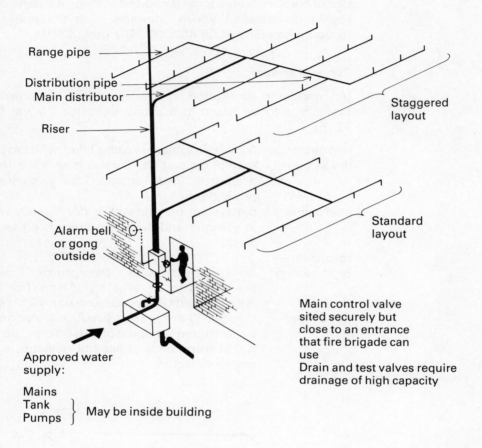

Range pipe

Distribution pipe
Main distributor

Riser

Staggered
layout

Standard
layout

Alarm bell
or gong
outside

Main control valve
sited securely but
close to an entrance
that fire brigade can
use
Drain and test valves require
drainage of high capacity

Approved water
supply:

Mains
Tank
Pumps } May be inside building

Sprinkler system FOC rules

Sprinkler layout requirements of the FOC Rules depend on the type of hazard being covered and the type of sprinkler being used.

The Rules stipulate (among other things):

maximum area of coverage per sprinkler ($9-21m^2$)
maximum space between sprinklers on one pipe (range pipe) (2.5–4.6m)
maximum space between range pipes (2.5–4.6m)
distance below ceiling (varies with ceiling construction)
horizontal distance from joists and walls, etc.

The hazard classifications are:

extra-light hazard
ordinary hazard
extra-high hazard : (a) process risks; (b) high storage.

Water supplies

In order to be sure that the sprinklers will have an adequate water supply under all natural conditions (i.e. barring earthquakes, etc.) the FOC Rules define five types each of which may be graded as 'superior' or 'acceptable' according to their detailed characteristics.

The five types are:

town mains
elevated private reservoirs
gravity tanks
pressure tanks
automatic pumps drawing from approved ground reservoirs or other sources.

For storage tank/reservoir systems the quantity of water varies with the hazard classification and the water discharge rate of the sprinklers (specified in mm/minute falling on the area covered by one sprinkler) between $9m^3$ for extra-light hazard up to $875m^3$ for extra-high hazard.

**Outline
design**

8.5
Constraints on the use of materials and the design of assemblies

---

UK LEGISLATIVE REQUIREMENTS

Standard and Statute
Fire Resistance
BS 476 pt 8 tests for
insulation integrity collapse

Material/element/assembly

element of structure

Building Regulations

Ditto and non-combustible

separating (party) walls

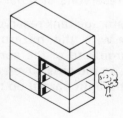

Ditto and non combustible

compartment walls and
floors and doors in
compartment wall

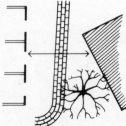

Fire resistance external wall

external wall not permitted
to be unprotected opening

Ditto and, if there is a stair or lift in the shaft, non-combustible

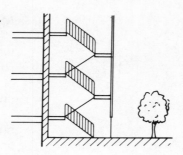

protecting structure enclosing protected shafts (excluding any external wall to the shaft)

Standard and Statute

Material/Element/Assembly

Fire Resistance
BS 476 pt 8 tests for
insulation integrity collapse

walls and floor separating small garage from house to which it is attached and any door in these walls

Building Regulations

Ditto

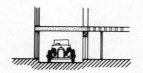

'large' cavity barrier (one whose surface can include a square of 1 m on a side)

Fire Resistant
BS 476 pt 8
Insulation integrity collapse

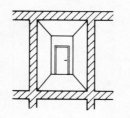

walls and floor-ceiling enclosing protected fire escape routes including doors

*Fire Precautions Act
Public Health Act §60
Licensing Act
Entertainment and Theatre
Licensing and * other
means-of-escape legislation*

Fire Resistant
BS 476 pt 8
Integrity collapse (not insulation)

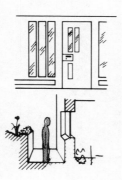

glazing in walls and doors enclosing protected fire escape routes

BS CP 153 pt 4 gives acceptable glazed area restricting radiation according to escape route width and mobility of occupants

glazing in external walls that is within 1m horizontally or 6m vertically below an external escape route

** Means of escape
Legislation*

* Ditto

* These standards are not explicitly set by statute but are commonly accepted by the authorities charged with ensuring that a reasonable standard is achieved.

Standard and Statute		Material/Element/Assembly
Surface flame spread BS476 pt 7 classes 1,2,3, and BS 476 pt 6 index $l<12$ sub index $i<6$ (called class 'O')	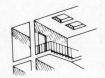	walls, ceilings and rooflights to rooms, circulation, or protected shafts
Building Regulations		standard varies with type of space, and use of building
Non-combustible		external walls close to boundary ($<$1m) or which are $>$15m high
Building Regulations		
		cladding to ditto. To be class 'O'
Fire resistant (when exposed to fire on the inside or the outside)	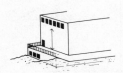	external wall of multi-storey "assembly" buildings adjoining ground or balcony/rooftop which is accessible to people who have no unprotected area within 7.5m of ground/balcony level (with stated exceptions E7(5))
Surface flame spread (Class 'O' if within 1m of boundary or index "l"$\leqslant$12 and "i"$\leqslant$6 if more than 1m from boundary)		
Building Regulations (England and Wales)		
Non-combustible		means of escape stairways including landings (and floors within a protected stair enclosure)
Building Regulations		
Ditto		fire stops
Ditto		chimney, flue, hearth, fireplace recess and material close to hearth or fireplace recess in wall or floor
Ease of ignition and penetration by fire BS 476 pt 3	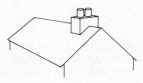	roof coverings and chimney discharge heights in relation to building use, volume, height, roof area and distance of roof from boundary

UK LEGISLATIVE CONTROLS FOR PREVENTION OF FIRE SPREAD THROUGH CAVITIES WITHIN BUILDING CONSTRUCTION

(1) Overall size of uninterrupted cavity limited by building regulations

Table to Regulation E14(4)

Maximum distance between cavity barriers

Location of cavity	Purpose group of building or compartment	Class of surface exposed within the cavity, excluding the surface of any pipe, cable or conduit	Maximum distance
Between a roof and a ceiling	Purpose group I and flats or maisonettes within purpose group III	Any	No limit
	Purpose group II and III except flats and maisonettes	Any	15 m and, in addition, area limited to 100 m²
	Any other purpose group	Any	20 m
Other than between a roof and a ceiling	Any purpose group	Class O	20 m
		Other than Class O	8 m

Note: These restrictions do not apply to the cavity within normal brick or block cavity wall construction although there should be cavity closures at the top of such walls and around openings in them

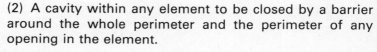

(2) A cavity within any element to be closed by a barrier around the whole perimeter and the perimeter of any opening in the element.

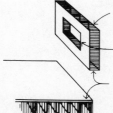

Where elements with cavities meet, barriers are required so that the cavities do not communicate

261

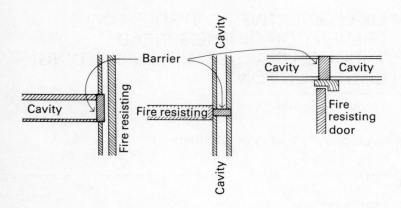

(3) Where a cavity abuts a fire-resisting element the cavity barrier should be in the same plane as the fire resisting element.

The requirement for cavity barriers does not extend to —

The solum or square between the ground
floor and the ground or oversite concrete.

Or the roofspace of a private house (purpose group I) —

But if the house has three or more storeys and the stair has therefore to be separated from the rest of the house by fire resisting construction the roof space must be separated from the stair. Thus:

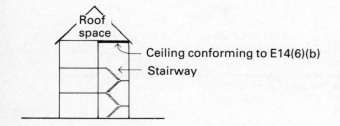

Roof
space

— Ceiling conforming to E14(6)(b)

← Stairway

{
Extends over all the stair ceiling
not made to be demountable
fire resistant to ½ hour standard
Imperforate (exceptions E14(9)(c))
Upper surface class 1
Lower surface index $I \leqslant 12$, $i \leqslant 6$
}

CONTROLS ON THE PROPERTIES OF SURFACES WITHIN CAVITIES

(1) Roof Cavities

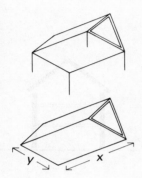

Purpose Group I and flats/maisonettes in Group III
No restriction on surfaces exposed inside cavity
No restriction on extent of cavity

Purpose Groups II or III except flats or maisonettes
No restriction on surfaces exposed inside cavity
Extent of cavity $x \leqslant 15$ m; $y \leqslant 15$ m; $xy \leqslant 100$m².

Any other Purpose Group — no restriction on surfaces exposed inside cavity: $x \leqslant 20$ m; $y \leqslant 20$ m.

(2) Cavities other than roof cavities:

Surfaces in cavity	Max. distance between cavity barriers
Class 'O'	20 m
other class	8 m

The control on surfaces in cavities includes all those surfaces such as structural members, water tanks etc. exposed in it, with the exception of pipes, cable and conduit.

Scottish Building Regulations on cavities

Maximum distance between cavity barriers = 8m
Maximum area between cavity barriers = 46 m²

Except:
Where all the internal surfaces are class O there are no limits

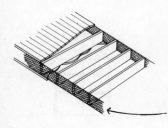

And
In the case of cavities between timber floor joists, barriers are required only at the ends.

INSURANCE STANDARDS FOR CONSTRUCTION

The fire offices' committee construction rules contain five 'standards', 'I' being the highest and 'V' the lowest. There are also three 'classes' of construction but these only apply to a limited range of buildings under the 'plastic tariff'.

The following is a brief summary of the 'standards' to give architects a general idea of what is involved. If instructed to design to one of the 'standard' it will be necessary to refer to the actual documents.

Standard V

Corresponds to conventional traditional construction with neither special fire resisting properties nor any special risk of fire.

Only walls and roof are subject to specific requirements:

External walls — Brick, masonry, terra cotta, cement concrete, blocks/slabs of solid or hollow brick, cement or concrete. Structural steel or iron frame not timber frame.

Material thickness or method of bonding not specified.

Party Walls — Brick, masonry, terra cotta, cement concrete, not less than 9" thick (230 mm), with no cavity, taken up to, or through roof.

Steel/iron frame to have 2" min. cover of one of the above materials.

Roofs — Requirements concerned mainly with the covering's resistance to fire penetration from outside. A range of acceptable materials is specified.

No control of roof structure.

Requirement for materials in, and form of, rooflights and lanternlights.

Standard II

The highest standard commonly found (Standard I being both onerous and expensive to comply with it is not often considered by building owners to be worthwhile)

Generally — Fire resistance (BS 476) of:
  2 hours — floor columns beams;
  1 hour — roofs.

Floors — Openings to be protected;
  Thicknesses are specified.

Roofs — Ability to contain a fire inside as well as resisting penetration from outside:
  Roof structure to have fire resistance.

The plastics tariff applies to premises in which plastics are produced, processed or stored. It does not apply where any of these functions are ancillary to the main purpose of the building.

  The class requirements under the tariff are couched in performance terms to a much greater extent than the 'standards'.

Determination of the appropriate 'standard'

The advice of the insurance company's fire surveyor should be obtained at the sketch design stage to check which insurance standards are likely to apply. Liaison with the client and his broker will be an essential part of any standard-setting operation.

Non-statutory

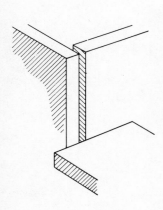

Joints and continuity of fire protection
If architectural design is all about the junctions between elements, much the same can be said about designing fire resistant assemblies.

  One of the most common faults in the fire protection of new buildings is the lack of continuity of fire resisting wall and floors.

  There are gaps at the junctions, holes left unfilled after services are installed, and cracks resulting from differential movement, shrinkage and so on.

Points for consideration

Wet construction: Shrinkage leading to gaps or cracks homogeneity (or the lack of it) air bubbles
construction joints with poor bond or cracks
cover to steel reinforcent

Dry processes: Joint design, is fire resistance considered
Joint filling, fire properties and longevity, tolerance and fit

Movement: Thermal — cyclic
Structural — cyclic in response to loading creep/settlement — progressive vibration

Accommodating services: Sequence of trades
Preformed openings versus cut, drilled etc. openings
Accessibility are fire stopping after services installation

Long term effects of 'environment' on selection of materials or assemblies for fire safety

Checklist:

Ageing   — effect on mastics, coatings, impregnation treatment, do their fire properties have a limited life?

Weathering   — effect on mastics, coatings, impregnation treatment, are the materials sufficiently protected?

Mechanical damage — how easily are the materials damaged both in themselves and in view of their location and the use of the building? Is a casing needed?

Maintenance   — how often will they have to be cleaned, repaired replaced, re-applied?
Does the detailing allow for maintenance access or replacement of damaged components?
What would be the effect or incorrect maintenance, e.g. painting over a surface that had a special fire-resisting treatment on it?

CHAPTER NINE

Detailed design and construction drawings

Drawings

OUTDOOR STORAGE FOR HIGHLY FLAMMABLE MATERIALS

Authorities involved

It is essential to involve 'interested parties' from the earliest stage when bulk storage of highly flammable material is proposed. These may be:

Health and safety inspectorate — factory inspector
Fire authority —   petroleum inspector
                    fire prevention branch
Local authority — planning and environmental
                    health departments
Insurer

Legislation which applies particularly to these installations:

Petroleum (consolidation) act 1928 and amendments
Highly flammable liquids and LPG regulations 1972 § 917
Fire certificates (special premises) regulations 1976
Health and safety at work act 1974, Section 2
(In Scotland building regulations make specific requirements for fuel oil storage tanks)

Guidance documents:

CP on keeping LPG in cylinders and similar containers Home Office/H & S Executive
CP on storage of LPG at fixed installations Home Office/H & S executive
H & S executive chemical safety series, new guidance

Notes CS/2 Storage of highly flammable liquids
      CS/3 Fire risk in the storage and industrial use of
           cellular plastics.

Basic considerations for flammable materials stores

The Store:

(1) Should be secure from accidential damage and vandalism.

(2) Should be of non-combustible materials (including the floor).

(3) There should not be any drains within or close to the store into which flammable liquid or gas could flow — gullies with petrol interceptors are required in car parking areas by most authorities.

(4) Should not have, or be within, a cellar (leaks and spills hard to clear/ventilate and fire fighting more difficult).

(5) Should be at ground level, preferably on solid ground.

(6) Should contain clearly marked and separated areas for full and empty containers (pressure bottles only, any crates or other combustible packing should not be stored here) a minimum, separation of 3 metres is recommended between empty and full cylinders of gas, or between oxygen, LPF, toxic, corrosive, or other highly flammable material.

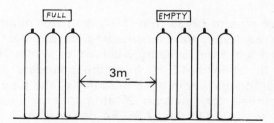

(7) Should have permanent natural ventilation (there should be baffles on the vent openings to keep out wild life, and matches/paper etc. which vandals might use to start a fire.

Metal masking plate over vent with substantial overlap, and minimal clearance (c. 20 mm) from wall

Metal mesh over vent inself as second line of defence and against animals

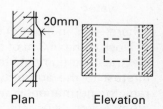

Plan   Elevation

(8) Should be sited away from escape routes from other buildings and from fire hazards such as high voltage electrical gear, boilers, furnaces etc.

269

Petrol storage tanks — underground

The design, installation and operation of petrol storage is subject to the approval of the local petroleum licensing authority and the following information must be regarded in that light:

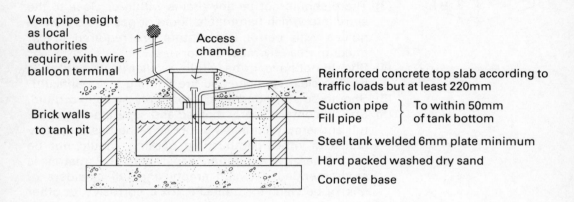

Vent pipe height as local authorities require, with wire balloon terminal

Access chamber

Reinforced concrete top slab according to traffic loads but at least 220mm

Suction pipe ⎫ To within 50mm
Fill pipe ⎭ of tank bottom

Brick walls to tank pit

Steel tank welded 6mm plate minimum

Hard packed washed dry sand

Concrete base

The vent pipe to be 38 mm (1½") diameter minimum. It may be required to have a flame trap. Its terminal must be at least 1.5 m from opening windows or vents. The pipe should be at least 1.5 m from the boundary and any electrical fittings within a 1.5 m radius of the pipe should be approved for 'division 2' atmospheres ('increased safety') according to the BASEEFA designation.

The licensing authority may also specify:
Fire fighting equipment
Methods of heating and lighting of buildings on the premises
Notices
Petrol interceptors and the method of draining surface water

Where — as in a petrol service station — there is an office or kiosk within 4.3 m of a petrol pump (or tank opening) the electrical equipment, loction of switches etc. will be of interest to the authority. For heating an oil-filled electric radiator permanently wired and without a thermostat or other switch, is usually acceptable (its power supply being switched at a remote point).

No basement or below-ground area should be entered within 1.5 m of any point vertically below the vent pipe opening.

Drawings

9.2
Detailed space planning and design

MEANS OF ESCAPE

Escape route components

An escape route can be considered as having four stages as one moves from a point in a room to a point on the open ground outside that is safe from the fire.

(Not all authorities, codes, guidance notes etc. use the same definitions for the stages.)

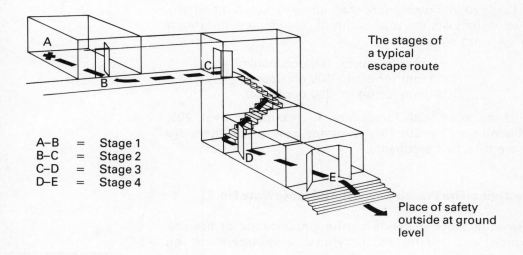

The stages of a typical escape route

A–B	=	Stage 1
B–C	=	Stage 2
C–D	=	Stage 3
D–E	=	Stage 4

Place of safety outside at ground level

In the following section the principle requirements/ recommendations for escape route planning are given, as they apply to a range of building types in each stage of the escape route (under UK legislation).

ESCAPE STAGE 1

From starting point (any point in an occupied or occupiable room to the room exit).

Hotels (Fire Precautions Act, Guidance Note No. 1)

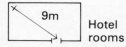 Hotel rooms

 High fire risk hotel rooms, e.g. kitchen

 From inner room to exit of outer room.

If either room is high fire risk the distance becomes 6m.

Large hotel rooms with 2 or more exits leading by separate routes to places of safety.

If the exits share a single dead end escape route the max. travel distance in the room is 9m or 6m if there is a high fire risk.

Actual travel distances (around furniture etc.) should be no more than 1½ times the recommended distances.

Large rooms need more than one exit. Discounting any one of the exits the total width of remaining exits from a large room should be:

760 mm for up to 100 occupants
1000 mm for over 100 occupants
1060 mm for up to 200 occupants

Plus an additional 75mm per 15 occupants over 200. Minimum exit width 760mm in any case where there are more than five occupants.

Factories (Fire Precautions Act, Guidance Note No. 2)

Travel distance depends on the classification of fire risk which is a matter of individual assessment of the circumstances.

Pointers to high risk   — Material causing rapid fire spread, or smoke production Unprotected stairways or vertical shafts

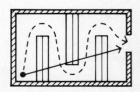

Large areas of flammable
surface
Dense occupancy
Handicapped or isolated
occupants

Pointers to normal risk   — Outbreak of fire likely to be
localised and slow to grow
Structure of building not
readily combustible

Pointers to low risk   — Few or no flammable
materials
Incidence of fire low and little
risk of rapid spread

Travel distance measured along actual line of travel

Escape in one direction only within room

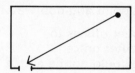

Risk	Distance
High	6m
Normal	12m
Low	25m

Choice of exits

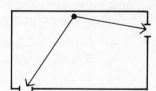

Risk	Distance
High	12m
Normal	25m
Low	35m

Escape from inner room

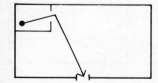

If inner room is	high risk	6m
If outer room is	normal risk	12m
If outer room is	low risk	25m

Note: outer room should not be high risk.

Rooms with more than 60 occupants must have more than
one exit.

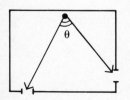

A second is only an adequate alternative if θ is more than
45°.

   From points in a room where θ <45° the travel distance
to the nearest exit must be less than the limit
recommended for escape in one direction only.

Minimum exit width normally 750mm but smaller wicket doors acceptable:

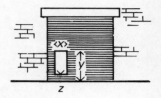

x = 500mm min., y = 1.5m min., z = 250mm max. and max. 15 people using it (2 or 3 max. if high risk area)

In large rooms the aggregate of exit widths minus any one exit should be:

750mm min. for up to 100 people
1100mm min. for up to 200 people

Plus 75mm for each extra group of 15, or part thereof.

Offices (Fire Precautions Act Guidance Note 3)

Travel distances measured in straight line between furthest point and doorway.

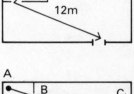

12m

From inner offices to
exit of outer office
(which should not be a
high fire risk)

Where there are alternative exits from the outer room (C_I and C_{II}) and these are to separate protected escape routes or are doors in compartment walls or final exits, then:

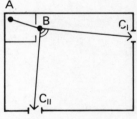

A – C_I or A – C_{II} is to be less than 45m
A – B is to be less than 18m.

Max. distance within rooms where escape is possible in one direction only.
 If there is high fire risk more than one exit is needed unless it can be positively confined to a point remote from the only exit.

12m

Exit width: Over 5   people — 750 mm up to 60 people
             60–100 people more than one exit,
                    aggregate of widths minus one exit
                    = 750 mm
             100–200 people more than one exit,
                    aggregate of widths minus one exit
                    = 1100 mm
             Plus 75mm for each extra group of 15 people
             or part thereof

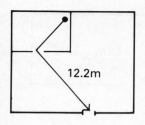

Offices (BS CP3, Chapter IV, Part 3)

Deemed to satisfy means of escape requirements given in EII of building regulations for England and Wales; travel distances measured along actual route travelled; inner offices without choice of exit from outer office.

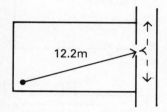

Office having a choice of route after leaving the room.
  Total distance to exit from floor by shortest route 46m.

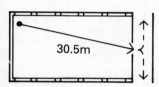

As above but on ground or first floor where escape via windows is reasonably possible.
  Travel distance 30.5m max. in section of route where escape is in one direction only.

Shops (Fire Precautions Act Guidance Note No. 3)

Travel distances measured along actual route travelled.

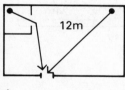

No alternative route
max. 12m within a room
or from inner room to exit from outer room
(outer room not to be high fire risk)

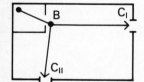

Where there are alternative exits from an outer room (C_I and C_{II}) which give onto protected routes separate from one another

   $A - C_I$ or $A - C_{II}$ should be less than 30m
   $A - B$ should be less than 18m

Number and width of exits as for offices (Fire Precautions Act)

Shops (BS CP3, Chapter IV, Part 2)

Deemed to satisfy building regulations EII England and Wales. Travel distance measured in straight line between room doorway and furthest point in the room.

Route with no alternative.
Max. 12.2m to point of exit to protected stair or final exit.

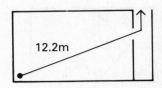

Choice of routes to points of exit (x) onto protected stairs or final exits separate from one another.

Distance measured in straight line but there should be no counter or other obstruction across the route which has an unbroken length of more than 9.1m.

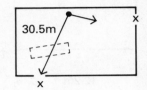

Schools (Department of Education and Science: Building Bulletin 7)

Fixed partitions ground or first floor.
x is either final exit or point of entry to protected stair.
No more than 160 children in the classrooms off the corridor.

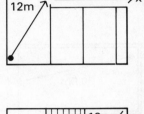

Open plan with or without rooms off it.
First floor — or ground floor with no escape possible through windows.
120 children maximum on this floor.

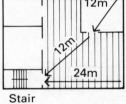

Stair

Number and width of exits in schools

(1) Except:

(A) Assembly or dining rooms likely to have over 100 occupants

No. of occupants	Min. number of exits	Min. clear width of each exit (mm)
100–200	2	850
200–500	2*	1350
500–750	3*	1350
750–1000	4†	1350

*Each exit to lead by separate route to place of safety
†3 of which to lead by separate route to place of safety

(B) Tiered lecture theatres for over 60 occupants.

(C) Room on upper floor opening straight into stair enclosure must have another exit leading by a different route to a final exit. This does *not* apply to 2 storey single-stair buildings of limited extend serving no more than 120 children on the upper floor.

(D) Laboratory or other high fire risk room where a single exit would be in a hazardous position.

Theatres & halls (GLC CP for means of escape in case of fire)

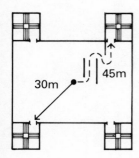

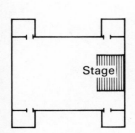

Travel distance

Halls with fixed seating — travel distance depends on seat layout, see page 00.

Halls without closely seated audience.

Direct distance to exit 30m max. measured in straight line but actual distance around obstructions (e.g. exhibits) should not exceed 45m.

Factors which might make greater distances acceptable:

Well separated exits to separated protected routes.
Clearly visible exits readily accessible past the contents of the hall.

Normally all exits are either final exits or must be points of entry to protected routes.

At least half the exits from an auditorium should be remote from any stage or platform.

Number and width of exits

Halls with fixed seating

No. of occupants	Min. no. of exits	Min. clear width of each exit (mm)
Up to 200	2	1100
200–300	2	1200
300–400	2	1400
400–500	2	1600

Plus an extra exit of 1600mm min. for every additional group of 250 or part thereof.

There should be at least two separate exits from every floor storey or tier half of which (at least) should be remote from any stage or platform.

Exhibition halls etc. with no fixed seating

As above for fixed seating, the number of people being calculated on basis of an occupancy factor, viz.:

GLC —
Dance hall	0.55m²/person
Exhibition hall	1.5 m²/person

Scottish building regulations —
Assembly hall, club	0.5 m²/person
Common room	1.1 m²/person
Concourse, dance hall	0.7 m²/person
Museum, art gallery, library	4.6 m²/person

Small general purpose hall without permanent seating (floor area not exceeding 165m²) (GLC Code of Practice)

No. of occupants	Min. no. of exits	Min. clear width of exits (mm)
Up to 50	2	760
50–75	2	760
75–100	2	760
100–150	2	900
150–200	2	1100
200–300	2	1200

Backstage areas requiring more than one exit

(A)   Rooms where travel distance to an exit exceeds 7.5m
(B)   Rooms occupied by more than 15 people
(C)   Rooms with direct access to stage or high fire risk area
(D)   Rooms off dead end corridors which are unprotected or over 7.5m long

E is room exit
X is exit to stair or
    place of safety
E – X <7.5m
or corridor to be
a protected corridor

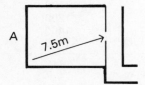

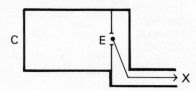

Theatres etc. with fixed seating

Seating layout to be agreed with licensing authority (this will include all layout variations where mobile bleachers etc. are proposed).

(Following guidance is based on Greater London Council Code.)

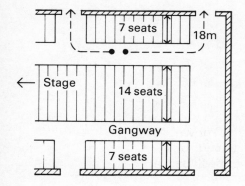

Conventional seating
No point in gangway more than 18m from nearest exit.

No more than 14 seats/row where there is a gangway at both ends of the row — but see below*.

No more than 7 seats/row where there is a gangway at one end of the row only — but see below†.

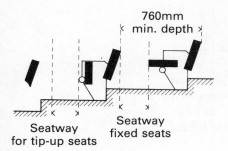

Typical section of seating
Where seats have back and arms seating area/person 760mm deep × 500mm wide.

Seats without arms or backs seating area/person 600mm deep × 450mm wide.

Seatway 300mm min. clear.

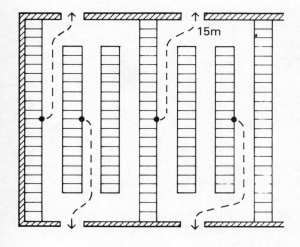

Continental seating
No seat more than 15m from an exit.

Gangways or exits are required at each end of every row.

Where there are gangways the exits must be positioned so people leaving seatway move away from rather than towards the stage.

The number of seats in a row is limited only by the travel limit and the width of the seat.

The clear seatway should be between 400mm and 500mm.

*More than 14 seats/row — up to 22 max. — if the 'seatway' (see below) is increased by 25mm for each pair (or odd number) of seats over the 14.
†More than 7 seats/row — up to 11 max. — if the 'seatway' is increased by 25mm for each seat over the 7.

Escape route planning within rooms

Furniture and fittings

Partitions
There are situations in which the final layout is not known until construction of the shell is well advanced or complete, or where it is known that the initial layout will be changed later.

If the first plan or shell is designed to the limits of permissible travel distance it may inhibit later changes — if legislation such as the Fire Precautions Act applies fundamental alterations may be required at this later stage.

Vision panels

(1)
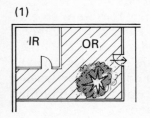

(2)
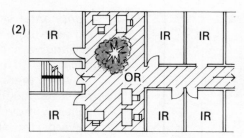

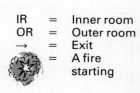

IR	=	Inner room
OR	=	Outer room
→	=	Exit
✹	=	A fire starting

Inner rooms, as exemplified in the plans above, are rooms within rooms. It may not be so obvious in the plan (2) as in (1) as to which are the inner rooms, but because the circulation space is combined with a working area, the occupants of all the rooms marked IR would have to escape through a space in which a fire could start.

A fire in the outer room threatens to cut off the escape of inner room occupants who therefore need to be made aware of the danger quickly. The accepted way of achieving this is to have windows — 'vision panels' in the enclosure of the inner office allowing the danger signs of a fire in the outer office to be seen.

Problem: Occupants of inner offices often consider themselves to be of higher status than occupants of outer offices and resent vision panels, feeling that minions may spy on them. Reflective glass may overcome this but it is usually adequate to fit ordinary glazing at high level as an early sign of danger will be smoke collecting at ceiling level.

Potential obstructions
Consider the following when planning room layout:

(1) Relationship of services to equipment
To avoid trailing leads which are potential causes of electrical faults and fires, as well as tripping accidents which not only cause direct injury and damage but can indirectly cause fires as a consequence of this damage.

(2) Mobile units
Trolleys, desks, bins etc. on castors or just humped about. Are there enough 'parking places' located so that they will be used, and so that the units will not be haphazard obstructions and not cause a fire hazard at some important point on the escape route? If the units are proposed by the architect has the client thought about ways of controlling their use?

(3) Unfixed seating
Stacking chairs, bleachers, seats on castors, folding seats. Are there adequate storage spaces when they are not in use? Are these spaces separated from escape routes? Have the authorities been consulted about all the alternative seating layouts? There are often requirements to fasten seating for public entertainments to the floor, or into groups to prevent it being dislodged (when it might obstruct the means of escape).

(4) Stock/goods/materials storage

Is storage space enough to prevent goods 'spilling over' into escape routes? This applies as much to display space in a school as to products in factories. Exactly what is to be stored? Highly flammable materials need separate, and probably lockable, storage. Even in apparently innocuous office spaces there can be a need to store large enough quantities of highly flammable material (e.g. duplicator fluid) to start a serious fire.

(5) People as obstructions

Is extra space needed at points where people will gather, e.g. vending machine, sales point etc.? If a queue forms will the exit route be obstructed and is the escape route from this area sized generously to allow for the sudden exodus of the queue *en masse*?

ESCAPE STAGE 2

From room exit to storey exit or to exit to protected route

Hotels (Fire Precautions Act Guidance Note No. 1)

Diagram of a hotel corridor forming a stage 2 route showing travel distance requirements for different room/exit arrangements.

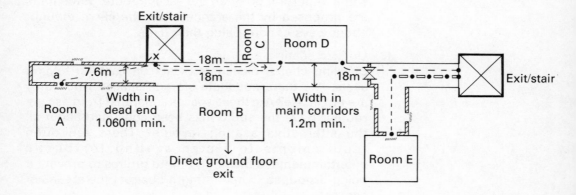

Room A: Only one route available — a dead end — max. travel distance 7.6m; walls/partitions forming dead end to be ½ hour fire resisting; doors from rooms other than lavatories into the dead end to be ½ hour fire resisting and self-closing.

Room B: Ground floor room with an exit direct outside to a place of safety; no limit on the travel distance by internal routes to other exit(s).

Room C: Only one room exit but a choice of routes in stage 2; one exit to be within 18m.

Room D: Room with more than one exit and with a choice of routes in stage 2. Max. travel distance 18m from any of the room's exits to the storey exit nearest to it.

Room E: Initially a dead end which gives onto a corridor in which there is a choice of routes. Max. travel distance in dead end portion 7.6m and total travel distance from room to nearest exit 18m. A fire door is needed to separate the alternative routes from one another at a point close to the junction with the dead end route.

Corridors should be divided by self-closing fire resisting doors into sections not exceeding 18m length.

Factories (Fire Precautions Act Guidance Note No. 2)

Travel distance depends on the assessed risk of the premises (see p. 273) as well as the escape route geometry.

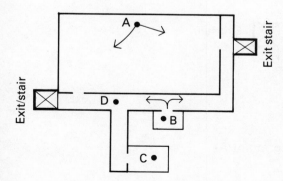

The guidance note gives recommendations for travel within rooms and total travel from within rooms to final exits and does not specify travel distance in stage 2 itself (other than by subtraction of the relevant figures).

The figures for travel within rooms are given on p. 273 but are repeated here for convenience.

(i) From points having alternative exit routes (e.g. points A and B)

Risk	Travel distance
High	12m in room 25m total
Normal	25m in room 45m total
Low	35m in room 60m total

(ii) From points where escape is possible in only one direction (point B and from C to D)

Risk	Travel distance
High	6m in room 12m total
Normal	12m in room 25m total
Low	25m in room 45m total

Any dead end sections of stage 2 routes should be in protected corridors with walls and self-closing doors to half-hour fire-resisting standard.

All stage 2 routes should normally be at least 1m wide.

Corridors which exceed 30m length should be sub-divided by fire-resisting self-closing doors to restrict the spread of smoke.

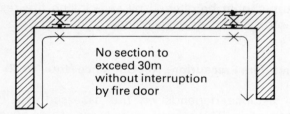

No section to
exceed 30m
without interruption
by fire door

Offices (Fire Precautions Act Guidance Note No. 3)

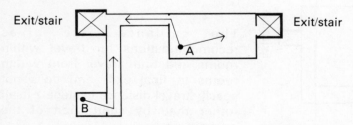

Exit/stair

Exit/stair

A

B

From points having a choice of route (e.g. point A)

Total travel distance including

	Stages 1 and 2	45m max.
	(Stage 1 only	12m max.)

From points having one escape route only (e.g. point B)

Total travel distance including

	Stages 1 and 2	18m max.
	(Stage 1 only	12m max.)

Where corridors are planned which exceed 45m length they should be sub-divided by fire-resisting doors that are self-closing, to restrict the spread of smoke.

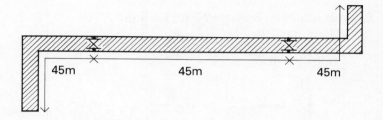

Normally main office corridors should be at least 1m wide.

Shops (Fire Precautions Act Guidance Note No. 3)

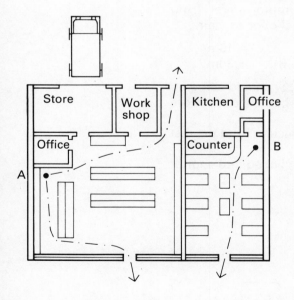

From points with alternative exit routes (e.g. point A).
   Max. travel distance 30m to nearest exit.

From points with only one exit route (e.g. point B).
   Max. travel distance 18m.

Where corridors are planned which exceed 30m in length they should be sub-divided with self-closing fire-resisting doors. (See also reference to Smoke Control p. 290.)

Schools (Building Bulletin 7 Fifth Edition)

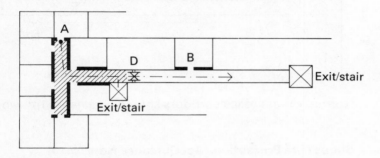

Classrooms off a corridor — maximum travel from classroom doorways to nearest external door or stair.

    Dead end routes (e.g. from A)   = 18m
    Routes with alternative (e.g. from B)   = 30m

Areas of dead end corridor (shaded ▨) should serve no more than 160 children on a ground floor and no more than 120 children on an upper floor.

A door should separate a dead end section from the rest of a corridor at point D.

Corridors exceeding 60m should be divided into shorter sections by self-closing fire doors.

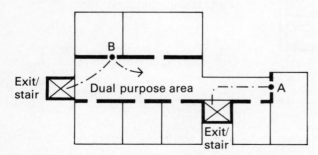

Classrooms off a dual purpose area (i.e. space combining circulation and another function).

Maximum travel distances from classroom doorway to nearest external exit or stair:

Dead end routes (e.g. from A)   = 12m
Routes with alternative (e.g. from B)   = 18m

No dead end (shaded⁄⁄⁄⁄⁄⁄) should serve more than 120 children.

Fire doors should be fitted across the circulation area to prevent undivided sections exceeding 45m long.

Theatres and halls etc. (GLC Code of Practice)

In the terms of the GLC Code there is no stage 2 travel from an auditorium or hall. The travel restrictions within the hall are given in the previous section on stage 1 and take the occupants straight to a final exit or protected escape route (i.e. from stage 1 to stage 3 directly).

Public areas other than the auditorium or hall (i.e. bars, foyers etc.):

Dead ends are not generally acceptable. If site restriction make them unavoidable maximum travel distance 12m.

Travel distance where there are alternatives 30m (measured direct — the actual distance around furniture etc. may be up to 45m maximum).

Every floor should have at least two exits.

Note on 'protected corridors'

The guidance notes to the Fire Precautions Act and BS CP3, Chap. IV Parts 1, 2 and 3 all recommend that dead end corridors should be 'protected'.

This means that the walls, and if need be, the ceiling, should resist fire spread from the adjoining rooms into the corridor for long enough to give the occupants of all the rooms served by that corridor a chance to escape.

If the room where the fire starts is occupied there should be no difficulty in warning people in the other rooms. If some of the rooms are likely not to be occupied — and particularly if they contain a fire hazard of some sort e.g. a distribution board or cooking hob — the area should be laid out so that these rooms are further from the way out of the corridor than the occupied and lower risk rooms.

287

An example of an entirely wrong layout from a fire safety point of view.

Pantry and electrics should be moved to the right-hand end of the corridor to lessen the chance of occupants being trapped.

Electrical
distribution/
used as
cleaners cupboard

To
exit

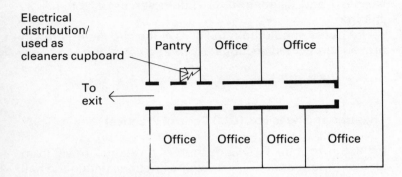

A half hour fire resistance standard (BS 476, Part 8) is normally adequate. This should include partitions, and any doors and glazing, flanking the corridor.

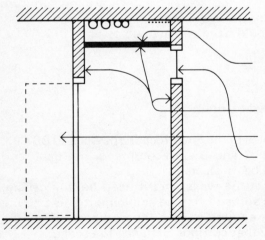

If services run in the corridor they should be of low fire risk and all their surfaces should have class 1 surface flame spread (BS 476, Pt. 7) or better, otherwise a suspended fire resisting ceiling should be provided.

Wall and ceiling surfaces to be class 1 or better

doors should be self-closing.

There should be some glazing (fire resisting) between corridor and occupied rooms to provide a warning that smoke or fire is spreading into the corridor.

Section through corridor and adjoining rooms.

STAGE 3 OF ESCAPE ROUTES

The vertical movement phase

Stairways

Stairways are of central importance to escape route design.

(A)   As the link with ground level and, ultimately, safety.

(B)   As a prime potential fire/smoke spread route.

i.e.   They must let all the occupants escape downwards (upwards in the case of basement stairs) quickly while preventing buoyant fire gases and smoke from spreading between floors.

The number and location of stairways follows from the standards for stages 1 and 2 given above and they therefore vary with the type of occupancy. However the basic fire safety design of stairways does not vary significantly from one occupancy to another and in this section we refer only to the protection of stairways on an occupancy-by-occupancy basis.

Building regulations (England and Wales 1976)

Where a stairway enables people to pass from one compartment to another it has to be enclosed by protecting structure and is referred to as a protected shaft. The key word here is compartment as it is important to distinguish and understand the difference between enclosure for compartmentation reasons and for means of escape protection: e.g. an office does not necessarily have to be compartmented so some of its stairs can be quite open through their full height. However, for means of escape purposes (the provisions of BSCP 3, Chap. IV, Part 3 and the Fire Precautions Act applying) some enclosed protected stairs are required. Thus in this case the legislation concentrates on factor (A) (top of this page) and ignores (B).

Protection of stairs

Where a stair enclosure is required for compartmentation reasons

Fire resistance of
enclosure   =   Fire resistance required by
regulation E5 for the structure
generally.

Material of enclosure   Non-combustible if fire
resistance of an hour or more is
required.

Fire resistance of
doors in enclosure   =   ½ hour in purpose groups:
III (other residential);
IV (offices);
VII (places of assembly);
or in other buildings half the
standard for the enclosure (½
hour minimum).

Where a stair enclosure is required for means of escape purposes only:

Fire resistance of
enclosure including
doors   =   ½ hour usually

But compared to enclosure for compartmentation there are additional measures to prevent smoke contamination of stairway.

Considerable faith is put in measures to protect stairways. Travel distance within the stair enclosure is not usually limited because it is assumed that it is a place of relative safety and there will be no impediment to travel. But for a stair to qualify as a place of relative safety the following standards apply in the U.K. (see also "Smoke Control in Fire Safety Design" by E.G. Butcher and A.C. Parnell, published by E. & F.W. Spon).

Hotels (Fire Precautions Act Guidance Note No. 1)

Minimum standards

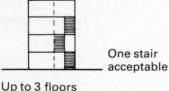

One stair
acceptable

Up to 3 floors
above ground floor

2 door
protection

At ground level
Either   direct access to open air
Or   protected route to open
Or   alternative routes from enclosure
           to separate final exits

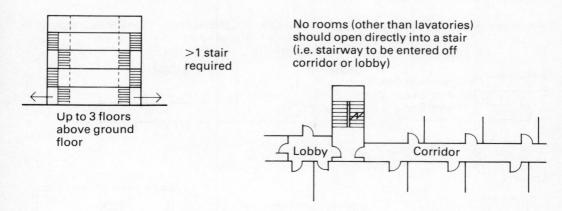

>1 stair
required

Up to 3 floors
above ground
floor

No rooms (other than lavatories)
should open directly into a stair
(i.e. stairway to be entered off
corridor or lobby)

Lobby   Corridor

Factories (Fire Precautions Act Guidance Note No. 2)

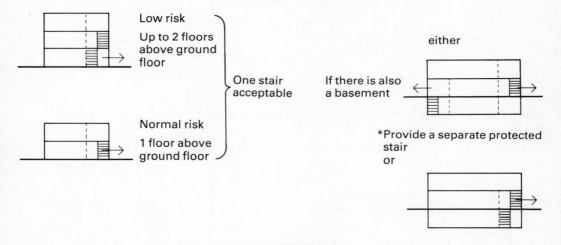

Low risk

Up to 2 floors
above ground
floor

Normal risk

1 floor above
ground floor

One stair
acceptable

If there is also
a basement

either

*Provide a separate protected
stair
or

*   Separate basement from ground floor levels with ½ hour.
Fire door at foot and head of basement stair or one
one-hour fire door at either head or foot of basement stair.

NB* Two stairs from basement will be the normal minimum
requirement unless it is a very small area.

In other cases more than one stair
is required

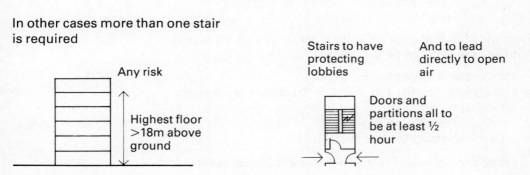

Any risk

Highest floor
>18m above
ground

Stairs to have
protecting
lobbies

And to lead
directly to open
air

Doors and
partitions all to
be at least ½
hour

Any high risk or

Normal risk (having more than one floor above ground floor)

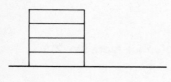

Stairs to be approached through lobbies or corridors

And to lead directly to open air

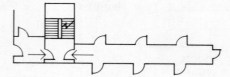

Low risk

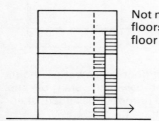

Any stair serving more than 2 floors to be fully enclosed.

The accommodation may open directly into stair via firedoors

Shops and offices (Fire Precautions Act Guidance Note No. 3)

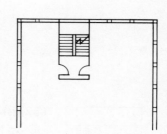

Not more than 4 floors above ground floor

Single stair acceptable with 2 door protection and direct access to final exit at ground floor

(A)   (B)

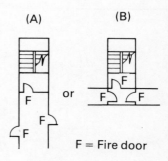

F = Fire door

Otherwise there should be at least two stairs so protected that they are entered only from:

      Protected lobbies (as (B) above)
or   Corridors (as (A) but without fire doors to corridor rooms)
or   WCs containing no fire risk
or   Lifts contained in stair enclosure

and they should lead directly to final exits at ground level.

292

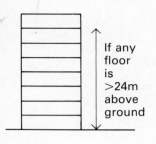

If any
floor
is
>24m
above
ground

The only doors onto the protected stairs should be to:

Protected lobbies
Lifts contained in the stairway
WCs containing no fire risk
Final exits

A minimum width for stairs should be 800mm but the width should be sufficient to cope with the flow of people. It should be assumed, in offices with two or more stairs, that one of them could be unusable in a fire, and the stairs' capacity would therefore have to be:

$$\frac{\text{Number of occupants on upper floor(s)}}{(\text{Number of stairs}) - \text{one}}$$

Basement stairs in general

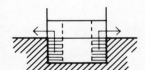

Basements should have at least 2 stairs unless they are very small (travel distance <12m).

Basement stairs should be separated from stairs to upper floors.

Exits from basement stairs should be positioned so that smoke escaping from a basement fire is unlikely to obstruct exits from upper storey stairs.

Some different ways of separating basement stairs

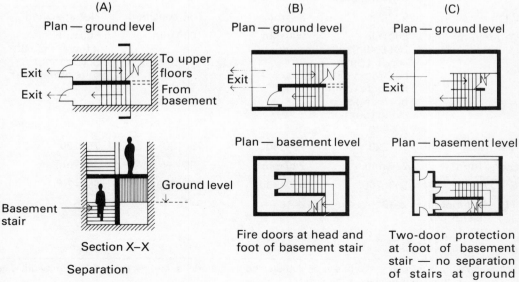

(A)
Plan — ground level

Exit
Exit
To upper floors
From basement

Basement stair

Section X–X

Separation

Ground level

(B)
Plan — ground level

Exit

Plan — basement level

Fire doors at head and foot of basement stair

(C)
Plan — ground level

Exit

Plan — basement level

Two-door protection at foot of basement stair — no separation of stairs at ground level

General matters of stair design

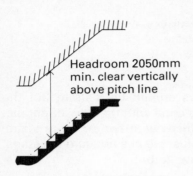

Headroom 2050mm min. clear vertically above pitch line

Building regulations control:

Pitch   = $P°$
Width   = W
Rise   = R ⎫ And proportion of
Going   = G ⎬ rise going
Height = H (in any one flight)
Landing = L (going)

The requirements vary with the type of occupancy involved.

Dimension	Occupancy Group			
	I or III	I or III	II or VII	II, III, IV, V, VI, VII or VIII
	Within or serving one dwelling only	Stair common to 2 or more dwellings		
Pitch	42° max.	38° max.	Not specified	Not specified
Width (mm)	800 min. But 600mm if serving only bathroom or WC or single room not being a living room or kitchen	900 min.	1000 min.*	800 min. If fewer than 50 occupants 1m min. otherwise*
Rise (mm)	75–220	75–190	75–180	75–190
Going (mm)	220 min.	240 min.	280 min.	250 min.
$G + 2R$ (mm)	550–700	550–700	550–700	550–700
$\dfrac{H}{R}$ = Number of risers† per flight	2–16	2–16	3–16	3–16
L	$\geqslant W$	$\geqslant W$	$\geqslant W$*	$\geqslant W$*

*Where W>1.8m the stair width has to be sub-divided by handrail(s) into sections of 1–1.8m width. The landing(s) 'L' must $\geqslant$ the widest sub-division.
†There should not be more than 36 risers in consecutive flights without a change of direction.

Spiral stairs

Should not be considered for use in protected stairways except where only a very few people (less than 10) are going to have to use them. These people should be regular users of the building and able bodied.

Handrails

Required for any flight over 600mm high to be securely fixed.

Height 840mm–1m vertically above pitch line to be terminated by a scroll or wreathed into the wall etc.

The last two steps at the bottom of a flight do not have to have a handrail.

Except where alongside fixed seating (as in a tiered auditorium) a handrail is required on at least one side of the flight.

If the flight is over 1m wide there must be a handrail on both sides.

If the flight is over 1.8m wide there must be a central handrail too, width of each section to be 1–1.8m and the rail to be terminated at the top of the flight with a vertical pole or member which is fixed to the ceiling or at a point that is at least 2.1m above floor level.

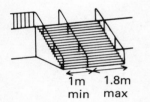

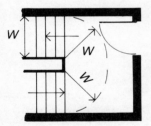

1m   1.8m
min   max

Landings

To prevent obstruction to the passage of people from floors above a door onto a stair landing should be arranged so that its arc of swing does not encroach on an arc of radius equal to the stair width swept from the bottom of one flight to the top of the next.

Materials within stairways

(A) Combustibility:

Building regulations require all materials used in the construction of stairways to be non-combustible except stairways:

(1) in a maisonette;
(2) in a storey for which the regulations' structural fire resistance requirement is less than one hour.
(3) in a Purpose Group III block of flats/maisonettes of no more than 3 storeys.

(4) that are accommodation stairs in a shop (i.e. not in a protected shaft);
(5) or an external stair whose overall height is less than 6m.

The regulations do not prohibit the use of a combustible material on the upper surfaces of stair or landing.

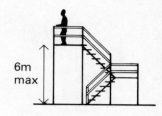

6m max

(B) Surface flame spread (Building regulations)

Walls and ceilings in a protected shaft should have a class '0' rating.

Except in a house of no more than 2 storeys where the walls can be class 1 and the ceiling can be class 3.

The object of these restrictions is to prevent a fire starting in a stair and to ensure that scope for fire spread is as low as possible. It is also most important that any protected stair will continue to be structurally sound for firemen who may still be using it when hot gas and smoke have entered the stairway and finishes could have started to burn.

Notes on external stairs

External stairs do not make good fire escapes:

(1) rainwater, ice and vegetation make them slippery;
(2) vertigo is quite common and is aggravated by open risers or perforated decking and balustrade openings at low level;
(3) external lighting, conveniently switched, is needed and needs maintenance;
(4) security is reduced.

Building regulations require external stairs which have a total rise more than 6m to be protected from the weather, but any external stair should be designed so that it does not become hazardous due to water, ice, snow, dead leaves, etc.

Fire or smoke coming through openings in the wall near the stair, such as windows (open or broken) or vents, can make an external stair impassable.

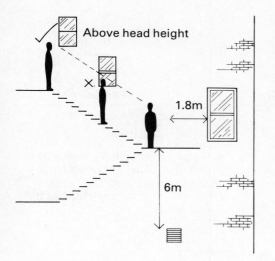

The rule of thumb generally applied in this situation is that no unprotected opening (this does not include doors to protected stairs or corridors) should be within 1.8m horizontally or within 6m vertically below, any part of the stair, landings, gangways etc.

But see also Part one, Chapter 3 on flame shapes outside window openings.

Where an external escape is subject to legislative control such as the Fire Precautions Act the authorities usually accept window openings closer that the distances given, if they have fire-resisting glazing to a half-hour standard. Good design should avoid such situations altogether.

STAGE 4 OF ESCAPE

Horizontal movement to final exit and a place of safety

Some routes from the ground floor will be direct from rooms or corridors etc. that are not protected areas. The travel distances governing them are those for stages 1 and/or 2. In stage 4 we are concerned with the continuation of the protected routes from upper (or basement) floors to the outside and then the route outside to the safe area.

The internal part of stage 4 routes should be:

(A)   Short — no distance specified in legislation or guidance;
(B)   Direct;
(C)   In a protected enclosure;
(D)   Devoid of fire risks.

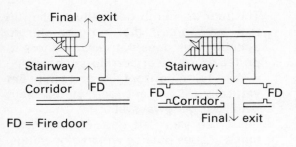

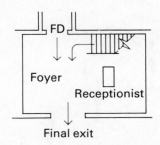

FD = Fire door

Acceptable

Not acceptable unless the corridor can be made into an extension of the protected stairway

To be acceptable the materials in the foyer must be controlled to the same standards of flame spread and combustibility as the stairway

The formation of a foyer or reception area is generally acceptable if the stair coming into it is not the only escape route from other floors and if there is no fire risk in the foyer. Scottish building regulations allow a ticket office or porters lodge there. The English regulations are not specific. The opinions of fire authorities vary — some see the supervisory function of a receptionist as a fire protection asset, others are worried about expansion of reception to clerical functions with attendant fire risks of paper, electrical machines and storage.

Where the geometry of the building does not allow a direct exit from the stair enclosure there should be alternative routes in stage 4 to the final exit:

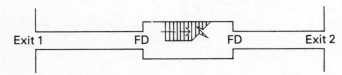

The routes should be separated by fire-resisting construction so that fire or smoke getting into one will not affect the other.

There have to be self-closing fire doors between the stair and each alternative route.

Stage 4 outside the building

In the same way that external escape stairways are vulnerable to the effects of heat smoke and flames from windows etc. close by, so can the stage 4 external route be affected.

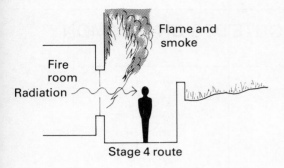

Flame and smoke

Fire room

Radiation

Stage 4 route

Possible solutions:

Remove openings (check effect on daylight and ventilation)

Protect the openings (radiation still a problem unless cill level can be raised above 1m so that people could crawl past — no help if more than a few fit people might have to escape)

Place a screen wall between openings and the escape (daylight?)

Move the escape route away.

The space outside must be detailed with the sudden efflux of people in mind. Incidents at sports stadia have shown that tonnage forces can be produced by the surge of a large body of people.

Paths

Firm non-slip and smooth enough to avoid tripping, well defined edges.

Width at least as great as the aggregate of the exits that give onto it.

Maximum gradient 1 in 12 over short distances.

Separated from roads by kerb at least, and where crowd pressure might force people into a busy road consider physical barriers high enough not to simply trip people up.

Consider the need for lighting.

Keep paths away from building walls, especially those of multi-storey buildings, to avoid danger of falling debris, breaking glass etc., due to the fire.

Railings

(Or walls) to guide the escapers and to guard and to mark changes in level or direction.

They should not hinder the activities of fire fighters.

They should be strong enough to take the lateral loads appropriate to the number of people involved.

SOME FEATURES OF ESCAPE ROUTE DESIGN COMMON TO ALL STAGES

Obstructions to smooth flow

The width of an exit route should never decrease as one progresses towards the final exit.

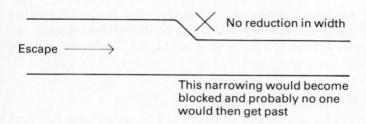

No reduction in width

Escape $\longrightarrow$

This narrowing would become blocked and probably no one would then get past

Where routes converge the width 'downstream' must take the total flow.

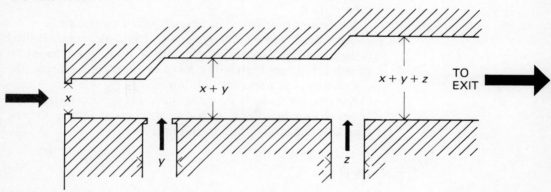

Where the density of occupation is such that the routes are likely to be full for more than a few seconds (e.g. in theatres or a large office) the 'downstream' width must be the sum of the 'tributary' widths.

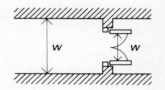

The widths quoted in stages 1 and 2 are minimum clear dimensions.

If there are significant reductions in width e.g. a doorway in a corridor the dimension 'W' should comply with the quoted minimum i.e. w, the corridor width, will be greater than the minimum.

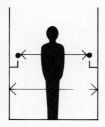

Different authorities have different attitudes to handrails:

Scottish regulations	— Projection of up to 100mm ignored
England/Wales regulations	— Measure least width between projections
Inner London	— Projection of up to 75mm ignored

Radiation

Openings, glazed or otherwise, onto exit corridors and sections of escape routes that are of restricted width, are potential 'sources' of heat radiation. This can be so intense as to make the opening impassable, even though no smoke or flames penetrate to the corridor.

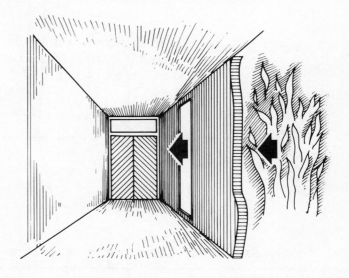

CP 153, Part 4, 1972 includes a nomogram which relates the size and shape of radiating area, corridor width, and speed of movement of the people escaping.

The example shows a mobility of 2m/s corridor 1.3m wide (assuming a fire of lower intensity).

Selecting a screen (opening) length of 6m gives a screen height of about 600mm max.

It obviously can be used in various ways, to find any one of the factors given the others.

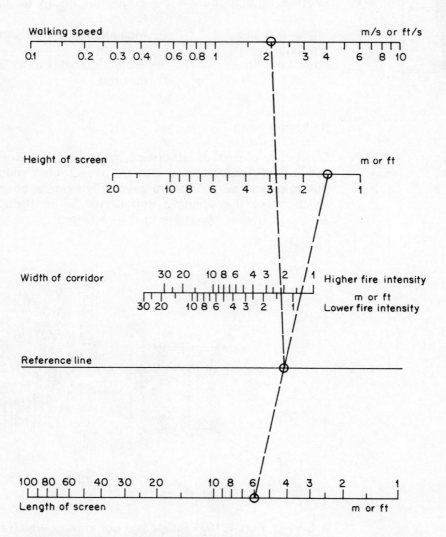

Nomogram for minimum width of escape route
bordered by a wired-glass screen

Doors on escape routes

Direction of opening:

To open in the direction of travel.

This is not so important where the number of people having to use a particular door is small, but if there are more than about 50 people 'upstream' the door should open in the direction of escape (it is quite acceptable for it to swing both ways).

Locking

Locks to be readily openable from the inside without a key e.g.:

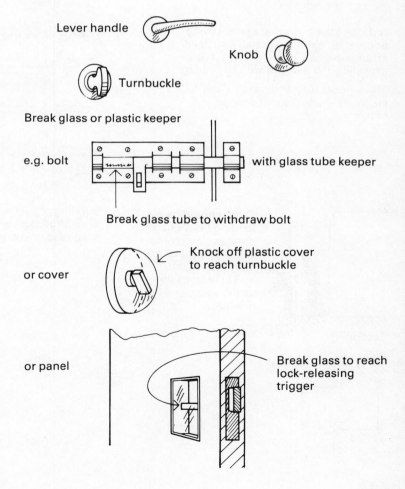

Lever handle

Knob

Turnbuckle

Break glass or plastic keeper

e.g. bolt — with glass tube keeper

Break glass tube to withdraw bolt

or cover — Knock off plastic cover to reach turnbuckle

or panel — Break glass to reach lock-releasing trigger

None of the above are suitable for doors through which large crowds may have to escape because they are relatively fiddly and only the simplest actions might be possible in a crush of agitated people — hence the push bar/pad panic latch which is operated by pressure at any point on the push bar/pad. The new BS improves resistance to unauthorized release of the latch from outside.

Door swings

Some examples to be avoided

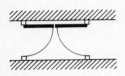

Although the swings are clear of one another on paper, in practice such an arrangement is difficult to negotiate, especially if the doors are self closing.

Move doors further apart to allow standing-space clear of swings, in between

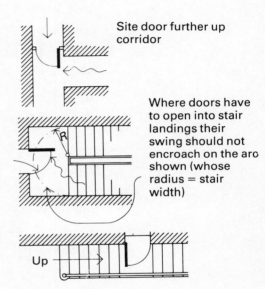

Site door further up corridor

Where doors have to open into stair landings their swing should not encroach on the arc shown (whose radius = stair width)

Up

Building regulations proscribe this sort of arrangement which should never be proposed anyway

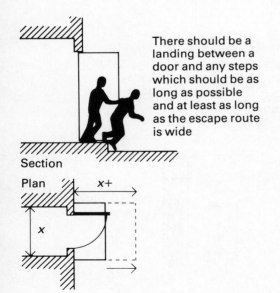

There should be a landing between a door and any steps which should be as long as possible and at least as long as the escape route is wide

Section

Plan

Sliding doors

Sliding doors are not normally satisfactory for use on escape routes. Logically they should present no more of a problem than an inward-opening door and as doors to rooms of low occupancy where the occupants are familiar with their operation, they should be acceptable. Also they have advantages for some handicapped wheelchair users.

Elsewhere unfamiliarity with their use and the difficulty of opening them when there is a press of people, rule them out in circulation areas on means of escape.

Automatic power-assisted sliding doors should be designed to fail safe i.e. in the open position.

Revolving doors

Revolving doors are not acceptable, usually, on escape routes and therefore have to be flanked by ordinary outward opening doors.

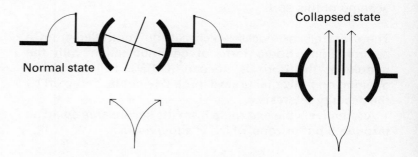

Normal state

Collapsed state

Revolving doors are made whose leaves fold under pressure to allow exit either side of the spindle but one must consider whether people would realize this was possible. Even with the leaves folded it is quite a narrow exit path.

Doors — security versus escape

Buildings were a conflict may arise:

Homes for the aged or young — whose 'clients' would be in personal danger if at large without supervision.

Prisons and detention centres — these may be exempted from normal means of escape legislation but the life risk remains.

Banks and depositories for precious objects.

Libraries — pilfering.

Shops, warehouses and factories — pilfering by
   'customers' or staff.
Data processing and storage areas — unauthorized entry.
Theatres, cinemas , etc. — where people may try to avoid
   admission charges.

From a security point of view direct access to the outside
from these places is undesirable.

Alarms can be fitted to doors so that their unauthorized
use is detected — but although this may deter some users
it does nothing to physically stop them.

If reliance can be placed on supervision for assistance in
case of fire, in homes for the young or old the exit doors
can be made difficult for the clients to open, e.g. by fitting
two lever-operated latches too far apart and too high or too
low for anyone who is not an able bodied adult, to operate.

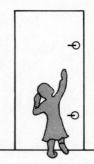

Consultation with the care staff to be in
charge of the establishment is obviously most
important before committing them to a
scheme of this sort.

There are electric locks which can be controlled from a
central point. Some form of communication with the
people at the door is needed (CCTV). Fail-safe locks
opening on power failure will probably not be accepted by
the security interests.

Alternatively the exit route from the secure area could be
through a buffer zone which is supervised.

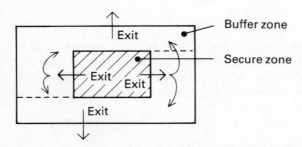

It would be prudent to divide the buffer zone into two or
more fire compartments (essential if there were any
significant fire risk in it) ---- = possible line of
compartmentation.

If the travel distance through the buffer zone was excessive
the secure area could be made a compartment of its own,
so that the distance is taken only up to the exit from the
secure area.

ORIENTATION AND ESCAPE ROUTES

(1) People normally try to leave a building by the way they came in unless there are strong visual clues to an alternative — such as a door in a wall which also has windows through which the ground outside can be seen. Even then if the need to escape is not felt to be urgent people seem to prefer to do the 'normal'.

(2) In large spaces the sight of some distinctive feature helps orientation.

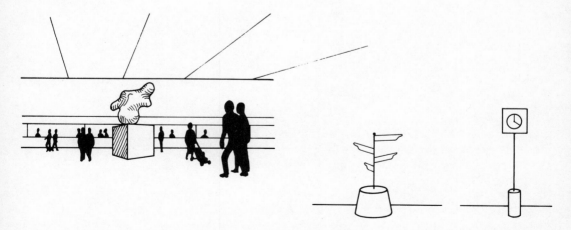

Such a feature can itself provide information about direction either literally or because of its shape or pattern.

(3) Lack of windows, repetitive detailing and finishes, symmetrical layout and large size are all disorientating factors.

   Lighting, colour and decoration can all be used as well as graphics to improve the situation where certain disorientating factors are unavoidable.

(4) In some buildings that are perceived to have a 'fire problem', e.g. foreign holiday hotels some occupants will be pre-disposed to note their route on their way in, looking out for 'landmarks' and signs of alternative ways out.

   Conversely, and more usually, people may be concentrating on other matters — catching a plane or finding a particular department for example — and they will have little idea of where they are or how they got there.

   Special efforts are needed to provide clues to orientation and clear information on direction, in buildings such as transport termini, hospitals, large public offices, theatres etc.

SIGNS

General

Signs associated with fire precautions should be considered as an integral part of the sign system in any building:

(A) So that there is consistent treatment throughout, e.g. the 'to exit' signs on escape routes do not vary in design.

(B) So that competition does not occur between different kinds of sign, e.g. so that an 'exit' sign is not swamped by an advertising sign.

(C) By creating a discipline for signs it becomes easier to locate the one needed.

(D) By considering signing as a system it should be possible with client co-operation, to minimize the use of *ad hoc* signs by the occupants.

The services of a specialist in sign systems may be needed.
There should be a brief for the sign system in any case, which should cover:

(A)	The range of functions to be performed by signs	— Mandatory signs Direction signs Identification of places and persons Advertising Instructions Etc.
(B)	Policy on location of signs according to function within particular spaces	— e.g. Zones for signs
(C)	Degree of co-ordination	— Lettering Type size Panel size Colour coding Etc.
(D)	Method and terminology for identifying parts of the building	— Titles Numbering Colour coding Diagrams Pictograms Etc.
(E)	Policy on future control	— How changes can be made Who makes them

Fire-related signs

Mandatory signs

In buildings subject to:

    The Fire Precautions Act (certificated premises)
    The Licensing Act

The Theatres Act
The Local Entertainment Licensing Acts
The London Building Acts and by-laws
The Cinematograph Acts
The Petroleum Acts
The Gaming Act
The Private Places of Entertainment (Licensing) Act
Scottish Building Regulations (to a very limited extent)

The enforcing authority may require signs indicating:

Escape routes and direction to exits
Location of exits
Fire doors to be kept shut
Fire doors to be kept locked
Smoking etc. prohibited
Maximum number of occupants allowed
Procedure in case of fire
Instructions on use of equipment, e.g. 'push bar to open' etc.

And they are usually considered to have the power to specify such details about the design of these signs as:

Letter height
Wording
Location
Colour
Illumination (internal/external)

Standards
Each authority has its own specification but it is to be hoped that standardization will eventually come about on the basis of:

BS 5499, Part 1, 1978:
'Fire safety signs, notices and graphic symbols — specification for fire safety signs'

and:

BS 5378, Part 1, 1980:
'Safety signs and colours — specification for colour and design'

There are also:

BS 2560 on illuminated exit signs, and
BS 4218 on self-luminous exit signs.

Some basic points from BS 5499, Part 1
Wording — agreed graphic symbols are preferred to text

   rather than | NO SMOKING |

say 'PRIVATE' rather than 'NO EXIT'

say 'EXIT' rather than 'WAY OUT'

Classes of sign —

Warning Yellow triangle
with symbol/text and
edge band in
black

Obligation Blue circle with
symbol/text and
optional edge band
in white

Prohibition White circle with
red edge and diagonal
band, symbol in
black

Fire equipment signs

Purposes: Rectangular with white text on red ground

To label appliance where its
function is not obvious or to
make its presence obvious or
to label water meter by-pass   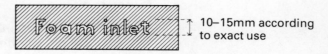 ↕ 10–15mm according
valve or hose reel valve   to exact use

312

Emergency signs (concerning escape routes)
Purposes:

(A)
To give instructions on how to
open doors or switch lights on
the escape route (the standard
gives several preferred
phrases)

Rectangular with white text on green ground

e.g.:   ͟I 5–50mm
according to
Written with capitals and lower   use
case

(B)
Indicate a way out that will be
available in an emergency

CAPITALS ONLY

e.g.: 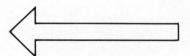 Letter height of
direction and exit
sign varies:

In public assembly buildings 100–125mm
Elsewhere — according to viewing distance

Up to 15m	Height	50mm
15–25m		75mm
25–40m		100mm
40–50m		125mm

Direction signs
The standard arrow shape is

The arrow should be used with the following meanings:

Straight on from here

Left on from here

Right on from here

Up and left on from here

Up and right on from here

Down and left on from here

Down and right on from here

The examples also show the preferred relationship of
arrow to left or right of text.

HELVETICA MEDIUM is the standard typeface in BS 5499.

Non-mandatory signs

In the UK many building designers and owners take
advantage of the Fire Services Act 1947 to seek advice from
the fire authority on the need for signs. This advice should
obviously be considered as one of the (important) inputs to
the problem of the design of the sign system as a whole.

MEANS OF ESCAPE: WINDOWS

The idea that the fire brigade will always be present to pluck occupants from the windows of burning buildings has to be discounted (especially if traffic hold-ups are likely).

No plans for fire escape should rely on this sort of traditional notion.

However:

(A) It should be made possible for fire brigade ladders to be set up to reach windows up to 24m above ground level.

(B) In certain limited circumstances escape through ground floor windows can be considered as an alternative route.

Requirements for ladder access (from Scottish Building Regulations E16)

Window — Min. width 550mm clear opening (a)
Min. height 850mm clear opening (b)
Max. cill height 1100mm above floor (c)

Highest floor		<11m	11–24m
x	minimum	1.5m	4.9m
y	maximum	9m	13m
z	minimum	4.5m	3m

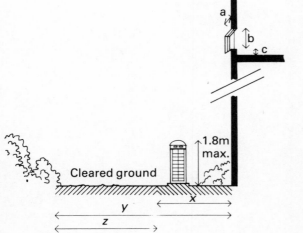

In zone x obstruction up to 1.8m high can be accepted.

Zone z should be cleared ground in front of the window, on which foot of ladder rests and being accessible from public road via a path at least 2.6m wide with 3.5m headroom and if floors are above 11m level accessible to a pump escape vehicle.

315

Escape via ground floor windows

The Department of Education and Science, Building Bulletin 7 (Fire Precautions in Schools) recognises that escape may be a possibility through windows from *some* ground floor rooms, for *some* types of student. The principle might be extended to other sorts of building where the same conditions can be met, i.e.:

(1) Occupants able-bodied and in approximate age range 10–55 years with no mental handicap;
(2) Occupants familiar with the buildings (i.e. not just visiting members of the public);
(3) Occupants subject to a measure of discipline i.e. their response to emergency is pre-planned with reasonable confidence of that plan being followed;
(4) Not suitable in large rooms where many people are gathered (upper limit about 35 people);
(5) Basic dimensional requirements:

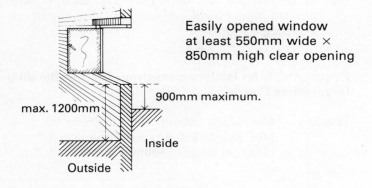

Easily opened window at least 550mm wide × 850mm high clear opening

900mm maximum.

max. 1200mm

Inside

Outside

9.3
Fire resistance of
structural elements

Drawings

The following examples of the BS 476, Parts 1 and 8 tests on structural elements are given to provide a general indication of performance.*

Since loss of stability is also a function of the stresses to which the element is subjected, none of the examples should be adopted without checking the loading conditions in the proposed structure against those in the test.

Similarly the restraint conditions in the test may have differed markedly from those in the proposed scheme. Load-bearing walls are generally tested with a load applied vertically while their vertical edges are free.

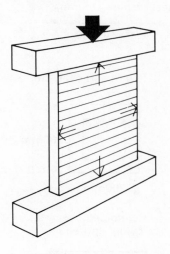

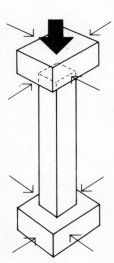

Column loading is axial (no eccentricity) and is kept constant during test.

Column head and base are restrained in direction and position.

* See also – Results of fire resistance tests on elements of building construction. HMSO 1975.

Beams and floor structures are possibly the most difficult in which to stimulate the effect of restraint and continuity. In most tests the panel (minimum size 3.05m square) or beam is simply supported with a flat bearing at the supports.

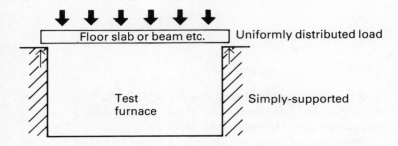

It must also be realized that although a member may endure the furnace heating cycle of a test it will not be given a fire resistance rating if it fails the subsequent re-loading test.

Fire resistance test results: columns

FROSI reference date and sponsor	Construction	Load		Stability (min.)	Fire-resistance grading (hours)
		Test	Design		
No. 4555 1968 C.J. Pell, Frischmann and Ptnrs	Reinforced concrete	60 tons	60 tons	120	2
No. 2361 1962 Lytag Ltd.	Reinforced concrete 'Lytag' aggregate	33 tons	33 tons	120	2

FROSI reference date and sponsor	Construction	Load		Stability (min.)	Fire-resistance grading (hours)
		Test	Design		
No. 4215 1967 Concrete Development Co. Ltd.	Prestressed concrete 292mm × 292mm	98 tons	98 tons	120	2
No. 3698 1965 Pell, Frischmann & Partners	Unprotected solid steel 6″ (150mm) × 6″	300 tons	300 tons	37	½
No. 5287 1971 Cementation Ground Engineering Ltd	15.7lb Universal section 6″ × 6″ Protected with 'Citex 89' spray applied to average thickness ⅛″	38.5 tons	38.5 tons	30	½
No. 412 1953 TAC Construction Materials Ltd	8″ × 6″ × 35lb BSB 5⁄16″ sprayed 'Limpet' asbestos	62 tons	62 tons	62	1

FROSI reference date and sponsor	Construction	Load		Stability (min.)	Fire-resistance grading (hours)
		Test	Design		
No. 488 1954 Cape Universal Building Products Ltd	8″ × 6″ × 35lb BSB ½″ 'Asbestolux' on 1″ × 1″ non-combustible battens	62 tons	62 tons	102	1
No. 1180 1958 Mandovol Ltd	8″ × 6″ × 35lb BSB ¾″ vermiculite/gypsum plaster on expanded metal lath with ¼″ MS stirrups	62 tons	62 tons	80	1
No. 4414 1967 Cape Universal Building Products Ltd	6″ × 6″ × 19.4lb rectangular hollow section ¾″ asbestolux panels with ¼″ asbestolux packing	51.5 tons	51.5 tons	100	1
No. 447 1954 TAC Construction Materials Ltd	8″ × 6″ × 35lb BSB 1″ nominal 'Limpet' asbestos on metal lath	62 tons	62 tons	120	2

Fire resistance test results: masonry load bearing walls

FROSI reference date and sponsor	Construction	Load		Stability	Integrity	Insulation	Fire resistance grading
		Test	Design				
No. 4954 1969 Thermalite Ltd	Aerated concrete blocks 'Thermalite' 3"	7 tons over 10ft length = 1568lb/ft min	7 ton 1220lb/ft min	30 min	30 min	30 min	½ hour
No. 1754 1961 Costain Concrete Co. Ltd	'Siporex' aerated concrete blocks 4"	1220 lb/ft min	1220 lb/ft min	120 min	120 min	120 min	2 hours
No. 2544 1963 Durox Building Units Ltd	'Durox' aerated concrete building blocks 6"	1680 lb/ft min	1680 lb/ft min	180 min	180 min	180 min	3 hours

9.4
Fire considerations in detailed design of services

Drawings

In all but the smallest and simplest installations detail design is normally in the hands of a specialist engineer. A detailed treatment of their work is outside the scope of this book.

The architect's function here is very much one of coordination. The following check-list is intended to assist in this.

	Location	Type	Statutory approval	Insurance approval	
Fire detection system:					If the system is to actuate other controls liaison required with designer/manufacturer of those other controls/systems to ensure compatibility and to sort out any 'demarkation' problems of design or installation.
Detectors	●	●*	●	●	
Wiring	●	●	●	●	
Power supply	●	○	○	○	
Control and indicator					
equipment	○	○	○	○	

If special power supply requirements affect ordinary electrical service design, e.g. special take-off at mains incomer, liaison with designer of that system

*The designer should be made aware of the conditions in each protected area so that the type selected will not be prone to false alarms.

General design points:

Maintenance — Are the user-maintained components accessible without difficulty?
— is there provision for maintenance of less accessible components, e.g. in-duct detectors?

If indicators or controls are brought to a central control room, consider integration into layout design of that room.

The fire authority normally want indicator boards to be at main entrance. There may be a need for slave indicators elsewhere.

	Location	Type	Statutory approval	Insurance approval
Fire alarm system:				
Call points	o	o	o	
Wiring	o	o	o	
Power supply	o	o	o	
Sounders	o	o	o	

General design points:

A detection system, if installed, would normally be designed and installed by those responsible for the alarm system also, and the points made under 'detection systems' above apply.

SPRINKLER SYSTEM

Generally the system will either have to conform to BS, CP 402.201 or to the insurer's rules.

The designer should have information on the precise occupancy of each space and any fitments such as storage shelves which could affect the efficiency of the system adversly. If spaces have multiple uses or are known to be likely to undergo a change of use, the designer should be told as much as possible about these uses and the changes in layout. Identify demountable partitions.

Settle position of main stop valve, consulting fire authority in the process, and position of alarm sounder.

If drains for sprinkler water-damage control are proposed liaison needed between sprinkler system and drainage system designers.

A check should be made with structural engineer if accumulations of sprinkler water are likely, that the floors in question are strong enough.

If there are any back up pumps or other equipment (such as certain types of pre-acting system) which need electrical power the requirement must be integrated with the electrical service design.

Diesel pumps will have ventilation and fuel storage/supply requirement which will need integration with other designers' work.

HOSEREELS

Location: in addition to insurance rules and statutory authority's requirements there is a practical limit of about 30m on the manageable length of a hose of this type.

Type: manufactured ranges make provision for many different fixing and unreeling arrangements — wall or floor, fixed or pivoting, open or concealed.

In selecting a type of reel consider:

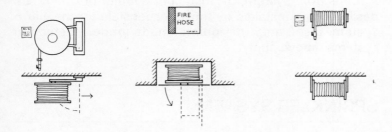

(1) That hose will not run out so easily if it has to come off the reel at an angle other than 90°. At acute angles it becomes very difficult. Cantilever type fixings exert very heavy strains, and with time they may work loose from walls of light concrete block. Either specify higher crushing strength or contrive spreader plates.

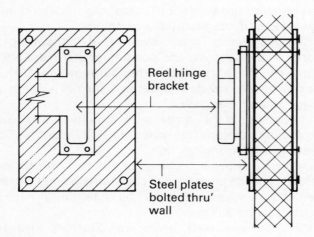

Reel hinge bracket

Steel plates bolted thru' wall

(2) Cunningly concealed hosereels are a nuisance if so tightly built-in that rewinding the hose is difficult. Maintenance requires that it should be fully unwound and examined. If rewinding is a problem maintenance might be neglected or the hose incorrectly rewound so that it was damaged or difficult to run out again.

(3) There should be a valve to isolate the hose from mains pressure fluctuations. Experience suggests that a simple, clearly labelled, wheel valve is more reliable than the 'automatic' type that is built in to reel itself so that unwinding the reel opens the valve.

(4) If mains pressure is not adequate pump pressurised systems are a possibility. However consider whether additional portable extinguishers would be more cost effective in the circumstances.

Fire brigade attendance time?
Fire risk?
Can a fire be contained in a small area temporarily by shutting the door?
Who would use the hosereel and would they be better to help the evacuation?

AUTOMATIC EXTINGUISHING SYSTEMS

Designer's brief — Kind of risk (flammable liquid, computers, archive material, etc.)

Volume and floor area

Disposition of fittings in space to be protected (false ceilings or raised floors, high partitions, cabinets enclosing fire risks, etc.)

Occupancy (numbers, night time/daytime variations, familiarity with their surroundings)

Ventilation (proposed mechanical/natural supplies, opening sizes and location, connections with adjoining unprotected spaces)

Before this stage:

(1)   The space needed to accommodate the system itself e.g. extinguishing agent storage.

(2)   The general mode of system operation,

(3)   And any general approvals for the system required from statutory authorities (or insurers)

— will have been settled with all concerned.

But points of detail remain:

(1)   Client (and staff representative bodies) approval of controls
Client and any statutory approval of system operation and safeguards in detail

(2)   Client and insurers detailed approval of system's effect on security

(3)   Liaison with electrical system designer over
(a)   power supply requirements
(b)   effect of extinguishant on ordinary electrical services in the protected area

(4)   Liaison with ventilation system designer over
(a)   Need to seal protected space before extinguishant is discharged
(b)   Effect of discharge over pressure on smoke control pressurisation system
(c)   Requirements for ventilation/purge of extinguishant before re-occupation

(5)   Liaison over equipment to be incorporated in central control room or monitoring point

EMERGENCY POWER SYSTEM

By this stage the architect's involvement should have become minimal, assuming that there is an electrical engineering consultant coordinating the design to ensure that supply equipment will have the capacity to provide the load, now that the load equipment is being specified in detail.

If there is not such a consultant the architect may be required to handle this liaison work.

The architect must ensure that any late changes in room or equipment layout are passed to the specialist designers, if it might have a bearing on their work and the architect will need to be told of any design changes or items requiring architectural detailing, e.g. combustion air intake for generation prime mover.

EMERGENCY LIGHTING/MAINTAINED LIGHTING SYSTEM

The type of system — central battery, battery/invertor, local battery, emergency generator — will have been selected.

The architect will be involved in the selection of luminaires, and the detailing of their fixing in some cases.

Check that system drawings and details have been approved by the relevant authority, e.g. where required for entertainments licensing. Submit to insurer if required.

DUCTWORK AND PIPEWORK IN GENERAL

Engineers' drawings must indicate the location of fire stopping around services and dampers within ducts, etc. wherever these pass through fire resisting construction.

Architect and engineer may have to look at methods of fire stopping and the construction sequence itself to ensure that effective barriers to fire spread can actually be built.

Drawings for building regulations approval, to show:

> Fire stopping;
> Cavity barriers;
> Surface flame spread properties of all surfaces within cavities;
> Fire dampers in ductwork;
> Duct material and method of jointing sections of duct;
> Fire resistance of builder-work enclosures to protected shafts.

Position air intakes and outlets to minimize chance of fire-smoke contamination of the building by way of either the mechnical ventilation system or window openings in external walls close to intakes/outlets of the system.

ACCESS

Consider access to service spaces:

> Doors probably need to be locked. Does the local fire brigade have a standard lock that should be used for some of these doors?
> Suspended fire-resisting ceilings may have to be removed in places for maintenance access. Does the chosen ceiling enable this to be done without damage and so that, when replaced, the original fire resistance is restored?
> Are service spaces adequately lit? Consider marking exit routes with luminous and reflective indicators.
> In-duct fire dampers and detectors need to be accessible for maintenance or repair.

COMMUNICATIONS

Matters for discussion with client and services engineer:

(1) Emergency call procedure, is there to be direct access to 999 or are those calls relayed by a telephonist?

(2) Does the telephonist require public address facilities, pageing of key personnel, or a fire alarm signal?

(3) If there is to be a control room how are responsibilities for communications to be divided with the telephonist?

(4) How are emergency calls to be made outside normal working hours?

(5) In extensive premises consider providing communications outposts for use by fire wardens (reporting on evacuation) and fire fighters, reporting to control.

(6) Public address for evacuation control requires very careful use as it can do as much harm as good. Work in the USA suggests pre-recorded messages very carefully worded, may be effective if the 'operator' has good information on the fire location and its development. It is generally deprecated in public assembly places in the UK, but in occupancies such as large shops and shopping centres it is probably a necessary adjunct to the fire alarm system, which the public will otherwise tend to ignore.

(7) In large multi-storey buildings the need for built-in provision for fire service communication should be discussed with the fire service, e.g. at inlet and landing valves of a rising main.

(8) Few fire authorities now accept direct connection by private land line to fire alarms on new premises (a few existing links remain in use). The alternatives are private line to one of the commercial watch services, or an automatic dialling unit. The latter will, when triggered by a fire alarm, make a call on 999 (or any other pre-determined number or numbers) and relay a pre-recorded message. They are not completely reliable, but may be cost effective even so.

It is likely that increasing electronic sophistication in communications equipment will lead to improvements in this field.

LIFTS

If there is a lift installation of any sophistication, its operation in a fire emergency should be specified to the manufacturer:

(1) Bring one or more lifts under central control?
(2) Bring one or more lifts under fire brigade control?
(3) All lifts to come to ground floor exit level and stop on receipt of alarm signal (from whom?)
(4) Protected twin power supply cables to motor?
(5) One lift of sufficient capacity for fire service use?
(6) Public address in lifts?
(7) Minimise openings between shaft and motor room?

Also consider:

(1) Access to motor room for fighting fire there.
(2) Provision of suitable portable extinguisher for motor room (e.g. for lift engineers use).
(3) Provision of ventilation, for smoke release, from motor room and from shaft.
(4) Basement motor rooms for hydraulic lifts can be successfully isolated from the lift shaft. Consider doing so to prevent smoke spread via shaft from motor room fire.

9.5
Detailed design of fire-resisting elements separating buildings or compartments within buildings

Drawings

In this section: Legislative requirements for materials in separating/compartment elements
Controls on construction of junctions
Permitted openings
Protection of openings: doors, shutters, glazing
Protected shafts

It is assumed that by this stage the location and performance of compartment walls and floors and of separating (party) walls, have been established on the basis of legislative and insurance requirements and good design.

MATERIALS

Requirements of England & Wales building regulations for:

Separating walls (party walls)

Entirely non-combustible (except for small uncompartmented buildings, see E8(7) and tables to E5).
Any beam or column forming part of the wall or any structure supporting the wall should be non-combustible.

331

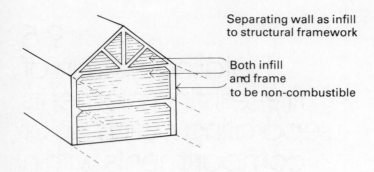

Separating wall as infill
to structural framework

Both infill
and frame
to be non-combustible

Compartment walls

Where the fire resistance standard is one hour or more
(*except* where this arises only because of the need to
separate purpose group II or III (institutional or other
residential) from some other purpose group) then —

Compartment wall or floor is to be wholly of
non-combustible materials —

Except for: (1) A floor finish
                 (2) A wall finish (complying with E15
                      for surface flame spread)
                 (3) A ceiling finish (complying with E15
                      for surface flame spread)

And the wall or floor must achieve the required fire
resistance without any benefit from any allowable
combustible material applied to it.

But in flats/maisonette blocks of no more than 3 storeys (in
purpose group III).

Only compartment walls in basement
and the compartment floor over basement
need comply with the non-combustibility
requirement (see E9(6)(a))

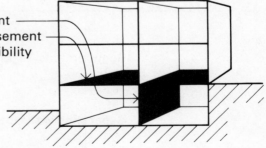

And in flats/maisonette blocks of no more than 4 storeys —
(in purpose group III)

Only compartment walls in the whole block
and the compartment floor over a basement
need comply with the non-combustibility requirement.

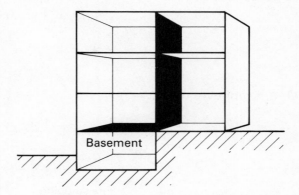

Basement

Exceptions to non-combustibility requirement

In both separating (party) and compartment walls and
floors combustible materials may be

> Built in to;
> Carried through over or across the end of the
> element.

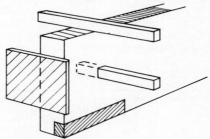

Provided that — This will not make the wall/floor
ineffective as a fire-resisting element

**Junctions with compartment walls or floors or with
separating walls**

Compartment or
separating wall

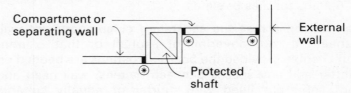

External
wall

Protected
shaft

Either fire-stop or bond-in at the junctions ✳

333

Roof–wall junctions

(1) Either take wall at least 375mm above roof measured at 90° to roof surface

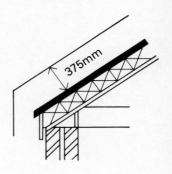

(2) Or run roof over wall if —

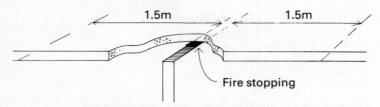

Fire stopping

    (a) The roof within 1.5m either side of the wall: is designated AA, AB, or AC and is solid or hollow slab construction and is of non-combustible material; and

    (b) the wall-roof junction is fire stopped.

(3) Or run roof over wall if —

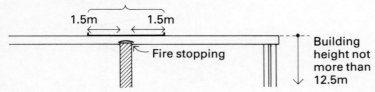

Non-combustible roof covering or asphalt in this area

Fire stopping

Building height not more than 12.5m

    Building purpose group III or IV or VII

Note:
Combustible material
— Boarding with or without sarking
  Wood wool with or without sarking
  Battens for tiles or slates

Can be run across the separating or compartment wall beneath a roof covering of asphalt or that is non-combustible provided the boarding/battens are bedded on mortar and any spaces between battens, wall head and roof soffit are filled with mortar or equally suitable material.

OPENINGS IN FIRE-RESISTING WALLS

Although openings can be protected they are potential weak points in a fire-resisting element and are controlled by legislation and by insurance rules.

(1) Openings permitted in separating walls

From amended 1976 building regulations for England and Wales.

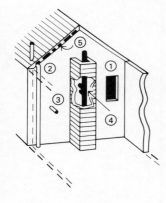

(1)　Escape doors of fire resistance equivalent to the wall itself.

(2)　Drainage vent pipe in accordance with E12(1) and N2(1).

(3)　Pipes other than for flue or ventilation, in accordance with E12, up to 150mm dia. depending on pipe material.

(4)　If the wall separates houses — branch or stack pipe if enclosed in a shaft/duct that is fire resisting and imperforate except for other water pipes (E12(3)).

(5)　Roof carried over the top of the wall provided openings are fire stopped at junction of wall head and roof (E8(3) and (4)).

(6)　External wall carried over end of separating wall provided the junction is fire stopped, or the walls are bonded together.

(2) Openings in compartment walls and floors

(Permitted (England and Wales building regulations 1976 and amendments))

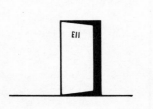

(1)　Access doorways to flats and maisonettes in compartment walls separating them from any space in common use. Doors to have at least ½ hour fire resistance and comply with E11.

(2)　Any door opening with fire resisting doors complying with E11 and of equal fire resistance to the wall.

(3)   Openings for protected shafts

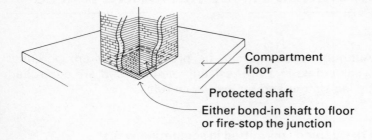

Compartment
floor

Protected shaft

Either bond-in shaft to floor
or fire-stop the junction

(4)   Openings for ventilation ducts not in protected shafts,
       suitably fire-stopped, with a fire damper in the duct.

There are metal
shutter and
intumescent honeycomb
types of fire damper
*both require access
for maintenance and
replacement*

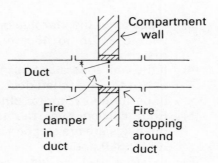

Compartment
wall

Duct

Fire
damper
in
duct

Fire
stopping
around
duct

(5)   Openings for pipes complying with E12 up to 150mm
       diameter depending on pipe material

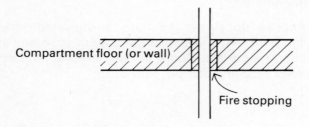

Compartment floor (or wall)

Fire stopping

See BRE current paper CP 38/77 by M. Curtis 'fire
spread and plastics pipes'

(6)   An opening for a chimney or flue duct complying with Part L and E8(5).

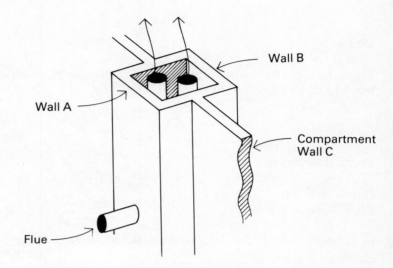

Wall B

Wall A

Compartment Wall C

Flue

Fire resistance of A + B = C

(7)   Openings for refuse chute access, complying with Part J.

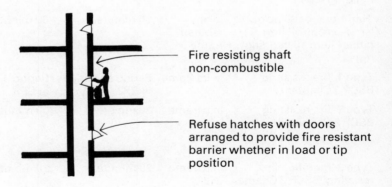

Fire resisting shaft non-combustible

Refuse hatches with doors arranged to provide fire resistant barrier whether in load or tip position

For guidance on the design of fire stops see also Building Research Establishment Current Paper CP 7/77 by F. Spiegelhalter.

PROTECTION OF OPENINGS

Doors

There is a confusing variety of terms and specifications used to describe different kinds of 'fire door'.

Some definitions:

Doors tested to
BS 476 Parts 1 or 8

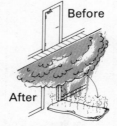  

Before

After

Door description	How tested	Collapse stability	Passage of flame loss of integrity	Loss of insulation
'Fire resisting' (reg. E1 table 1 item 14 building regs.)	In its frame	Period specified in E5 etc.	Period specified in E5 etc.	No requirement
'Modified fire resisting' fire check or 30/20 (reg. E1 table 1 item 15 building regs.)	In its frame	30 minutes	20 minutes	No requirement
'Half-hour' or 30/30 or 'smoke control' (reg. E1 table 1 item 16 building regs.)	In any rebated frame	30 minutes	30 minutes	No requirement
Type 1 'fire resisting' BSCP 3 Chapter IV	In its frame	Period specified in CP3	Period specified in CP3	No requirement
Type 2 'fire resisting' BSCP 3 Chapter IV	In a frame with a 25mm rebate*	30 minutes	30 minutes	No requirement
Type 3 'modified fire resisting' BSCP 3 Chapter IV	In a frame with a 25mm rebate†	30 minutes	20 minutes	No requirement
Type 4 'smoke check' BSCP 3 Chapter IV	In a frame with a 25mm rebate‡	30 minutes	20 minutes	No requirement

*In use the door need not have a rebated frame and can be single or twin leaf and single or double swing.
†In use the frame should have at least a 12mm rebate. Either a single leaf single swing, or a double leaf opposing swing with rebated meeting styles.
‡In use the door need not have a rebated frame and can be single or twin leaf with any swing *and brass or aluminium butts may be used.*

Scottish building standards regulations — fire door definitions

BS 476 Part 1 1953

Door description	How tested	Collapse	Passage of flame	Insulation
Fire resisting*	In its frame and with either side of door exposed to fire	Period specified in Table 6	Period specified in Table 6	No requirement
Fire resisting†	In its frame and with either side of door exposed to fire	Half the period specified in Table 6 for the surrounding wall — or 30 mins. whichever is greater	Half the period specified in Table 6 for the surrounding wall — or 30 minutes whichever is the greater	No requirement
Fire check‡	In its frame and with either side of door exposed to fire	Period required by reg. D5	20 minutes where D5 requires 30 min. 45 minutes where D5 requires 60 min.	No requirement

*Refers to doors etc. in fire division or separating wall other than type†
†Refers to doors etc. protecting openings etc. in:
(a) Fire division wall enclosing stairway or liftshaft;
(b) Separating wall between a flat and common access way;
(c) Duct enclosure carrying through a separating wall or floor, or fire division wall, or compartment floor.
‡Applies only if D5 calls for no more than 1 hour, single swing only. If D5 calls for 30 minutes and the doorways open into lobby or corridor from a stair enclosure (E9), the door can be of any type, without rebates, so long as any glazing is in wired glass panes not exceeding 0.4m² per pane: (BS 476 testing not required).

BS 459, Part 3: fire-check flush doors and frames

The standard's specification for minimum dimensions for fire resisting doors is widely used to assess the acceptability of doors for which BS 476 Parts 1 or 8 test results are not available.

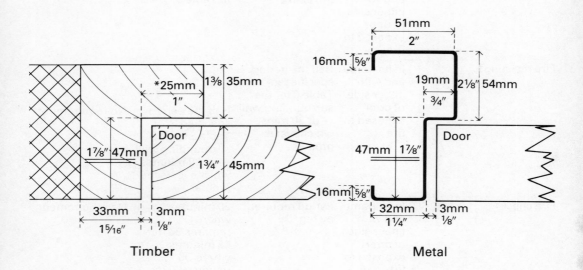

Timber   Metal

Minimum dimensions for half- and one-hour door frames.

Note:
Dimensions underlined Refer only to half-hour resistance and for one hour become 2¼" (57mm).

*The stop may be glued and screwed to a half-hour frame but must be worked from the solid for a one-hour frame.

The standard also specifies:

> Door size
> Suitable timber and plywood
> Suitable plasterboard
> Suitable asbestos coverings
> Adhesives
> Door construction
> Frame construction
> Finish
> Hanging and fastenings

Fire doors: further information

Since BS 459, Part 3 was written more research has shown that the fit of door in frame is just as important as the size of rebate. Also intumescent material has become available which can significantly improve a door's performance.

Langdon-Thomas has suggested the following guidelines: (Langdon-Thomas, G.J., *Fire Safety in Buildings*, Adam & Charles Black, London, 1972)

30/20 Door

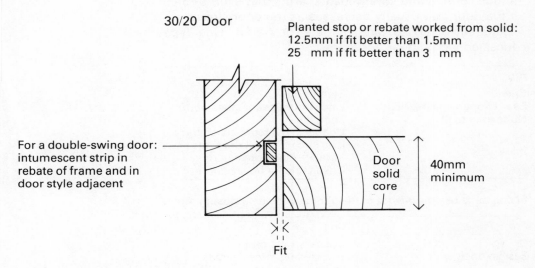

Planted stop or rebate worked from solid:
12.5mm if fit better than 1.5mm
25　mm if fit better than 3　mm

For a double-swing door: intumescent strip in rebate of frame and in door style adjacent

Door solid core

40mm minimum

Fit

30/30 Door

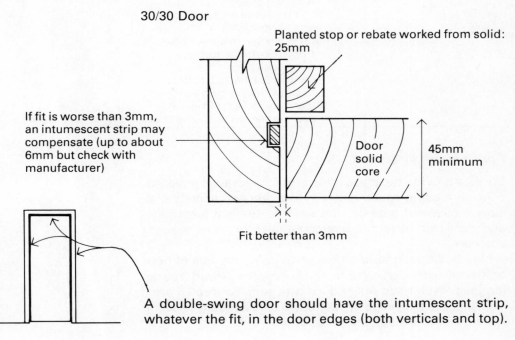

Planted stop or rebate worked from solid:
25mm

If fit is worse than 3mm, an intumescent strip may compensate (up to about 6mm but check with manufacturer)

Door solid core

45mm minimum

Fit better than 3mm

A double-swing door should have the intumescent strip, whatever the fit, in the door edges (both verticals and top).

Door closers

Fire doors can only limit fire spread if they are closed. People can not be relied on to close them, hence the need for closers. There is a wide range of devices to choose from, at a wide range of prices.

Simple devices

Various springs and spring-loaded arms that exert a force on the door that usually decreases as the door closes.

Generally fixed to face of door or frame. One type concealed within door and frame.

Pro	Con
Cheap	Slamming
Easy to open against closer	Latch bounces and does not
Quite easy to fit	engage
	Unable to overcome latch force
	If no latch, may let draughts or
	fire pressure, open door
	Unsuitable for heavy doors

Rising butts use the weight of the door to provide a closing force.

Pro	Con
Cheap	Not easy to fit properly
Easy to open door	Low closing force decreasing
	with age as bearings stiffen
	Unable to hold unlatched door
	against draughts
	May not begin to close door
	from intermediate open
	positions
	Frame may have to be cut away
	to allow full opening action so
	that gap exists for fire
	penetration when door is shut

Spring hydraulic devices

Springs provide the closing force but a hydraulic governor controls closing speed and may provide two speeds with slow movement near closing point to prevent slamming, and increased torque to overcome latch or resist draught pressure.

May be fitted in floor below pivot point, on face of door or frame with closing arm, or concealed within special hinges or within top rail of door with semi-concealed arm.

Except for the hinge type greater concealment is at the expense of more difficult installation.

Pro	Con
Progressive action without slamming adjustable for door weight Positive closing force	Expensive Poor adjustment or abuse can set up forces that damage door and frame May be difficult for weak people to open door Skill required for installation and adjustment

The expense and difficulty in opening are serious objections in buildings such as residential social services homes for the handicapped, the elderly, and young children.

Automatically activated fire door closers

To overcome some of the inconvenience of closers there are an increasing number of devices which only close the fire doors on an alarm signal being given.

A low voltage AC energized coil attracts a plate or rod attached to the door. An alarm signal breaks the circuit and the closer shuts the door

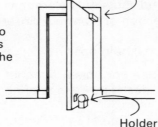

Closer

Fail-safe holder needs adjustment and may vibrate, puts strain on door hinges and closer fixing, expensive electrical work

Holder

(1) Conventional spring hydraulic closers with:
(a) Electromagnetic hold-open devices

(b) Pneumatic hold-open devices

Very similar in layout to the electromagnetic system except that the catch holding the door in the open position is controlled by air pressure rather than electricity.

The air line is claimed to be cheaper than electrical wiring to instal and adjustment problems are said to be eliminated.

A special pump is required and relays to control it from the fire alarm system.

In both cases 1(a) and 1(b) doors can be shut by hand, individually, at any time.

(2) Special fire door automatic closers
(a) Spring hydraulic free swinging type

The closer is attached to the doorway architrave but its arm is not fixed to the door. In everyday use the door swings freely and there is no self-closing action.

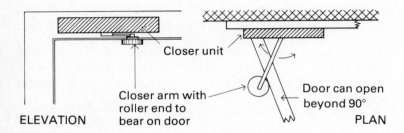

Closer unit

ELEVATION

Closer arm with roller end to bear on door

Door can open beyond 90°

PLAN

The unit is connected to the fire alarm/detection system. A solenoid in the closer which inhibits the closing action will be de-energized ay an alarm signal (or power failure) so that the closer arm swings round, picking up the door in whatever position it may be, and shuts it. The arm has the speed governor and latching action of a normal closer.

(b) Spring hydraulic with integral hold open

Many ordinary closers will hold a door open at about 90° but then the door must be part closed by hand to bring the closer into action.

This special unit is connected to the fire alarm/detector system so that if the door is opened beyond a certain point a solenoid restrains the closing action and the door is held in that position.

An alarm signal (or power failure) de-energises the solenoid and the closer takes over. The effect is similar to the action of the systems described in 1(a) and 1(b) above.

(c) Spring hydraulic with integral fire detection

The electronic components of smoke detectors having been compressed onto a single integrated circuit, some manufacturers have combined detector and a closer similar to 2(b) above, to give individual fire door closing.

A weakness of the other centrally-controlled systems is that appreciable quantities of smoke may have spread before the doors close. Also by closing *all* the controlled doors at once the hindrance problem is created just when maximum ease of movement is needed for evacuation.

Roller shutters

Proprietary steel roller shutters are available which provide fire resistance for an hour and more when tested to BS 476, Part 8.

Care is needed both in design and construction of the shutter installation to ensure that there are no weak points around the edge of shutter or its roller box.

Possible weak points

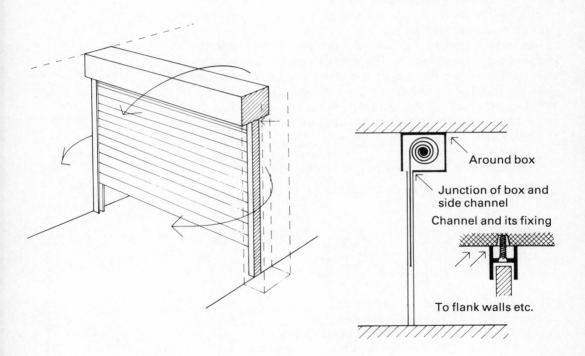

Around box

Junction of box and side channel

Channel and its fixing

To flank walls etc.

The exact details of the installation tested for the manufacturer ought to be compared with the installation proposed.

Are the same edge channels to be used (a more beautiful aluminium channel would fail almost certainly)?

Is a slot needed to accept the shutter foot when closed?

Could the shutter be by-passed by failure/reduction/differential movement of the building elements to which it is fixed? A slender timber post would char away. A metal post might bow and leave gaps.

If the box is within the ceiling is there proper fire stopping around it?

345

Shutter operation

Normally arranged to close by descending under gravity with spring counter-balance to control descent speed.

Being slow to open the shutters are normally held open when the premises are occupied and are closed automatically in case of fire, or manually when the premises are closed, e.g. at night.

A common usage is to protect openings in the compartment walls between parts of large shops, while allowing free-flow of customers.

Similar openings for conveyors in industrial premises are often shutter protected.

Automatic shutter release is normally either electro-magnetic or a fusible link. The former can be actuated by signals from fire detectors or the alarm system and would thus be quicker to respond than a fusible link. With the latter conditions in the vicinity of the shutter may be unendurable for unprotected people before the shutter is released.

Shutter propelled by fractional HP electric motor

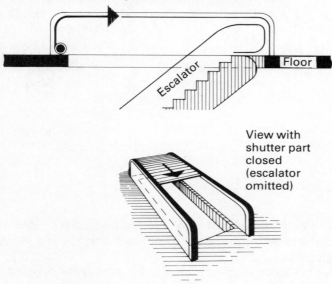

Floor

Escalator

View with
shutter part
closed
(escalator
omitted)

A special variant of the fire shutter is the motorized horizontally closing type used to protect and enclose floor openings for escalators.

Generally they are not accepted for enclosing stairs through compartment floors because of their necessarily slow operation and because mechanical failure would allow rapid upward fire spread.

Sliding doors

Sliding doors are the main alternative to shutters for the fire protection of large openings for which side-hung doors are inappropriate.

As with shutters, sliding doors of this sort are too heavy to open and close constantly and normally stand open.

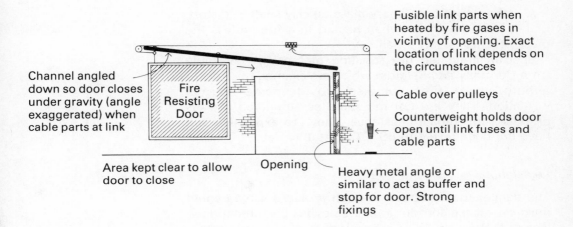

Fusible link parts when heated by fire gases in vicinity of opening. Exact location of link depends on the circumstances

Channel angled down so door closes under gravity (angle exaggerated) when cable parts at link

Fire Resisting Door

← Cable over pulleys

Counterweight holds door open until link fuses and cable parts

Area kept clear to allow door to close

Opening

Heavy metal angle or similar to act as buffer and stop for door. Strong fixings

A typical installation might be in a theatre protecting openings between say workshops and stage area.

The door must be very carefully installed to ensure that it closes reliably but leaves the least possible gap between door face and the face of the wall surrounding the opening.

Because of the difficulty of reopening such doors by hand they are only expected to function in the developed stages of a fire, hence the relatively slow acting fusible link. Their function is related to structural protection, rather than means of escape, to prevent large scale fire spread.

It is unusual to find sliding fire doors, in ordinary room doorways, replacing side-hung doors. This is because it is difficult to achieve even 30 minutes resistance in a sliding door that can be easily opened by hand.

Sliding doors would be difficult to open with a crowd of people pressing to escape and are therefore unsuitable on means of escape routes. However where the numbers are very limited or where there are wheelchair users who find sliding doors easier to manage, a case might be made for them.

Glazed openings

BS 153, Part 4 describes two types of glazing —

> 6mm wired glass;
> copperlight (akin to leaded light glazing but with copper cames);

which can resist collapse and the passage of flame for up to an hour in BS 476, Part 1 or Part 8 tests. They provide no insulation.

All other types of ordinary glass quickly shatter, distort, or fall from the frame when heated in a fire, unless the piece of glass is very small.

Special laminated fire resisting glasses are available from Germany and Belgium which are claimed not only to endure severe fires but also provide some thermal insulation. They are not the same as laminated glasses produced for impact resistance. They are expensive and have not been tested to BS 476, Part 8, to date.

Legislation

The danger that radiation through a glazed screen could make an escape corridor impassable, has been mentioned (see p. 302). The building regulations require compartment and separating walls and protected shaft walls to satisfy the insulation criteria of BS 476, Part 1 or 8 so that even fire resisting glazing is not likely to be acceptable in openings in such internal walls.

However, the regulations make no insulation requirement for fire resisting doors so that some glazing is permissible in doors provided the criteria of BS 476, Parts 1 or 8 are satisfied for resistance to collapse and the passage of flame for the appropriate period.

Glazing in fire resisting elements

Small vision panels:
(in doors of 30/20 fire resisting standard)

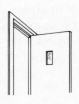

6mm thick plain glass (float/plate etc. unwired)

Not exceeding 0.065m^2

One pane only

Larger panels:
Half hour (30/30)

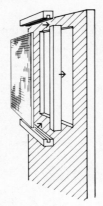

6mm thick wired glass

Individual panes not exceeding 1.2m² each

Frame:

Metal

Min. melting point 900°C

Where there are not beads, or are beads of lower melting point there must be a way of retaining the glass, proved by test

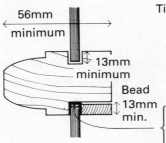

56mm
minimum

13mm
minimum

Bead
13mm
min.

44mm min.

Minor reductions in section away from critical areas such as rebates can be accepted

Timber

All members at least 56mm deep × 44mm wide

Rebate if worked from solid, at least 13mm deep

Beads, at least 13mm wide, may be protected with metal capping melting above 900°C or intumescent paint

Or use beads which withstand 900°C and are non-combustible

For 30/20 fire resistance beads may be of unprotected timber or use metal capping with melting point above 650°C.

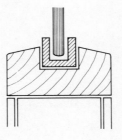

'Composition'

Proprietary materials based on mineral fibre are available in channel and bead form for use with metal or timber frames

See manufacturers' advice and tested examples for details

349

One hour fire resistance

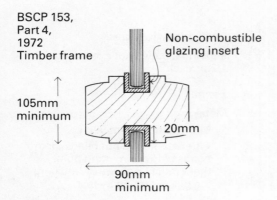

BSCP 153,
Part 4,
1972
Timber frame

Non-combustible
glazing insert

105mm
minimum

20mm

90mm
minimum

6mm thick wired glass

Individual panes not exceeding:
0.5m^2 each if construction in BSCP
153, Part 4, 1972 is followed

1.2m^2 each if construction tested for
manufacturer of 'Marinite', or
equivalent, glazing channel is
followed

Frame

Timber

    All members 90mm deep ×
    105mm wide minimum

    Rebates 20mm to take
    non-combustible glazing inserts
    that withstand up to 980°C

Metal

    Minimum melting point 980°C

The code was written before products such as 'Marinite'
were available, which made 1 hour fire resistance easier to
achieve.

A note on plastics glazing material

The superiority of polycarbonate over glass, for impact
strength has lead to its regular use in some types of
buildings, e.g. schools.

It should be remembered that this material has not got
any fire resisting qualities and if a proposal to replace
Georgian wired glass with polycarbonate, is being
examined check first that wired glass was not originally
specified on fire resistance grounds.

PROTECTED SHAFTS

If levels 1, 2, 3, 4 each constitute separate compartments any shaft connecting them which allows the passage of 'persons, things or air' between compartments has to have a protecting enclosure so that fire and smoke can not spread quickly from one compartment to another.

Building regulations:

England & Wales 1976   E10
Scotland   D10 & 12, E9

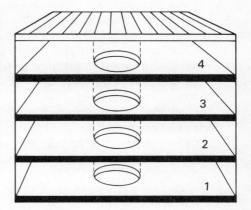

Openings in protected shafts

Permitted by England and Wales building regulations.

(1) For a pipe (excluding flue pipes and ventilating pipes other than SVPs) conforming to E12;
But —
if there is a stair in the shaft there must not be a pipe conveying gas or oil;
And —
if there is a gas pipe the shaft must be ventilated direct to open air.

(2) For doorways with fire resisting self-closing doors:
  (i) If shaft is partly or wholly above ground and the building is Purpose Group III, IV or VII, then half hour doors:
  (ii) Otherwise half the period of resistance required for the protecting structure.

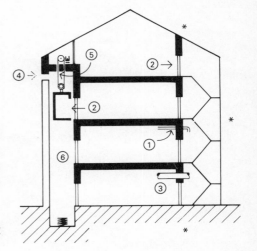

*An outside wall or roof or a floor laid directly on the ground is not subject to any of the requirements for protecting structure to a protected shaft.

If part of a protecting structure is also a compartment wall/floor or is a separating wall, the requirements for protecting structure do not take priority over those for compartmentation or separation.

(3) For ventilation ducts;
  But
  (i) If there is a stair in the shaft there must not be a ventilation duct;
  (ii) Any ventilation duct must be fitted with dampers to prevent fire spread via the duct from one compartment to another;
  (iii) The material of the duct or its lining should not contribute to the risk of fire spread.
(4) Where the shaft contains a lift there should be permanent ventilation to open air of at least $0.1m^2$/lift, at the top of the shaft.
(5) For lift cables to enter a motor room — smallest possible openings
(6) Lift shaft may not also contain pipes for gas or oil or ventilation ducts (Hydraulic lifts may need special consideration).

FINISHES, FITTINGS AND FURNITURE

Some notes on the surface flame spread properties of timber and plastics

Test BS 476, Part 7   — Classifications 1 to 4,
(see Chapter 4)   4 being the most
                                      rapid/extensive flame spread

Timber: Timber untreated usually rates class 3 but treatment by surface coatings or impregnation can achieve class 1.

Building regulations (England and Wales, and Scotland) include also a class 0 for materials that: are non-combustible throughout; or have a surface that is classed 1 by BS 476, Part 7 and (with its substrate if any) when tested to BS 476, Part 6 has indices $(I) \not> 12$ and $(i_1) \not> 6$.

Some impregnation treatments enable timber or timber-based material to achieve class 0 standard.

References Fire resistance of timber elements; flame
                    retardant finishes — *Architects Journal*
                    Timber Review, 15 August 1973
                    Flame Retardant Treatments for Timber
                    TRADA, February 1976

Note: An interaction between certain impregnation treatments to enhance fire properties, and subsequent kiln drying at elevated temperature has been observed to reduce the structural strength of the timber very significantly.

Plastics

The use of plastics for surface finishes is very widespread. The building regulations (England & Wales, and to a lesser extent Scotland) make special provision for these materials. Defining 5 'types' of plastics and controlling their use.

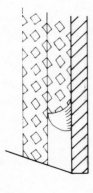

Generally materials and coatings of less than 1mm thickness are disregarded in any assessment of fire properties, if they are fully bonded to the substrate, as their influence is minimal in comparison to the substrates.

The use of foamed plastics sheet such as expanded polystyrene as a ceiling finish is deprecated. The fire performance varies with formulation thickness and fixing method and should use of the material be being considered the following references should be studied.

References: *Fire hazard of expanded polystyrene linings*: Fire Research Note 827 May 1970: Morris, Hopkinson, Malhotra.
Expanded polystyrene in building design: Expanded Polystyrene Product Manufacturers Association: June 1976

For information on the chemical and physical properties of plastics in fire refer to Part One of this book.

Furniture

The use of foam plastics in furniture upholstery can cause dense smoke production in fires that would otherwise be classed as minor.

Regulations: Regulations have been made to the effect that all upholstered furniture sold in the UK should pass a simple test of resistance to ignition (using a match and a smouldering cigarette as ignition sources). For a transitional period items that fail the test may be sold if warning labels are attached to them (*The Upholstered Furniture (Safety) Regulations 1980,* HMSO)

Materials

Polyurethane is the most commonly used upholstery foam.

Neoprene foam, though more expensive than polyurethane, has superior resistance to ignition by small sources and burns less rapidly.

Recently in the USA production of polyimide foam began. This material is said to be highly resistant to ignition and when it does burn gives off little smoke, and much less heat than polyurethane. It is less dense than polyurethane, for a given resilience, and its cost is said to be similar to polyurethane.

The design or selection of furnishings and fittings probably has as powerful effect on life safety as the measures embodied in the building regulations. A considerable amount of research has been done on various aspects of the problem. In Britain the work of Palmer, Taylor and Paul at the Rubber and Plastics

Research Association from 1972 to 1975 was reported in Building Research Establishment Current Papers 18/74, 3/75 and 21/76. These papers, especially the last one should be read by anyone who is designing or specifying furnishings.

Shape
The shape of a chair can be as important to fire safety as the materials of construction, where resistance to ignition by cigarettes and matches is concerned, and these are two of the most common causes of fires.

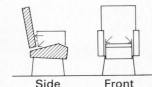

Side   Front

The designer should avoid traps for cigarettes or matches, which tend to occur at the junctions of back sides and squab.

A gap between these elements would be one possibility, or the covering could be fitted overall so that there were covers protecting the junctions.

Effect of special fire problems on detailing

Explosible dusts and explosions

A number of industrial processes are 'dusty' ranging from timber sawdust through flour to metal dust resulting from grinding operations.

General checklist
A surprising number of these dusts can ignite and burn with explosive force if sufficiently finely divided. The detail design of spaces in which these hazards may exist can help to reduce the probability of an explosion. The points to consider are:

(1)   Make provision for the removal of the dust at source, e.g. the 'cyclone' collector units commonly used in woodworking shops to control sawdust or suitable traps on drainage where washing down is the technique adopted. If collected dust is to be stored care is needed to ensure that this store is not a hazard to the rest of the premises.

(2)   Avoid details which encourage dust to gather, i.e. inaccessible ledges and very rough surfaces, and generally make cleaning as easy as possible.

(3)   Ignition can result from flames, sparks or contact with surfaces of sufficiently high temperature. The services engineer has to be briefed on the safe limits for the type of dust in question both with respect to open flame equipment and to processes, pipework or equipment where high surface temperatures are generated.

Pressure relief

The overall layout of premises in which explosions are a possibility has been discussed at the preliminary design stages.

Research following the Ronan Point disaster suggested that, for gas explosions at least, the maximum over-pressure generated could be significantly reduced (from 4–5 p.s.i. to 1 p.s.i.) by installing 'back relief' panels very close to the likely ignition point. The panels have to be in an external wall at a point that is reasonably unlikely to cause injury. For example it would be wrong to have say a gatekeeper's office right outside the relief panel.

The area and weight or pressure at which the panel ruptures, affect the maximum pressure developed by the explosion in the building. Taking the maximum acceptable overpressure and the size and shape of the room as starting points it is possible to calculate the size of panel needed and the pressure at which it must rupture or become unfastened.

References: *Dust Explosions in Factories*, Health and Safety at Work No. 22, HMSO, 1970.
Fire Research Notes Nos. 830 and 961 K.N. Palmer, DoE Building Research Establishment, Fire Research Station.
BRE Current Paper CP 26/71, Mainstone, Fire Research Station.

Petroleum and heavy flammable vapours

Classification of flammability hazard areas has been referred to in section 8.4.

There are three other main points to consider:

(1) Heavy flammable vapours should be dispersed so as to keep the concentration of vapour in air below the flammable limit (as the most explosive concentration for light hydrocarbons is about 3% vapour in air this is not easy). <u>Avoid</u> sump-like areas where falls meet

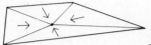

or pits

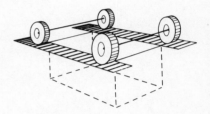

If these features are necessary for other reasons consider means of ventilation or special 'drainage' for fumes to a safe place.

(2) Petrol or other flammable vapours must not be allowed to enter the sewers or surface water drainage system.

All gullies in an area where heavy flammable vapours might be released should be fitted with traps of the petrol interceptor type.

(3) Falls should be contrived to lead heavy vapours away from ignition hazard or fire risk, e.g. machinery or vehicles with spark ignition internal combustion engines in the first case, and storage tanks or waste collection area in the second case.

CHAPTER TEN

Pre-contract procedure work on site

Hand over and building in use

10.1
Fire precautions during construction

The site is the general contractor's responsibility during the construction phase. Architects would be unwise to become involved in the minutiae of the contractor's fire safety arrangements, as this might expose them to liability.

However the architect should point out anything he considers is deficient and could well ask the contractor for a statement of the precautions that will be taken. This should be done at the start of the contract. The points which might need to be covered are:

Supervision	Steps to prevent unauthorized entry and arson; Control of high fire risks: welding, flame cutting, grinding, blow torches and heating devices, the use of highly flammable materials, smoking
Fire fighting	First aid fire fighting equipment; Means of calling fire brigade; Fire brigade access up to and inside the part-built structure; Water supplies for fire fighting; Possibility of early commissioning of fire protection systems in building
Safety	Arrangements for fire alarm and evacuation; Training in use of fire fighting equipment; Fire prevention training
Storage	Segregation of ignition risks and highly flammable material; Control of LPG and oxy-acetylene, equipment and storage of empty cylinders

Insurance will normally be covered in the preliminaries of the main contract.

10.2
Supervision by the architect and other consultants of the work on site and commissioning

A great deal of the success of fire safety measures installed in a new building depends on the quality of workmanship by the installers. Many of the works are covered up by finishes or hidden in voids. Integrity of fire resistance depends on good fit and conscientious finishing-off. Treatments such as intumescent coatings require very thorough preparation of surfaces.

This all calls for close attention to detail. Clerk of Works and Site Architect/Engineer should keep a close watch on this work before it is covered up.

Where specialist sub-contractor work is involved the main contractor may not be well qualified to assess the quality of work. A certificate that the work complies with the manufacturer's recommendations or the appropriate code or standard should be obtained from such specialists.

Copies of such certificates should be passed to the client in case the fire authority want to see them under Fire Precautions Act certification procedure. Licensing authorities equally could have an interest, e.g. in the fire retardant properties of soft furnishings in a theatre.

Programming must allow enough time for the commissioning of fire safety systems, most of which is best done when the building is complete. A pressurization system can only be tested properly when the building is heated and any mechanical ventilation or automatic control system has been balanced. Ideally its performance in different wind conditions should be checked too.

Automatic detectors require a settling-in period. Even if the system is commissioned when the main heating and ventilation is working there are likely to be some false alarms when the building is first occupied and arrangements should be made in advance to deal with them.

10.3
Hand-over and the building in use

The amount and complexity of the documentation given to the client obviously varies with the size and sophistication of both building and client. Many of the topics covered below may not be appropriate in a particular case.

THE SITE AND SURROUNDINGS

Site plan showing:

Points of exit from building and any external routes from these points.

Roads and hard standings needed for fire brigade access.

'Firepaths' for fire brigade access to other parts of the building.

Location of fire hydrants.

Function of any outbuildings or external plant.

Location of any main service controls outside the building — water, gas, electricity, fuel oil cut-off for external tanks.

Location of inlets to rising mains, foam inlets, replenishing inlets for bulk CO_2 or other extinguishing agents.

Open water or stored water where provision has been made for fire brigade access to obtain water for fire fighting.

Zones deliberately left vacant because of blast or radiant heat hazard, or from which ignition sources must be excluded because of gas or petroleum, etc. hazard.

Location of external pipes or tanks containing flammable material.

Note any external walls which are combustible, if it could be dangerous to put any building, hut or plant close to them.

THE BUILDING(S)

Layout plans and sections showing:

Compartment walls and floors

Fire resisting structure to protect escape routes

} With the standard of fire resistance indicated

Exits from each floor and any protected routes to those exits;

The purpose for which all main spaces were designed;

The occupant capacity to which assembly rooms were designed;

Fire alarm call points;

Location of hosereels & extinguishers;

Areas covered by automatic detection systems and the location of the control and indicating equipment;

Areas protected by extinguishing systems, and the controls;

Fireman's lift(s);

Rising main(s) wet or dry with landing valve position;

Emergency telephone points;

Refuge areas.

FIRE SAFETY SERVICES

Plans, diagrams, descriptions, specification, etc. to explain the workings of specialist systems. Name installer and manufacturer of all major components and consumable supplies.

Detection system and any devices activated by it;

Extinguishing system;

Alarm system;

Emergency power;

Emergency lighting;

Emergency communications and control;

Pressurization or natural smoke control arrangements.

The maintenance requirements of each system or component are best obtained from the manufacturer, hence the importance to the client of full documentation.

10.4
Maintenance and materials

Attention must be drawn to places where special materials or components have been used for fire protection purposes, and detailed information given about them.

It is not always obvious that special material has been used — for example:

Intumescent coatings;

Surface flame-spread retardant paints;

Fire resistant glass (some new types are visually indistinguishable from ordinary plate).

Obviously the occupants must be told that these sorts of material are there for a purpose and must not be altered.

Index

DATE DUE

APR 30 '84			
DEC 17 '84			
APR 25 '85			
SEP 24 '86			
OCT 10 '86			
FEB 23 '94			
APR 23 '95			

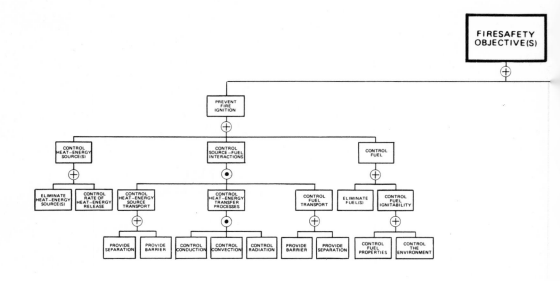

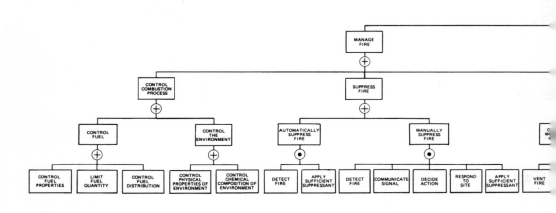